The story is set in Western Australia. The spelling and grammatical style are typically "Australian". The Australian terms are explained at the end of the book.

Western Australia is experiencing a financial boom due to the mining industries, and oil exploration. Consequently, the tradesmen and blue collar workers can earn high salaries and out spend the established rich. Most high schools in Perth are private. Increased wages mean the tradesmen can now buy a place for their children in the elite schools usually reserved for the children of a higher socio economic class. This creates turmoil and changes for all involved. The reader has a ring side seat to that drama as Anna Lennox, psychologist, braids it with the varying degrees of criminality of the offenders, the politics of the Ministry of Prisons and Corrections and her family life. The results are explosive.

# Gael McCarte

# THE CON

Fact◆ion
...fiction based on fact
an imprint of GEA Press

THE CON
Copyright © 2010
By Gail Julie Buesnel


Library of Congress Control Number: 2010939769
Buesnel, Gail Julie
THE CON
ISBN 978-1-935434-53-5

Subject Codes and Description:
1. :FIC050000: Fiction: Crime  2. PSY014000: Forensic Psychology
3. SOC004000: Social Science: Criminology

This is a work based on professional experience gained as a psychologist in the Department of Corrections (in Australia). The names, characters, case histories, places, brands, media, and incidents are the author's creation as part of a work of fiction. The author acknowledges the trademarked status and trademark owners of various products referenced in this work of fiction, which have been used without permission. The publication/use of these trademarks are not authorized, associated with, or sponsored by the trademark owners. The places that do exist are used fictitiously.

The Press does not have ownership of the contents of a book; this is the author's work and the author owns the copyright. All theory, concepts, constructs, and perspectives are those of the author and not necessarily the Press. They are presented for open and free discussion of the issues involved. All comments  and feedback should be directed to the Email: comments4author@aol.com and they will be forwarded to the author for response.

Cover design by Barton Green

Printed in the United States of America

Published by
**GlobalEdAdvancePress**
Under the **FACTION** imprint
**www.globaledadvance.org**

# There are a few people I'd like to honour

Sandra Fleury, my friend and colleague,
for her dedicated service to the Department of
Corrective Services.

~

My dear husband and children,
for their ever present support.

~

Charles Andrew Woods, explosives expert,
for his guidance.

~

Olivia Nelson, editor and writer,
who assisted me with her editorial expertise and support.

~

I honour and thank the many nameless faceless employees
of the justice department and law enforcement agencies
who work with those in prison and those identified as
'offenders' within the community. You are the true heroes.

~

I also acknowledge the many who have transferred their
skills to legitimate pursuits from crime.

~

10% of my profits from this book in any of its versions will
be given to Puppies Behind Bars (PBB). Prison inmates
raise service dogs for the disabled and explosive detection
canines for law enforcement. They place trained service
dogs free of charge, with wounded veterans, special needs
children and disabled adults, and more than 240 explosive
detection canine units. Thank you for supporting inmates'
contribution to society by purchasing this book.

# Table of Contents

# 1

## Lachie Counts

"*Mum, why do they pronounce ninth as 'neye-nth' when there is no 'e' in it? Shouldn't it be 'nin-th'?* If he could engage her in meaningful conversation she might not notice he was still in bed.

"*You are right lovee, now pop up*".

"*Mum shouldn't third be three-th?*"

"*Why lovee?*"

"*Well you have fourth and fifth, why not three-th?*"

"*Why indeed?*"

"*And Mum, same as second, it should be two-th*". He added pleading to his voice to keep her engaged.

"*Mum, and fifth, when did five become 'fif'? How did that happen? Shouldn't it be 'fiveth' not fifth? Ppfffttt who ever said 'four, fif'?*" He was still in bed. He lay dead still.

"*Pop up poppet*".

"*Mum really shouldn't first be 'oneth'?*"

"*What?*"

"*I think it should be one-th, two-th, three-th, fourth, five-th, sixth, seventh, eight, nineth.*" Recognising the familiar garden path she was headed down Anna knew what to do.

"*Lachlan Arthur Maximilian Lennox*".

"*Yes Mum*".

*"Get your skinny little 9 year old bag of bones up, NOW".*
*"Yes mum."*

He resisted facing the morning storm without his blankets or roof. He wanted to marinate in the warm bed but his mother had used his four names. He jumped up. She made his bed while it was still warm so he would not snuggle back into it. As he was showering she heard him ask the soap *"Why is Jimmy short for James? It's not shorter and anyway shouldn't it be 'Jammy'?"* She never did know if the soap answered him. She was just glad he did not ask her.

*"Stuart Frederick Stephen Lennox you need to get up babe"*, Anna reminded his 14 year old brother. Using the formal 4 family names worked on Lachie, she tried it again. Stu stumbled into the shower in his parent's bathroom. He did not welcome the morning or the foul weather. Between childhood and manhood Stu intuitively located the parental radar and flew under it. But there was no escaping when his 4 names were used.

Lachie's bed hugging was making her late. She hated being late. Most days Anna caught the train to work. There was no time for station to train hopping today. She could not drive the family car as Max needed it. His company supplied vehicle was undergoing unplanned repairs and public transport did not take him to his office. These multiple dilemmas had one solution. The family would commute together. Max offered to drive Anna to the office and take the boys on to their respective schools to save time.

Both boys ran through rain then tumbled and tripped into the back seat of the family car. They sat in their neatly pressed rain spotted school uniforms, hunched over their back packs. Anna swore as Max drove into the curb at the traffic roundabout and the car ricocheted backwards. Her expletive escaped more out of a genuine startle reaction than any intention to be coarse. Annoyance rose quickly to her throat when she thought Max may have damaged the car tires.

*"You have to watch your language in front of the children."*

*"I am watching it"* she said.

*"Anna, that's a ridiculous thing to say, ever since you've had* **that** *job, your language has deteriorated to toilet level. So has your attitude. You are cranky and this 'tough Wonder-Woman-crime-buster' facade is getting old."* She was silent. Words were irrelevant, no way to win this argument. Besides she refused to have this conversation in front of the children.

*"Dad, mum said 'frigging' yesterday"* the child's voice in the back seat offered. Anna reached back and pinched him, she winked at both boys.

*"Anna, listen to him, he's now speaking like you."*

If Max knew the words that flew into her mind he'd really have something to stress over.

*"It's your job, you really have to work on not letting it affect you like this, where are your boundaries? The culture of your clients is bleeding into your family life and all over us,"* Max continued. Anna wanted to respond,

*"And what do you even know about boundaries? The day we don't spend every cent of my wage is the day I know I can stop working with low life,"* but she did not. She had learned not to take these thoughts too seriously. They soon passed. The subject was likely to soon change.

*"Can we have some decent music instead of that crap?"* a teenaged voice growled. The Stuart Sphinx had spoken. Bingo.

Subject change, maybe object change would be more like it.

*"Son, don't use that word. Which radio station do you want?"* The language police refocused. Kid approved music filled the vehicle.

Lachie was dropped off first. When he walked through his school gate he looked like one of the 'turtle boys'. You have seen them. They walk with their head and neck extended in front, a bulging back pack that covers them from strained neck to thumped thighs. It looks like a turtle shell. And below, thin knobble kneed legs that keep the load moving. 'Turtle boys'.

Next Max stopped the car at the set of lights closest to Anna's office. Anna Lennox, Forensic Psychologist, hopped out, dragged her brief case on wheels from the boot of the car. She ran the short distance, through punishing rain to the office of the Ministry of Prisons and Corrections in Fremantle, Western Australia.

*"Morning Anna, get caught in the rain did we?"* The all too cheery voice of the security guard greeted her through his first morning cup of fruited tea. Anna wondered if he really thought she cultivated the 'just showered in my clothes' look.

*"Yep Jason, wet again. When the Directorate provides parking for me, I will drive in and won't have to run blocks through this drenching rain."*

*"Well we all have to do it, budgets you know. You were the last on, I am the 4th last, and I still don't have a parking place either. If you get voted 'employee of the month' you will get a reserved spot. I have had it twice already. What sort of a day do we have today?"*

*"If they all show up, it'll be a busy one"*. She had a new name for Jason, 'PP' from the movie Pink Panther. On her less kind days, she thought of him as a spoof of Inspector Cousteau. In accordance

with departmental policy she handed him the typed list of scheduled clients. His log book recorded those who attended, those who
did not, and how long each stayed. He refused to use a cyber diary,
or a blue inked pen. If he could have seen the future he may not
have been so meticulous with the visitor log.

The Ministry of Prisons and Corrections in Fremantle stood on
Abernathy Street. It was half way down the hill that overlooked
the 1850's limestone convict built Fremantle Prison. Anna worked there 2 days a week, and in the Ministry's community based
centre in Port Stirling, to the south, the other 3 days of the working
week.

Fremantle was a major working port historically and currently.
Century old buildings with sparse windows nudged up against
modern well lit glass fronted department stores. Silent stone
church steeples, wrought iron trimmed hotel verandas, the railway
station, the historic custom's house competed with coffee shops
and book stores for attention. Crowds often filled the leafy streets
in search of a cold drink, a hot meal, or a good show from the
street performers. Bronze statues captured a moment in time in the
subject's life as crime arrested development in an offender's life.
These statues were peppered throughout the town in leafy, shaded
and well sunned areas.

The comings and goings of the port mirrored the lives of the
offenders. Ships, mismatched collections of characters from varied
times and beginnings, lives frozen in place, lives on the move, no
real place to put down roots and grow, only a place to berth.

Her life was becoming more crowded. She loved Lachie's
questions, most of the time, but sometimes she wanted to turn him
'off'. Stu was too quiet. She wanted to turn his 'on' button on.

When the offenders were not occupying her attention, the boys took up the space in her heart and head. Max, not so much these days. It wasn't always that way.

An unexpected benefit of her working south was that the hour driving to the Port Stirling Centre gave her time to think, or not think. As she held the steering wheel she considered non psychological, non family thoughts or no thoughts at all. The trip which took her over an hour, give or take, took the European settlers 3 days by oxen drawn cart. She would have gone insane lurching to the oxen's gait surrounded by Lachie's questions for three days?

Anna's secondment as part of the team of forensic psychologists treating community based individual offenders was a new position. She had worked with offenders in various situations within the Prison and later in the community based offender group program division. Her long held goal was to do individual intervention with offenders. This astonished those who sought safer climbs. She applied for the position three months ago, through the intranet. The resultant Department's letter informing her that she was considered to be 'non competitive' was disappointing. She was shocked out of that disappointment when Liz contacted her two months ago. The newly appointed Principal Forensic Psychologist, Liz asked,

*"Anna, do you still want to work for us? I can offer you a year's contract. I have reviewed your qualifications, your education and stated clinical approach. Your prison and program experience has given you a balanced view of what is possible with our clients. As far as I am concerned that puts you in the lead and takes you out of the non competitive to the highly rated category."* Anna was stunned at Liz's praise. She took a moment to recover and responded,

*"Thank you. I was shocked at the 'non competitive' rating I*

*received from the panel. I would be honoured to join your team and a year sounds good"* said Anna, *"give us both time to see if the fit works. My work with offenders in groups brought its satisfactions but the opportunity to deal with offenders on a more personal and individualised basis appeals to me."*

Liz asked her why she had entered this field. Anna choose not to self disclose. How do you tell your boss that your only reason is a driving compulsion to understand psychopaths? No family history of crime or interventionists, no crushing trauma to be understood, no feral lover, just an urge, since girlhood to understand the bad guys. Despite the power of the compulsion it rang shallow with the telling. And at this point in their relationship Anna did not want to wade in shallow water. Anna simply said,

*"I am fascinated with the latest research on the connection between neurology and behaviour. Knowledge in this sphere will direct our intervention as we increase our understanding of the aetiology of aberrant behaviour. I am eager to take advantage of this opportunity, in the light of that research. I am sure I can add to the great work already being done."* As obfuscated an answer as it was, Anna's answer pleased Liz. Anna asked her about the Department's mandated role to offer support and consultative services to its clinical staff in rural and remote areas.

*"We have not gotten there yet, I am new to the job, but I certainly appreciate your interest and will make a note of it. When we are able to offer those services I will talk to you about your being involved."* Anna looked forward to supporting her more isolated colleagues. Her manager at the group program's division released her for a year. This launched her into the team of psychologist working with community based offenders.

Despite the rain, Lachie's arithmomania, the rushed trip with
the boys in the car, the tire bounce, Max's lecture and her damp
clothing she was glad it was Monday. She enjoyed her days in
Fremantle. She was challenged by the opportunities her new role
presented. She never knew what a day would bring. Charlotte, the
acting manager, was the one constant. She was entirely predictable,
they all knew the mayhem encountering her could inject into their
day. Most had become quite adept at avoiding her.

Before she had time to pat her hair dry with the rough government issue recycled paper hand towels in the female's bathroom, a
voice announced over the intercom,

*"Mr. Williams is at reception for Anna".*

*"Mr. Williams, good morning, how are you?"*

She welcomed him into her small office, through the door with its
generic sign 'Staff Psychologist'. Seated on the Government issued
chairs they heard her government issued computer reformatting
itself or whatever it did noisily when first booted.

*"I can't stay long I have an appointment at the Clinic I need
more* (metha) *'done than I am getting I am fine I'm doing good
really call me 'Jack' I feel like I am in school if you call me 'Mr.
Williams' you get caught in the rain or take a late shower?"* All
one sentence, words running together, spoken without inhalation,
inflection or punctuation.

Jack Williams was not one of the offenders she wanted to see
for the full therapy hour. The feeling was mutual. He was not one
for mandated chit-chat. Jack's few existing teeth were unseen. His
teeth long ago fled the frontal gum area, both top and bottom of his
bite. He looked to be 20 years older than his documented age. His
body aroma announced his presence before his physical presence

did. He traded in a particular brand of determined indifference. He was indifferent to the negative impact his criminal activities had upon others and indifferent to the potential impact of rehabilitative intervention upon him. Anna decided against chatting with this toothless man about the circumstances of her morning.

*"Mr. Williams we have to discuss your offending behaviour and how to implement a relapse prevention program. Increasing your methadone is only one plan to consider. There are others. Let's talk about your discussing those other options with Dr. Tan?"*

*"Let's not. The doctor knows what he is doing. All that crap that you call 'offending behaviour' happened so long ago. Whatever I did was minor league, a purse here, a wallet there, hardly 'criminal'. 'Sides I have changed, I am on the 'done. It wasn't me that done that snatch and grab stuff, it was the drugs, or in the early days – the booze. I am not using now. You see the pee test results. As much as I would like to I just can't keep chatting like this today. Really. I will see you in a couple of weeks and we can talk about whatever then. You should dry your hair before you catch cold."* At least he breathed this time. He was fully committed to leaving. She was fully committed to letting him. Leave he did.

PP looked at her questioningly, Williams was leaving after 5 minutes, *"The last psych saw clients for over an hour"*. Anna thought *"It's bad enough I live with the language police, now I work beside the time cop"* but she answered,

*"So I hear"*.

She wrote cryptic notes on Jack Williams. She needed to alert the Probation Officer to the fact he gave no indication of desiring to change or of truly engaging in the therapeutic process. She emailed her *"Jack has attended his 5 sessions but the total time in attendance was 45 minutes."* The response caught her off guard,

*"At least he attended I can tick that box, I don't have time to do the paperwork to violate him"* wrote his Probation Officer.

*"He has been scored as highly likely to re-offend. Doesn't that concern you?"* asked Anna.

*"Re-offend? If he does re-offend he will rip purses and wallets off the old drunks in the park. They will be too drunk to know who did it. Not exactly high crime. Charlotte does not support us violating the petty criminals, even if they are at risk of re-offending."*

*"Are you telling me you are going to let him skate?"*

*"Skate? What, where, he attended, end of story."* Click. Call over.

*"End indeed"* Anna muttered to the dial tone on her hand phone.

The next scheduled client did not show. That offender was a house burglar. He was a specialist, a highly self-trained thief who crept about in the dark of night. He was skilled at instilling terror into the good people in town who had the misfortune to wake when he visited. He snuck or broke into occupied houses and stole precious and hard earned items from easily awakened sleepers. Fully awake they could beat him silly or at least gouge or scrape his DNA from his body for future analysis. He functioned with that threat, nightly, yet rain kept him inside during the light of day.

The absent offender was tall, and toothless. If she had not moved quickly at their last meeting he might have walked right over her. Like the platypus his body appeared to be a collection of bits and pieces left over from others. He had a size 17 head on a size 10 neck, size 20 hands on size 10 arms and of course, size 13 Wide feet on size 10 legs. He walked hunched over, actually he lurched rather than 'walked'.

*"I do not understand, given his physical anomalies, how he was actually nimble and athletic enough to operate as a proficient night stalking thief,"* Anna later commented to his Probation Officer.

*"Well, believe it, he is proficient, or, at least he was. He has managed to escape the daily grind of ever doing an honest day's work in his 40 years of adult life,"* the Probation Officer responded. Anna marked the night burglar as 'pre-contemplative'. He was not yet thinking about changing his career or ways. His name was Bartholomew Alexander Mew; he went by 'Bam'. Anna thought if he went by the end of his first name and the beginning of his second he could be called 'Mew Mew' and that translated to 'Cat'. That fit given his choice of professions, but 'Bam' it was. She shook her head. She sounded more like Lachie than Lachie himself.

The third, or as Lachie was now saying 'the three-th' scheduled offender called to cancel; she did not have an umbrella and could not go out in 'this weather'.

*"I don't have an umbrella either but I came out in it"* Anna grumbled inwardly. Her shoes were still damp from her morning rain run. She could not say what she was thinking to the offenders. She rescheduled her. PP commented

*"Not many showing today Anna".* There was a ring to that. The unspoken part was *"if you were worth your level 6 pay perhaps the client actually attend and stay longer like they did with the last psych."* Short of giving the offenders free heroin shots, door-to-door taxi rides, or umbrellas she did not know how to get them to attend.

She finished her reports and notes about the no shows, refiled the files and walked bare footed to the lunch room for coffee. Jason hovered by the refrigerator, surrounded by a small flock of

Probation Officers and office staffers. The conversation stopped mid syllable as she entered. She inspected the orphaned mugs in the kitchen. The Department did not supply mugs for staff to use. The latest donation was from a staff member who brought in a dozen discarded mugs of various shapes and colours. Anna knew enough to scald it first and scour out the tea stains. Cockroaches reigned supreme in there at night and she had no intention of drinking from their unwashed throne. The coffee pot was empty so she made herself some teabag tea. It was obvious to her that they had been talking about her lack of time with the offenders. What was she supposed to do, rope them to the 'bloody chair'? She didn't want to care what level 3's and 4's thought of her, but she did.

Her next client was a caricature of the typical criminal, bald head, earrings, goatee and tattoos. He was a patched up member of the bikie gang known as 'The Mob'. The Mob was believed to be a less violent, loosely organised gang. They were not known to practice unilateral punishment. The Mob was considered to be a collection of wanna be's who sat astride huge throbbing motor bikes. They were not taken as seriously as other motorbike gangs. But their appearance was scary enough to qualify them as real bikies.  The Mob's members assisted each other's high end burglaries. They did not have an organized arm of drug manufacture and supply. That did not prevent the individual members from building their own drug empire.

*"Yeah I earned 50 grand a week as a drug dealer now I can't get a frigging $15.00 an hour job to feed myself"* stated Warren Leigh Conaughton, 'Warro' for short, Mob member.

*"I need to ask you how you feel about almost having completed your orders successfully. That must be a relief. From the record you*

*have not reoffended, and you seem to be doing well."*

*"Not so fast, did I just hire you as my ghost writer? If not, you do not get to rewrite my life story."*

That comment annoyed her. All readily identified stupidity pre-packaged as a humour annoyed her. She referred him to the educational officer to discuss retraining options. She did not have the energy, or inclination today to attempt to convince this ethically bankrupted offender of the value of integrity. She arranged to meet with him the following week.

Perhaps he had a point though. Ethical Anna would have been lucky to clear $50 grand a year after taxes and she contributed to the greater good with her master's degree and passion 'to help'. This unethical high school dropout claimed he earned 52 times more than she did, destroying lives. Something was wrong with that picture.

As the rain eased the rest of 'the scheduled' arrived. The day blurred into a litany of all too familiar stories and unfamiliar faces. Morale at the Centre seemed to be slipping to an all time low. As she left the office she bade Jason goodnight with *"See yah PP"*. Jason's confused look was priceless.

The homeward bound train was crowded causing Anna to stand for the entire journey home. Clutching the overhead strap she lurched and bumped against others in concert with the train's motion. Broad-shouldered young men sat while she stood. Even healthy school children who were mandated to stand for adults if they rode on subsidised fares, sat. The school children avoided her eyes when she tried to give them 'that look'. Obviously they had mothers too and were accomplished 'look' avoiders. The rain had eased and the weather was suddenly pleasant. Her walk home from the train station refreshed her.

*"Daddy said I am not to swear like you do,"* her youngest, Lachlan, offered while she was preparing the evening meal. *"Did he?"*

*"Mum I was wondering why they call apartment apartments, they are not apart, they are together. Shouldn't they be 'togetherments'? And then they call them flats. They are not flat; they are stacked one on the other. I think they should be called 'stacks'."*

Lachie realised Anna was not listening to him, so he tried a different tack,

*"Mum what do fish drink?"*

Anna did not feel obliged to entertain Lachie's Thesauristic diatribe or his verbal puzzles. They had ploughed this field at least 4 times. She gave him a quick cuddle, kissed the top of his head, rewashed her hands for her food preparation task and diverted his attention with *"How was school?"*

*"Crappy."* How could she reprimand him? She knew his language deterioration matched hers. It didn't dismay or even seem that bad to her. She remembered 'crappy' days at school too. The 'these are the best days of your life' routine, referring to school was never true for her.

*"What happened?"*

*"Well mum, you know that kid I told you about, the one with the organs outside of his body? Well mum, actually he thought I was staring at him. He got so angry that he threatened to belt me and shove me down the stairs, and he was swearing at me."*

*"What did you do?"*

*"I told him to get stuffed".*

That seemed like a remarkably restrained response to her. She knew Max would not see it that way. She was too tired to turn it into a parental lecture so she tried the humanitarian self discovery approach.

*"You said that? Does that sound like a kind thing to say to a kid whose organs are on the outside?"*

*"All the more reason to stuff him".*

Max arrived home at that point. He did not understand why Anna and Lachie were giggling. Anna made no attempt to explain it. Moments like that lose their humour in translation.

*"You are late,"* was the only alternate greeting that came to mind.

*"Is that all you can say? How about 'Hi darling'?"* snarled Max.

*"Nothing I say is frigging right, whether I swear or not,"* her thoughts ran loud.

*"How are you darling?"* she asked.

*"Fine, the day was intense, what about you, the criminals show up?"* asked Max in a slightly less confrontational tone.

*"Let's not talk about them, tell me about 'intense'."* Anna switched topics.

Not one to miss the opportunity to explain or describe himself and his mastery over every situation he launched into the answer. She climbed in her head and drifted away.

*"What date is the wedding?"*

Good grief! Something that demanded a response. *"When did he stop talking about himself?"* her head voice demanded.

*"I don't know"*, she lied. She would be burned at the stake before she became his conduit to reality. *"You can find the invite on the frig"*. Then she thought but did not say, *"where all the invites*

*for the last 17 years have been, even though this is obviously news
to you."*

When did she become so angry at him? When did she give up
trying to make it work for her as well as him? What was wrong
with the 'us' in them?

Anna had watched the televised version of Queen Elizabeth's
international celebration of her 50 years as monarch some years
ago. One brief snippet of the interaction between the Royals took up
permanent residence somewhere in her trivia memory bank. Prince
Charles, the pride of Britain waxed eloquent about his mother in
his speech. The Duke, standing beside her, within the same hearing
range as she, asked her *"what did he say?"* Well, no one could
answer that. No one ever knows what Charles is saying, you know
that. The Duke, in front of the entire world, asked his wife to be
his conduit to reality. He expected Her Royal Highness to leave the
glory being bestowed upon her, interrupt one of her finest hours to
interpret for him what his own son said, about her.

As incidental as it was Anna often thought about that exchange.
It fed her prejudices. She watched her father and other older men
disconnect and only fleetingly re-enter the world around them
via their wives. When she asked her father about family plans he
typically said,

*"Talk to mum about it, she knows about that stuff".*

Anna abdicated the role of husband conduit; Max would have to
do his own connecting.

• • • • •

# 2

## *Charlotte*

*T*uesday found Anna traipsing her way down Abernathy Street in Freo. Seven offender appointments were booked, seven offenders showed. Bam was her 2nd client. He was a carryover from the day before when he failed to show in the rain. He apologised for letting the rain keep him from his session. He was grateful she had time to see him today. He did not know the secretary had rescheduled him without Anna's knowledge. Anna felt no inclination to explain that to him. Gratitude and apologies were rare from this mob of mandated attendees, it caught her attention. Anna tried to assist him to determine effective goals for himself. Of course there was the usual and obligatory 'Bonnie and Clyde I will die in a hail of cop bullets' fantasy to dispense with. It took 20 minute to pass that hurdle. Anna was astounded to hear Bam's goal.

*"I want to write, my teacher said I was good at it."*

He checked himself out of school at age 12 so that teacher-pupil conversation must have occurred over 30 years ago. Anna was not sure if it was still valid or if the statute of limitations had run on that praise. Suddenly he seemed more childlike than ominous, more desperate and unskilled than truly 'criminal'. Anna stopped this line of thought. She reminded herself that he had spent his life time stealing hard earned property from others. She needed to stay aware of his highly honed criminal skills. She reminded herself that he had never done an honest day's work in his entire life. She doubted that his limited fund of knowledge and lacklustre grammatical prowess was sufficient enough to serve him well as a writer. It was her role to encourage any effort toward industry so she worked to assist him to build on this interest. As she spoke to him about his goal an unspoken argument raged in her mind. She tried to convince herself that half the population spoke like Bam. Most of those she passed on the street, on any given day, did not know a preposition from syntax. Who said someone writing in 'the commonly used language style' could not sell his work? After all William Hung sold millions of songs to those who did not know, or care he was off key. Not everyone sings or hears 'on key'. Self coaching over she forced herself to focus. Bam seemed pleased to be taken seriously, and equally pleased to design homework for himself. He left determined to locate a writing class for himself, at night of course, as that was when he functioned best.

Anna needed to clear her head after Bam. Fortunately the 11:00 am offender was 10 minutes late. She was hungry. The client's lateness gave her the opportunity to bolt down her lunch early. Bits of blue cheese freckled her keyboard as a testimony to her haste and hunger. Blue cheese notwithstanding Anna found Andrew Johnson to be an exceptionally frustrating client. Andrew was her 'three-th' client for the morning. He always got the better of her. What really got to her most about that was that she smiled about it, without exception. She found that to be particularly irritating. He was fishing and she took the bait. She knew he was the master at negating any and all of the potential therapeutic impact of their meetings. He was humorous and personable, even charming. She found herself laughing and letting him off the 'stay-there-and-talk-about-how-you can-change' hook.

In his typical 'let's talk about anyone but me' routine he mentioned the fact his sister in law was pregnant or rather *"preggers"*. Anna knew Andrew's brother was in prison and had been for 2 years. As there were no conjugal visits she asked how his wife could be pregnant. Andrew looked at her with total disbelief. He spelled out the answer for her, slowly, as you would to a small child,

*"I guess she found someone to do 'the m-a-n thing'"*. Anna's embarrassment flushed her neck and face with a creeping red-pink. She absolutely hated it when that happened. Andrew on the other hand, absolutely enjoyed his hit. He waited in silence, revelling in her discomfort, watching the red patch creep its way up her neck. He was smiling.

*"Let's talk about you Andrew. How are you are doing? You said you were struggling with mood swings last time. How have your moods been this week?"*

*"I have had better days, but having said that I do basically feel chipper, thanks. What? So is there a problem with me being chipper now? I am the eternal optimist, I do what I do and I don't actually believe I will get caught. Usually I am right. Sometimes I am not. The only problem with that is I can't go to my kid's show and tell at school. You know other kids take in their dads. Firies\*. Coppers\*. Ambos\*. All uniformed up, telling young eager kids to grow up to be like them. I couldn't really do that could I? 'Look at me bambinos I am a burglar, not just any burglar but the best frickin' burglar I Perth', nah the missus would not like it if I did that... What?"*

He enjoyed flaunting his alleged criminal behaviours. Anna was not sure how proficient a burglar he was but she did know that if she tried the usual focus tactics with this client it would be as ineffective as their time together had been so far.

She tried to hook into his self interest and use that to inspire him to live less recklessly. She reviewed the negative consequences and the dangers of crime. Andrew said,

*"Everything is dangerous Anna. Even gravity. I am right you know. You fall off a building and gravity will kill yah. In fact I have read that in 95% of the fatal falls it's the gravity that kills yah. Ssssheeesh, and gravity is all around yah. No one escapes it, ever. How dangerous is that? How come you have never warned me to stay away from gravity? What kind of a therapist are you?"*

She did not want to smile but she did even as she tried to focus him on the reason he was there, on the various ways therapy could help him. She made the near fatal mistake of saying what they were doing today was not therapy.

*"What do you mean this isn't therapy? Don't you think it is therapeutic for me to make you laugh? Or, blush? Even I need to know I still got 'it'. Ms. Lennox you need to stop drinking the decaf version of life. Besides if there is a God, and if He is watching all we do, we might as well make what we do entertaining for Him."*

Maybe he was right. If God did need entertaining she was sure He would pull up beside Sean over her any day. She let Sean run with the remaining time they had. He repeated full roasted caffeinated accounts of family weddings. He brandished the topic of the competitions that exists between the members of his large Scottish family. He said there is the,

*"'My daughter is uglier than yours competition' which always goes along with, 'but she had a more expensive wedding dress than yours did' competition. And the, 'my daughter had more courses to*

*eat at her wedding that nobody can remember than your daughter did at her wedding' competition".*

He said that the first born babies in his family always come in 7 months. It's a tradition based in a reproductive genetic flaw. It's the one and only contagious genetic abnormality. He knew that because even in the brides who marry into the family, regardless of their ethnic origin had their 1st baby early. But the 2nd babies and all those who follow always come in the usual 9 months. It was a time honoured family tradition.

He verbally careened in and out of family outings, and his more memorable crimes, real or imagined. It was a rerun but it was funny. Anna hoped it was therapeutic for him because she certainly felt better at the end of that session than she did at the end of many others. Even Liz enjoyed the stories when Anna retold them during supervision. Andrew's avoidance was pervasive. Yet she knew she had granted him implicit permission to avoid dealing with his own life. That permission was by proxy contagious and extended to him from unexpected quarters, like Liz.

Andrew was at the end of his orders. All that was left for Anna to do was to send in his final report and hopefully never see him again. Even as she wrote it she knew it was too much to hope for. As she handed Barbara his final report she wondered, was he the one to do the *"m-a-n thing"* with his sister in-law? Then she wondered why she had not wondered that before.

As Anna waited for her next client the phone rang, it was the expected client, the mason. He was wild and woolly. Intense. Unpleasant. If Andrew was coffee, he was fully caffeinated mug of cappuccino coffee, sweet and frothy. The mason, on the other hand, was a short black double shot of bitter coffee. No sugar. No froth. He telephoned Anna to tell her he was *"damned annoyed"* at having to take time off work to see *"some stupid shrink"*. He railed against the judge who ordered him to attend counselling. He threatened that if she forced him to attend he would *"do his block"**. Anna responded,

*"I did not write the orders, a judge did, look it's your choice, but if you do not attend you will be violated as you have only attended 1 session in 3 to date."* He seemed to unplug from his anger when she suggested he not bring his *"block"* with him to *"do"*.

He arrived 10 minutes late, in a work shirt and shorts, his legs were 'cement grey'. His work boots shed dry cement and yellow sand in her office. He reeked of stale sweat. His hair was long and wild. Usually the missus cut it but he was not likely, given their situation, to sit quietly while she had scissors at his neck level. He was thin and scrawny. He looked like he was wearing himself away with the hard manual labour he slogged at 6 days out of 7.

The mason threw himself into the chair and told Anna 'the block' was parked outside but he knew where it was and if he needed it he would get it, and he would 'do it'. He then railed on how it was *"not fair"*, on how he was *"not really a criminal"*. True enough his only charges related to an assault on his wife, and his subsequently violating the restraining orders she had been granted to protect her. The mason was adamant that Anna needed to understand that it was his missus' fault anyway. The missus knew how to press his buttons, she knew what would upset him, and she did it – frequently. She was *"The Great Button Pusher of Perth"*. And, *"Anna if you had done your job and read the reports you would know all of this"* he accused.

*"Besides"* he grunted, *"I pick my women like I drink my beer, bitter and cold."*

Anna did know 'all this'. She had read the reports. However her JDF did not require her to memorise them. She resisted informing him of that fact. He knew she had spoken to his missus, he had given her permission to do so. She had read the judge's admonition to her against entrapping and enticing her husband to violate the restraining orders. In fact, given the history of their matrimonial bait and 'gotcha' interactions, the judge warned her that it would be unlikely that she would be granted another restraining order.

The mason could have requested that the restraining order be lifted. The court transcript reported that he had told the judge he wanted the missus *"to feel safe"*. Anna doubted she could teach him to be self protective or rescue him from his misplaced and warped sense of matrimonial chivalry. If stupidity was a crime he was guilty, and in his case when stupid rained stupid poured.

Trying to make him understand that regardless of what the missus did, he was responsible for his own reactions, fair or not, was mission impossible. Anna knew she did not get through to him. He didn't need a therapist, he needed a mother. He left the session feeling as mistreated as he did when he arrived. He left with as much anger as he had brought to the session. And he was in as much danger of violating the restraining order yet again and ending up back in jail as he had been prior to the session. His 'in' button was broken. Sometimes successes were thin on the ground. Anna sighed.

As the work day ground to its conclusion PP slipped a note under her door reminding Anna that it was time for the team meeting. The staff gathered around the table listening to the same jokes about offending behaviour. They were all sleep-deprived. Exhausted or not they must remain vigilant. They were wary of Charlotte, the manager's tongue. She could verbally slice staff into pieces in 20 words or less. She left their bits flailing on the floor. She was highly skilled at it and practiced her art frequency. She was not particular where she engaged in her tirades, in the hallways, the lunch room, in front of an audience, in seclusion, or in the public parking lot. If it had to be said, she said it.

The staff-meeting jokes deflected away from staff politics and focused the staff upon topics other than their fear of her. The talk stayed within safe parameters. They laughed too loud at managerial jokes, gave Charlotte too much credit for her masterful supervision, *"if it wasn't for Charlotte's help with Mr. Evans I would not have known what to do…"* To counter the rising cynicism she felt Anna began thinking about the bald 'Warro' and his claim to earn 50 grand a week. Anna wondered what 50 grand a week, tax free, would look like and what she would do with it. She was startled to realise she had doodled a money tree.

The names and faces of the Probation Officers at the table changed regularly. As the more experienced officers left, younger uninitiated officers arrived to take their place. They were eager to help the criminals and contribute to the Greater Good. They soon discovered the energy it took to negotiate Charlotte. Their focus shifted from saving the world from criminals, or criminals from prison, to political survival within their own careers. No one was deluded. It was a game that was played in earnest, based on her predation toward young world changers. Everyone knew the rules. When the game got the better of them, they did the only thing they could, they quit. They returned to the florist shop, or the service station, or the family business. They left with their regrets over the money and time they had poured down the drain of their future by earning a degree in criminology or related field. Some lasted a year, most less than 6 months.

Charlotte took her permanent level 8 spot at the head of the very long Government issued table and ruled supreme. She fixed her attention upon one officer after another in seeming random, pouncing first upon one then another and back again.

The various offenders and the stories Anna had encountered that day in her office replayed through her mind. She sat absently and wordlessly in the meeting trying to encapsulate the last few hours. Finally time to leave. And leave she did, quickly, tugging on the handle of her office on wheels, dragging it over the curbs and sidewalk, tossing it into the boot* of her car.

•••••

# 3

## Cory Henderson

*I*t was Tuesday evening. Anna had one of her weather headaches, the kind that preceded a storm. She was scheduled to work in Port Stirling the next day and did not relish the thought of driving impaired by pain. It was late August, almost spring in the southern hemisphere. The weather bureau, not given to over statement, had predicted 'unsettled rain'. At 10:00 pm, unannounced, the sky exploded. Frequent erratic lightning slashed at the earth and sky producing a disco strobe light effect. The residents below startled at its deafening rifle crack. The rolling ever increasing roaring-sleep-chasing-kid-scaring-heart-stopping-window-rattling din of thunder rocked the earth. This riot of multiple explosions shook their home. Anna, Lachie and Stuart stood, in their pyjamas, by the open second floor window, generously sprayed by the rain ricocheting from the ground level veranda roof below. They were entranced and awed by the chaos raging around them. Words weren't necessary. Max slept on. It was a gift.

The morning television news displayed visual images of the city's nocturnal experience. It was a stunning, far ranging violent sky show. Some areas had received 50 mm of rain; others were thrashed by ferocious rain and wind. Streets were strewn with tree limbs and anything else the wind could tear free, grab and hurl. A rare tornado tore through the Western suburbs and reduced a school to brick and steel rubble. Metal sheeting had been ripped from walls and rooves and now hung perilously, swinging erratically from overhead electric wires. Huge metropolitan areas were without electric power. Theirs wasn't one of them, although the blinking digital clocks attested to the fact that power had been lost and restored quickly through the night. They did not know it when they bought their home but they were on the same electrical grid as the nearby hospital. When power was lost and restored their grid received it first.

Headache free Anna drove south to Port Stirling. The grey/black sky was illuminated by the full arc of a vibrantly coloured rainbow. The weather was grovelling to the inhabitants below, begging for forgiveness to atone for its temper tantrum a few hours earlier. The rainbow apology stretched above the freeway like a long-lasting arch, tantalisingly close but resolutely untouchable. The colours were intense. The rainbow was directly in front of her. It was her constant companion travelling with her for most of the drive. She hoped it was an omen for the day.

Crystal was a frighteningly beautiful child. She was 19, and had a 4 year old daughter. Crystal was slender, with the body of a 13 year old. Her clothes were juvenile in style, her makeup and hair from some teen magazine. Her beauty was riveting. She was curled up, well as curled as anyone could get in that Government issued chair. In a flat monotone voice she told a horrid tale of childhood abuse, neglect and abandonment. She recited it as if it was someone else's story, or a grocery list. Not once did she look at Anna. Although addicted to amphetamines her hands were still. Her facial complexion gave evidence that it was clearing with healed over scabs and new skin. While she shifted in her chair as though she was uncomfortable she did seem to be improving physically. She said she had not used drugs in a few days.

Her story revealed that she had ditched school at the beginning of 8th grade. Anna did the mental computation quickly, and ascertained that due to her being held back 2 grades Crystal left school at age 14. She was 'taken in' by some kind street soul who promptly pimped her and introduced her to drugs. Crystal would not have been able to identify when the concrete set, cementing her to that situation, but cement her it did, physically, mentally and emotionally.

A scruffy female associate accompanied her to care for her daughter while Crystal was in session. Paid help was an unattainable concept at this socio economic level. Her daughter broke free from her bored warden and bashed her tiny fists and feet against the other side of the door. She screamed for her mother. Crystal did not notice. Anna tried not to be distracted by the racket, the child's screaming voice and sobs as she begged for her mother, but she could not concentrate. Anna had to end the session to preserve her own sanity. They rescheduled.

A newly assigned Probation Officer appeared in her doorway,

*"Since you have a few minutes can we chat?"* 'Chat' was not exactly what Anna wanted to do. Her head pounded from the noise and chaos. She needed to analyse Crystal's story, and formulate an effective treatment plan before her next session. Instead she chatted. The Probation Officer spoke about inconsequential stuff and an offender with minor offences. Anna knew it was not about the offender but about the Probation Officer. A recent staff transfer from Fremantle, she was reaching out to connect with a familiar face. And to be welcomed and safe to do so in a Charlotte free

environment. Anna's attention peaked when she said she was from rural Kalgoorlie. The Probation Officer was disoriented by the move to the city. It was not the work load as the Kalgoorlie staff often worked hours beyond what they were paid. They learned to adjust their practices in order to serve the Aboriginal community. They worked together as a unit. It was a different kind of team work than she had encountered in the city. She liked the 'Kalgoorlie way' better. Anna could understand her point as this Probation Officer had not experienced effective team work at Fremantle. Anna hoped she would fare better in Port Stirling.

During the break between clients Anna walked to the new foreshore in Port Stirling. There were several strip malls lining the streets which were massively unremarkable in design and presentation. As it was a new area many store windows sported 'For Sale', or 'For Lease' signs. However one that was inhabited and welcoming was Franny's Korner. She baked muffins, not ordinary muffins. These muffins had to be laced with something addictive. They were huge and bursting with fruit. Franny was a dear, always cheerful, no matter what the weather or the profit margins. Anna ordered a large chunky muffin, raspberry, bananas and chocolate bites. Who would think of putting raspberries and bananas and tiny chocolate bites in the same muffin, crowning it with large chips of brown sugar? Only Fran and only she could make it work. The aroma of the various coffee blends, the fresh baked foods were compelling.

Fran chattered about the recent storm. Her home, which clung to the hillside by the Indian Ocean, took the full blast of the wind and the horizontal rain. The damage caused by water blasting through her windows and up under her eaves was minor but annoying. She'd handle it. She then switched the topic to her soon to be business neighbour. He was a well known local photographer who would sell his wares from this store front. He had computer enhanced pictures of the area, the ocean, the sand dunes, the birds and sea life, the glorious sunsets on canvas, stretched over large frames. She would display his framed and stretched photographs. He would let her put two tables on the pavement in front of his store. He had offered to decorate her window like it was the back wall in a 1950's diner. Anna was pleased the store front neighbours were getting along so well but did wonder why Fran was discussing their business agreement with her. She figured it was an occupational hazard. Once others knew she was a psychologist they often immediately thought she was interested in the minute details of their lives. If only they knew.

Anna found a table by the window and sidled into the chair. Beneath the brilliant blue photographed and stretched rendition of the nearby sandy beach of Geographe Bay she savoured the warm early spring sun. She delicately removed each sugar chip from its muffin place individually with her tongue, then she invited the totality of the muffin decadence and the Irish Cream latte to radiate her senses.

Another session, another offender. The young man sitting in front of her had doe's eyes, black, and meaningful. His eyes ambushed you and compelled you to dive in. No they dragged you in. Smiling. He was handsome, with perfect facial symmetry, a thick shock of black hair and an unassuming air. Dangerous. Maybe.

He was dressed in a dark blue gabardine shirt and black jeans, but he wore them like a high end suit. His highly polished dress shoes had slick leather soles. He was slender and moved with the grace of a ball room dancer, even though he did not dance. His appearance was an anomaly. His feet looked like they were going to a wedding. His clothes looked like he had come to fix the leak under the sink. He moved as if he was doing neither. His expression said he was really, yes really, interested in what Anna had to say. He was not flirtatious, or trying to disarm her with sensuality, he seemed to connect intellectually and emotionally to her intervention.

It was an unusual session, to say the least. This offender actually asked for help. He seemed to track and comprehend the content and process of their exchange.

Anna checked the referral form in his file to see how long she would have to work with him. Two years, one year beyond her contract, at least they had time to do some significant work. Unlike many of the time crunched officers; Katy his Probation Officer had actually completed the form this time. He left with a list of eagerly received out-of-session assignments. Cory Henderson turned back to flash Anna a smile and to mouth *"thank you"*. She felt exceptionally pleased with herself. In the line up of those who had to see her or be violated was one who wanted to be there, and wanted to work on his issues. Amazing. Maybe.

Had Anna met him elsewhere she would have thought of him as a tradesman, who happened to have had a run in with the law. Meeting him as a client of the Department of Prisons and Corrections she was inclined to define him as 'an offender', end of story. She wondered how this reframing of the clients affected her treatment of them. Criminals, offenders or tradesmen? Did it matter how she categorised them?

*"Perhaps something does happen to us in criminology that stops us from facing the fact that there is no demarcation between 'us*

and 'them'. Is that why we set them in a different category than we do ourselves?" Anna asked herself. She grinned when she realised she was unable or unwilling to answer her own question.

That night in the darkness of their room as they held hands between their bed sheets Anna talked to Max about this. He said he had often wondered how, or if she could forever compartmentalise her clients and put them in boxes where she or he or the boys did not belong. He said he had long wondered if her work would impact her view of the world, or him, or herself. She dismissed what she called 'his philosophical ranting'. They had better things to do than talk.

●●●●●

# 4

## A Mixed Bag

Thursday was Port Stirling's turn again. It was scheduled to be a busy day. The new security guard there was a jolly fellow, far too pleasant to be a guard of any kind. Like PP, he could defuse tense and potentially conflicted situations with his affable, casual approach. Her case load was a mixed bag and thanks to the security guard was relaxed and ready to talk. Most of her clients today were at the light to mid end of the offending continuum. Except two who were seemingly placed in her case load just to keep her clinically interested. They were her first and last scheduled clients of the day.

The first was an unlikely, well seasoned, habitually violent female thug. At first glance few would identify the young female seated in front of Anna as a habituated criminal. The many psychiatric reports in her file revealed a mixed history of offending and multiple mental health diagnoses. She was British born. Her parents migrated to Australia when she was 3 years old. The father soon abandoned them and fled back to London, alone. Her mother was overwhelmed with raising two daughters in a strange, brown land. She was little more than a child herself when the client was born. Her mother slid down the neck of a wine bottle and stayed there most of her hours. The children were left to fend for each other and themselves.

When the client was 8 years old her father travelled back to Australia. During one of the many brutal altercations with his ex wife, he held a knife to her mother's throat. The client had witnessed it, but just left the room. She ignored her mother's terrified screams for help. She walked outside into the garden area and rode her bicycle on the driveway outside her home. She kissed her father 'goodbye' when he left for the last time. She did not go inside the house to see if her mother was dead or alive until well after sunset. She only went inside the house then as she was hungry. Her mother was alive but bleeding, rocking and crying, holding a dish rag to her throat. The client made herself a jam sandwich and watched TV. She ignored her little sister's pleas for food.

Schooling was a nuisance to her. She never did engage with the academic process. She had no intention of allowing it to interfere with her daily plans. Her skills were low, yet her presentation and vocabulary made it appear she was well educated. As a young teenager she was diagnosed as having Attention Deficit Disorder with Hyperactivity. She was medicated with dexamphetamine. Then the diagnosis was changed to depression with anxiety, yet her appetite for speed remained. She was creative at using and inventing various resources to procure it.

She was of slight build, and even though 5'10" tall, appeared much smaller due to her light frame. She looked scrubbed and clean, and almost demure. Her finger nails were immaculately kept, every nail was filed to the same length and French polished. She moved with the grace of a ballerina. She spoke with a slight English accent. Nothing about her indicated her potential for violence.

When she was not speaking, she puckered her lips together tightly. She then forced air into various areas of her mouth, one at a time. She moved air in and out of the skin covered cheek cavities. If she was not talking her face became bored and needed something to do.

Empathy or even awareness that she should consider or care that anything she did had a negative impact on others was beyond her capacity. Two years previously she had slashed her younger sister with an effectively sharp knife. She struck her sister's liver and pancreas, leaving her ill for life. When asked how she felt about that the client stated *"I'm fine, it doesn't worry me"*.

Anna was sure that she should be assessed to rule out Reactive Attachment Disorder or Aspergers/Autism but the Probation Officer was reticent to order such an assessment. In a perfect world Anna's first choice would be to order an assessment by the only effective treatment centre Anna knew for these disorders, but it was in Seattle, Washington. The department had no financial ability and no real will to remediate this disorder. In fact, the department was not sure it was a bona fide diagnostic category. Secondly the officers had all been warned that although it was only part of the way through the financial year, all funds for external testing had been exhausted. They could not afford bus fare for her to travel to Perth to see a psychiatrist let alone Seattle.

Anna emailed back and forth to various funding sources for her young English client for two weeks. She consulted with the centre manager in person and the disbursement officer by telephone. She lobbied hard to procure effective assessment and intervention for her. This frenetic activity ceased when the Probation Officer notified Anna that the client had re-offended. She was now a guest of the women's prison. No one would post bail for her so there she remained the prison's guest, awaiting trial. This was another violent random crime committed as she pursued funding for her 'medication'. She followed a wealthy shopper to her vehicle. As the shopper began to load her bought goods into the rear seat of her expensive vehicle, the young English thug struck. The victim was lucky to have survived. The client was unlucky. The attack was recorded on non self erasing, non grainy security surveillance tape. While the presence of the cameras may have upset her, Anna was sure she would feel 'fine' about the damage she had inflicted on the hapless shopper's body and soul. She wondered how the victim felt.

Stuart called Anna during her lunch break. *"Mum can I stay at Tom's place tonight?"* He had soccer practice after school itself. This made it a long school day for him. Anna answered,

*"No son be home before I get there. It is a school day tomorrow so you cannot be hanging out with friends tonight".* He responded

*"Mum, did you forget that tomorrow is a pupil free day, no school?"* Anna said *"Oh okay son, I did forget that. But it is not a work free day for me, I will need you home to watch Lachie, please be home at 10:00am. I will stay there until then. Call me tonight before you go to bed."* He would, he did. She cancelled her early morning clients.

Stuart arrived home on Friday at 10:00 am as promised. Once Stu was safe at home she left for work, arriving later than usual. The two boys arranged to go to a movie in the city and call her when they arrived back home. Anna felt uneasy when the boys travelled on trains or any public transportation since she began work with the Department. It was there that she had learned how many offenders, of necessity, rode the trains and buses during the day, on Department issued TransPerth passes. She was soon distracted from that thought as it was a busy day in Port Stirling. Only five offenders were scheduled due to her shortened day.

The first name in Anna's appointment book was Thomas Gilroy. He was one of the least complex clients in her case load. He was a petty thief, on community based orders as his crimes did not rise to imprisonment. Anna was surprised to see Crystal in the waiting room. Crystal had organised an emergency session. She had called the secretary in Fremantle and begged for the first opening as her last session was cut short due to her daughter. She promised to arrange off site care for the child. She was in luck; unbeknown to Anna, Thomas had cancelled his session. Crystal saw Anna's surprised expression and quickly explained the situation.

*"I am glad you could see me today. I do need to talk, really talk"* she said. Her skin was clearer than it was yesterday. Her most recent urine test had come back negative for drugs. Anna marvelled at the recuperative value of a week free from drugs, especially methyl amphetamine.

Crystal accurately chronicled her story. She quietly described trauma focused and abusive parents. This time she told it as though it was her story and she actually connected with it. Her vocal volume remained low. She hyperventilated when discussing the years of sexual abuse and emotional and parental abandonment. She suspected that her mother was a 'working girl'. Wordlessly she punched her thighs with her clenched fists after she disclosed that at 10 years of age she was told that her mother was indeed a prostitute. Her mother offered to teach Crystal 'the trade'. At ten years of age! Crystal's verbal output remained barely audible. Anna dare not ask her to increase the volume.

When Crystal was 14 years of age she fled parental prostitution.

However prostitution waited for her with outstretched arms on the street amongst her new found very best 'friends'. She convulsed with sobs at session's end. Anna kindly warned Crystal that the session exhausted her and she suggested she *"take it easy"* for a day or two.

The remaining four offenders scheduled or rescheduled for the day attended their sessions, on time. Each was a particularly challenging case. One in particular concerned her for diagnostic reasons. During her late and brief lunch Anna consulted with Port Stirling Mental Health on his behalf. All the signs indicated this offender was entering a manic phase. One of Anna's favourite Professors often said *"mania and crime are sisters that drag each other down the same path"*. This client had almost killed his family during his last manic phase. Anna needed to act quickly to prevent his entering another full blown episode.

The client required psychiatric oversight to lessen his potential for re-offending. He needed medication, and maybe even hospitalisation. And he needed them now. He had no private funds or insurance, so he'd have to use the public system. Anna knew she could not suggest a diagnosis to the psychiatrist, protocol demanded that she only describe symptoms. The doctor was the only one qualified to make the diagnosis and plan the intervention. A master's level therapist had no business telling a psychiatrist how to diagnose a client. She talked to the duty doctor. He did not seem to understand the urgency Anna felt. She explained the offender's episodic violence during what looked like manic phases. She explained that she had noted intertwined periods of what looked like depression, pending further diagnosis of course. She begged the ear on the end of the phone to listen to her. The duty doctor's anger escalated. He had an identified enemy. A government paid psychologically trained master's level pushy employee.

The voice on the phone told her to write her concerns and a list of the presenting symptoms and send them to him. He would then decide if, or which course of action to implement. Anna stayed pleasant.

She used the rest of her lunch hour to hurriedly list the history and presenting symptoms and fax it with the release of information signed by the offender. The voice called back, they made him an appointment. Tomorrow. Anna visibly shook with relief.

Her client load was becoming more complex than she could have imagined. Where was Thomas Gilroy when she needed him? She had read about her last client but she would not have predicted his presentation. His criminality outdid the English girl's by spades. He was a well dressed and muscular forty year old male. He had long blonde hair tied in a neat and brushed pony tail. Surf and sun had tanned and life had etched his face, making his face appear older than his stated age. He had an ever ready smile. He wore a tight fitting short sleeved shirt. To advertise his attributes he had rolled up the already short sleeves to expose his killer biceps and associated biker tattoos. His jeans were equally tight.

Tony Trapone spoke with a lyrical almost musical tone with a slightly gritty element. It could be described as 'sexy', 'really sexy', even 'hot'. His self introductory approach was ingratiatingly pleasant. He portrayed the sense that he was entirely comfortable with himself and believed that he was the consummate good guy. He was skilled at instilling that belief in others. At least, for the duration of the first meeting. He had piercing blue eyes and a practiced flirtatious demeanour.

Anna introduced herself and asked how he would react to being counselled by a forensic psychologist. Tony said that the forensic part was not an issue but the fact that she was an attractive woman might be. He watched carefully to compute Anna's response to that comment. Had Anna not read his record she may have been charmed, instead she was alarmed. He noted it.

Anna was pleased Crystal had cleared the building as she knew she would be vulnerable to Tony's version of predation.

Tony was an entrepreneur who founded and developed a vast state wide empire within the security industry. Tony had named his company 'The Guardians'.

It was a duly certified and legally registered company. He was tight lipped about his dealings and the activities of The Guardians. Unbeknown to Tony a specialised Organised Crime Police task force had compiled a thorough brief explaining the extent and nature of his business dealings, brutality and crimes. The brief had been couriered to Anna a week ago. It read like the script of a block buster movie. She was riveted to it through to the end.

Tony's trained army of uniformed security guards operated as the bouncers at night clubs. They were the keepers of the peace at special events. They operated the metal detecting doorways in secured buildings, such as the Courts and the personal banking areas of banks that pander to the wealthy.

When The Guardians were assigned to guard the entrances to various venues their placement had little to do with securing the building or event. Their presence was strategic placement of personnel. They knew which drug dealers to allow into events and which to keep from attending. Those who belonged to Tony's network were given priority; those who paid Tony a sizeable fee received a second tier registration entrance. Those in neither group were not admitted. Ever.

It was great press when the investigative reporters blazed headlines about the many drug dealers identified and kept out of the family event by The Guardians. Such headlines told the good people that they were safer because of The Guardians. They reiterated to the drug world that only those who belonged to, or paid Tony the required fee would be admitted. Non payers risked being exposed by the unwitting reporters. Such reports reassured the readers, on both sides of the issue that The Guardians were in control. The family events, or rock concerts, or private parties, or night clubs were no safer from drug lords with The Guardians on watch. The dealers who were present had bought their ticket. This negated the possibility of turf wars. Tony was in control, at least of this domain.

Tony had another army of trained security system installers. They lay kilometres of electrical cables and outfitted alarms in the most opulent of Perth's homes and businesses. They particularly focused on the Western suburbs where real estate was the most expensive in the country. Here the lords and ladies of society demonstrated their wealth in bricks and mortar and verdant manicured gardens behind wrought iron electric gates. The Guardians knew where the wires were should they need to be cut at any time. They knew how to install and maintain the impressive state of the art tamper proof alarms they sold. They also were the only ones who knew how to neutralise them with the touch of a key on a computer keyboard kilometres away.

Additionally they wired and rewired the security systems of the club houses, businesses and private homes of gang members.

Rivals could cut but they could not disable the security systems in facilities guarded by The Guardians. In the establishments likely to be targeted by rivals The Guardians ran blinds and double blinds to disguise and protect the actual operating systems. Any errant computerised access to the security systems was equally protected.

Tony employed his adult step son, Gary to break into the prestigious businesses or homes and trip the alarms. He would be chased away by the ever vigilant Guardians, who were parked just around the corner. Gary returned to the home or business a few minutes later, dressed in his Guardian uniform, looking more like a Police Officer than a criminal. He encouraged that client to call the local newspaper and tell them what happened. He advised the homeowner that a rash of such burglaries had happened in that immediate area. He explained that the homeowner now had a duty of care to ensure that the neighbours who were not protected by a Guardian alarm system understood that they needed to be. The traumatized homeowner was often open to suggestion and desperate not to have his neighbours experience burglary. As occurs in traumatized settings the rescuer is idealized and over trusted. Gary was that rescuer, and due to the circumstance his instructions took on the power of a hypnotic suggestion. His directions were usually followed. If the distressed homeowner could convince others to become alarmed and protected by The Guardians (did they not respond immediately?) it would mean something good came out of his own distress.

In the unlikely case that the homeowner was resistant to the idea Tony's executive assistant made sure that the reporters of local newspapers knew who it was that saved the day. The reporters at the major newspapers were not usually interested. The reporters at the local suburban newspapers were bored and leapt at news that made them look 'investigative'. Tony called them his 'print whores'. He didn't care if it was front page or page 6 as long as it was printed.

Tony and his armies were bikies. Some were bald with red beards and others presented as respectable businessmen. Others looked like hard working tradies, which they were. Some were mules, some were nominees, some were patched up members but all were Tony's boys at heart. And they were genuine bikies, bona fide, no imitations tolerated.

Tony's third army was the drug arm of the business. This was a tightly controlled network of home bakers who specialised only in amphetamine production. The youngest baker was a 17 year old virgin high school science nerd with acne whom no one would suspect of such activity. Tony's oldest baker was a 68 year old grandmother who had recently acquired the ability to make good gear. Tony's outfit was organised with military precision. The bakers were assigned to distributors who then worked on their own customer base. Each segment of this business stream was protected by The Guardians. Tony made many millions a year from this arm of the business. It was more lucrative than the security business. The business side of the Guardians was labour intensive to oversee. Tony needed it as a legitimate front through which to launder the excessive riches 'amphets' amassed for him. With the introduction of the 'unexplained wealth taxation law' he had to explain to the taxation department the origin of his fortune. One of the most influential accounting companies in Perth prepared that explanation.

Tony's long criminal history described a vicious warrior who ran his own war of weapon procurement and drug distribution. He lived hard, he partied hard and he put many of the women who had loved him in hospital or women's refuges. When one of his ladies begged entrance into a refuge she was turned away and dissuaded by the Police from insisting on admittance. Her being there would endanger the staff and other clients. The confidential and suppressed addresses were not suppressed to him. Tony knew the location of each refuge.

When Tony was aged twenty two he lived in the gold fields' area in Kalgoorlie, Western Australia. His female partner disappeared. The story he told was that she had just taken off, gone, left him with her two boys, Gary and Phillip. He had raised them. What else could he do? What else indeed? After all they needed a home. Their old man was a drop kick; the little boys had no one but him, Tony.

Anna knew it would be a rare woman who would go interstate never to be seen again, leaving her two young sons with a non relative. Anna thought a more likely end to that story was that their mother's mummified or desiccated body would one day be found down a dry, hot, abandoned mine shaft in Kalgoorlie. This was the one story about his life that Tony would tell, up to a point, and as he did he oozed testosterone.

He described himself as

*"A good mate who liked to ride a Harley for recreation, and that was it "*. Anna knew that was not a fraction of 'it' but today her goal was not confrontation but to attempt to establish non sexualised rapport with this highly sexualized offender. She soon realized she had her work cut out for her.

Tony had been arraigned on organised crime charges when it was discovered that many of the richest of Perth's homes were systematically robbed. They all had one thing in common, they were protected by a state of the art, newly installed, tamper proof Guardian Security System. Tony was arrested. With that one arrest an empire collapsed. Or so the Police said. His armies were unemployed. Temporarily.

The Police loudly congratulated themselves on the televised nightly news and in print media headlines. But before the local newspaper could print the full glory of their victory Tony had sold his list of clients and home and business security plans to an alternate 'brother' club. 'Sold' is too permanent a description for what happened, it was more 'rented'. Once Tony took care of the little legal misunderstanding the list would be 'sold' back to him, the rightful owner. But between now and then he needed to cleanse the records of any 'misperception' his security empire was involved with drugs. The only thing that had actually changed, and that change was temporary, was the name of the mongrel at the top of the dog pile.

Anna left the office quickly; she later described her exit to Max as 'fleeing'. She shook out her hair, removed her shoes and suit jacket and sat. The breeze cooled her face and arms as the creep meter imbedded in the back of her neck settled. Once she felt released from Tony Trapone she started the engine and drove to Fran's store. She picked up half a dozen fresh baked muffins and drove home, bare footed, windows down, radio blaring.

●●●●●

# 5

## Sunset at the River

13 year old Stuart and 9 year old Lachie enjoyed the movie. They safely negotiated the train home; they played computer games and kicked the soccer ball around through the late afternoon. The fact they could be trusted in this manner made Anna proud. Anna, Max and the boys took the food from the table, and the fresh muffins, placed them in a picnic basket and transported the lot to McCallum Park. The evening weather was gentle; the breeze wove them together. Spring in this part of the world was Anna's favourite season. Max and Anna relaxed on a blanket on the grass across the river from the city of Perth. The boys wrestled each other, talked to other people's dogs and intermittently kicked a soccer ball. They laughed and squawked. All was well with the world.

Sunset is a sudden affair in Australia. Day leaves no lingering 'farewell'. You have to be quick not to miss it. One moment the sun is there, the next a spectacular but brief rotation of brilliant colours, reflected from the sky to buildings, to the river, next to the first star and then the inky sky. Darkness falls, without warning. Perth at night is gracious, not dazzling like New York, it is not incessantly busy like London, not magical like Seattle, but gracious. Tonight Anna knew why her American friend Cindy called it 'the pretty city'.

Dogs came by walking their owners, families ate, children

played, adults gossiped and the lights of the city slipped their image into the Swan River. The world of offenders seemed decades away. It was a fitting entrance to the weekend.

During the drive home the boys were verbally sparring and Anna switched off. Then Lachlan introduced the topic of his new teacher. At first Anna did not connect with what he was saying. But something in his tone caught her attention.

*"Mum my teacher is mean; I know she does not like me. Today I had a spelling test. I am always slow at writing in cursive so I printed the answers. That is how I got the test finished before she rang the bell. I got 105 out of 100 because I was the only one to know how to spell the bonus word 'arachnid', a-r-a-c-h-n-i-d."* Lachie then described that when she received his paper Ms. Hopkins removed him from the class, marched him outside and 'yelled' at him until he cried. Lachie said that he knew she wanted him to cry. She would not stop yelling until he did. He did not want to cry but he could not help it. He began to cry again, Anna reached back and held his hand. Anna decided to talk to the teacher, Ms. Hopkins, the next Monday.

The following day was Saturday. They had a funeral to attend. They had been advised of the need to attend, late, in fact the telephone call did not come until Friday evening. A major player in Max's circle of colleagues had passed. He was 75 years of age and died at his desk, sitting bolt upright. It was 2 hours before anyone noticed he had died. Max did not know the deceased well. Anna did not know him at all. He was the founding CEO of the company. It was expected, even demanded that Max and his wife would attend the funeral. The fact it was on a Saturday was inconsequential. Anna's sister came by early to take the boys to tennis practice and

Max and Anna set off for a funeral.

Anna and Max found a rare shaded parking space at Karrakatta Cemetery. They located the funeral procession for Bernie. They stood more quietly than respectfully by the gorgeous, spotless black funeral cars in the cool of the morning. Max was shocked to learn that Bernie had been in the military. He later wondered why it surprised him as Bern was of 'the age' that most of his generation 'went to war'. The Australian flag draped casket, the solemnity of the mourners, the deliberately comforting design of the gardens around them, added to the ambience.

Max and Anna joined the 50 or so others equally obligated to attend. The attendees dutifully walked behind the funeral cars. The procession wound slowly down the long drive to the chapel. Max was not one to spend time in cemeteries and he had certainly not spent much time in this one. The combination of well established trees, of varying textures, the roses, the plaques commemorating a life, aged 18, aged 23, aged 88 provided a rich canvas upon which to paint one's own idea of the departed, or even departing itself. Could a life of 18 or 23 or 88 years be so unremarkable that it was adequately marked with a metal plate half the size of a small envelope?

Suited, hat wearing and overly respectful women guided them with gloved hands to a wooden pew type seat in the chapel. It really was a remarkable building. A garden with a glass roof protected mourners from the prospect, or even the concept of rain. The focus of the room was an ornately bordered frosted glass sky light above a semi circle enclave where the casket silently lay. Light fittings looked enough like angels to comfort the faithful but enough not like them to offend the irreligious as they threw a softened glow. A purpose built building to comfort all and offend none of the dead or the grieving.

The eulogy was as canned as the music, although it was not polite to say so. The memorized often spoken words recited by the overly reverent women could have been spoken over anybody and been accurate.

*"Remember him when he laughed, remember him when he cried, remember him when he was splendid and remember him when he was not. Just remember him. To those who liked him the family says 'thank you', to those who loved him the family says 'celebrate him'."*

Bern was a nasty bastard and Max had problems thinking any one really loved him, although it was not proper to give voice to such a sentiment. A well dressed blonde woman was sobbing. Snotty, noisy, nose blowing sobbing. Why on earth was she so distraught? She worked in a branch that was at least 30 kilometres away from Bern, she had little to do with him socially, or did she? At the final receiving line Max heard her tell the 'not grieving' widow that she was projecting herself into the future imagining how it would be when her own husband died. That explained it. Her tears had nothing to do with Bern and everything to do with herself. Max thought it was rather loud and ill placed narcissism. He checked himself, was he thinking like Anna, 'narcissism'? It was the first time he recalled using that word.

This was a funeral for the non religious. No comfort in heaven, no prayer, no talk of the love of God. Just syrupy, oft spoken 'paid for' secular words and overly reverent bought sentiment that was later described by those who attended as *"simple yet classy"*. When she heard them say that Anna thought *"meaningless and bought and paid for"* more aptly described it. She kept that thought quarantined, even from Max.

As they walked back up the long drive way to their vehicle Anna said

*"I think that is an azure blue sky".* She was not really sure what 'azure blue' was but when she had seen it written or heard the phrase spoken it seemed to describe the brilliant blue that canopied them today. She knew it was a diversion. The funeral was as void of real sorrow as her own heart over the final goodbye to Bernard Leigh Conaughton. She knew if Lachie was there he would say the sky was really anything but blue, according to the colour spectrum. The colour that was missing was the colour the object appeared to be. How do you shut a kid up when he crawls into your head and comments from inside? It's hard enough to shut him up when he is on the outside?

*"Want lunch?"* asked Max.

*"Sure."*

Lunch it was in a Tudor style cafe overlooking the Swan River. The company was pleasant, the service was non intrusive, the crunchy rolls were stuffed with delicious fresh salads and chicken and the coffee was hot. The air was fresh and cool; it felt like cider and was intoxicating. What a wonderful lunch for a Saturday? They delayed their home going.

●●●●●

# 6

# A Dilemma with Dr. Tan

*"I* have a new P.O., this is the 3rd new one this year, can't *this department get its shit together?"* Was it two weeks already? Time flies, there was the virtually toothless Mr. Williams. Monday came too soon.

*"Mr. Williams let's talk about your offending behaviour."*

*"Wha'?"*

*"Your offences,"* stated Anna.

*"You can hardly call them 'offences', it's not like I am a criminal or anything."*

*"Mr. Williams, the Statement of Material Facts states you..."* started Anna.

*"Oh shit you don't believe everything you read do you, the coppers\* write what they want. Haven't you read the papers lately? The cops are totally corrupt, especially around here. A stash of cash and firearms disappeared from the middle of the cop shop across the street. Now who do you suppose took that? I will tell yah, it was no one who looks like me,"* spat Jack Williams.

*"Mr. Williams regardless of what others do we need to discuss your offending behaviour."*

*"Its 'Jack', I already told you. Look, I really do have to go. The doctor is adjusting my 'done again."*

*"Up or down?"* asked Anna, more dutifully than out of genuine care for this toothless man.

*"Up - a bit, just temporarily, to help me through this, he said there is no need for me to do this the hard way. He understands what it is to come off drugs, he realises how good I am doing to be this far into recovery. It's all good, I am doing good."*

*"Mr. Williams will you sign a release for me to contact him?"* she asked.

*"Yeah, next week."*

*"No, now."*

*"I don't want you two yarning\* about me behind my back"* quipped Jack.

*"Sign here, you are releasing me, to discuss your case with Dr. Tan, and him to consult with me."*

Williams signed the form, took the pen with him and left. Anna typed an email to his doctor, requesting to discuss the case with him. She scanned the release to Dr. Tan and had some coffee.

She checked her email, Charlotte had cyber summoned her to her office. That was quick. Her shoulder blades snapped together and a hot knifed slice through her upper back. She went with her coffee.

*"Anna, Dr. Tan just called me, apparently you forced an offender against his will to sign a release so that you two could confer."* Silence. Anna felt no compulsion to respond, she knew how this was going to go. She was just grateful the encounter was occurring in an office and not on the stairwell. She was not even that interested in Jack Williams to care. She was doing what she thought she needed to rather than what she wanted to.

*"Dr. Tan refuses to honour the release, he does not want you interfering in his case management of this offender, and wants me to respond to his distress over your actions. He wants my written*

*assurance that you will shred the release and cease from pressur
ing anyone in this manner. You need to understand your boundaries.
You have overstepped the line. It is hardly professional. No matter
how well intentioned you are, you never force an offender to sign
such a release. What were you thinking?"*

Silence. No need to fuel this fire, it had a fuel source of its
own.

*"Look interested, keep the scorn out of your eyes,"* she coached
herself.

*"Dr. Tan is well respected by the Directorate. He is one of the
few psychiatrists who will work with the Department. It's almost
impossible to procure psychiatric services for our guys. Who would
want to work with clients who scare them, threaten them or steal
from them or their staff? Dr. Tan will contact the Directorate about
your highly unprofessional behaviour. He asked the Directorate
to formulate a protocol to protect firstly, offenders, then secondly,
medical practitioners, from the scrutiny of overly officious master's
level therapists. The Directorate will look unfavourably upon any
action that threatens the contract we have with him."*

*"I will consider your input Charlotte, right now I have another
offender scheduled and need to prepare"* offered Anna, desperately
trying not to allow her voice to crack or her neck and face to
colour.

*"Your avoidance and silent insolence will not help you Anna,
you cannot..."*

*"Excuse me."* Anna left mid ridicule. She knew Charlotte did
not usually stop until she, like Lachie's 'mean' teacher had struck
tears, and anguish. Anna did not have the energy for either. She
knew how few psychiatrists wanted to work with the clients the

Department referred to them. In fact she had tried to convince a former colleague to assess her clients. He was a brilliantly skilled diagnostician and was on top of the latest research findings. She knew they needed his services. He was not interested in being frightened or robbed. How could she forget that? That side of the issue had completely eluded her. The politics of this position were new to her. She decided she best apply herself to learning about it, and fast.

One of the Probation Officers realised that Charlotte had done something 'Charlotte' to Anna and gave her a comforting smile. Jason's voice was gentler when he told her that Mr. O'Connor was waiting for her.

*"Morning Mr. O'Connor, how are you today."*

*"Great compartmentalisation Anna,"* she silently congratulated herself and focused on the surly offender in front of her.

She knew Charlotte and Dr. Tan would not let this go. She would have to give them tears and anguish at some time, but not today. She was barely present during the session with Sean O'Connor. She hoped her notes accurately reflected what occurred. She had mindlessly noted some of their interaction. There was no way she could reconstruct the session at a later time.

After Sean came Bam. He asked her to call him 'Bamster', so she did. He had located a night writing class. He brought in some writing to show her. It was more like calligraphy. The letters were meticulously formed, neat, perfect in every way, at least to the untrained observer. She felt herself slowly reconnecting with her present. She was amazed as Bam seemed to genuinely revel in her singular attention and her approval. She took time to look at him. He dressed like an oversized school boy. He had polished his shoes and they were the 'college' type Stu and Lachie wore. A neat ironed shirt was visible beneath a woollen vest. He was aware she was actually 'seeing' his clothes. He felt compelled to explain and told her he had been shopping at the Salvation Army thrift store. He appeared to be as pleased with his purchases as anyone would be with expensive garments.

The content of his writing was rudimentary, almost primitive, but it had charm. It was a biography of his mother's childhood. After her Dr.Tan incident, her lost hour with Sean she found Bam to be a welcome interlude. Each day has its surprises.

Her last session cancelled. Anna decided to drop by her youngest son's school and talk to his teacher personally, rather than discussing her concerns over the phone. She called ahead to let the school know she needed a few moments of Ms. Hopkins's time. The school receptionist would advise the teacher.

The red brick school building was over 100 years old and seemed to have been grown in its place among the arching ghost gums. It looked a lot quainter from the outside than the shabby, poorly designed interior indicated. It was 'picturesque' in a historical postcard way, but it was decidedly not functional. It was not air conditioned. Children were stuffed into rooms with small windows, sweltering in the above century summer heat in early December and February. The well timed summer holidays gave the children and teachers reprieve from the scorching Western Australian summer of mid December through to January.

Anna drove into the school parking lot as classes were ending. Lachie's class had been outside for an activity and was now filing into the building, ready for the home going routine. Ms. Hopkins strode into the hallway. The children formed two columns and pressed up tight against the sides of the hallway. The line ended at the doorway to Lachie's class room. There was adequate space between the children for her to pass along the hallway. Hopkins started screeching,

*"You naughty children look how crowded this is, how can I get by? You make everything so difficult for me."* Anna wondered which hallway she was in. She thought the comment should be *"What good children you are look at the lovely lines you have made, and you left such a nice space for me to walk".* The children visibly shrivelled under Hopkins' scorn. Anna decided that Ms. Hopkins' approach was not situational, it was character based. She knew there was no remedying it. She excused herself from their meeting.

She called Max and said they needed to talk about enrolling their youngest in the same school Stuart attended. They had no budget for the fees and uniforms for this expensive school. Their original plan was to wait until Lachie was in Year 8 and entering high school. They had long ago decided both boys would attend private high school. The one state school in the area had a wretched reputation academically and behaviourally. He could not attend the one acceptable high school in their general area as they lived outside the catchment boundary lines. They were not financially prepared to pay private school fees from the end of Year 4. They had to make a way as they should not, could not leave Lachlan with Ms. Hopkins. Anna telephoned St. Benedict's. It was an excellent school. As Lachlan was wait-listed they informed her they may be able to get him in. The dean of admissions promised he would check the register and get back to her tomorrow.

After dinner, when the dishes were done, and the boys were

showered and in bed and they were lying down in the quietness of their own room Max asked

*"How were the criminals?"*

*"The correct word is 'offenders' and the offenders are easy, it's the office politics that stinks. And staff morale it's the lowest I have encountered anywhere. Staff leave as soon as they arrive, and I can see why."* She was surprised that she actually did want to talk about this.

*"You can't fix the morale of others. You never were one to tread lightly; you need to be more politically astute. I hope you do not get yourself stuck in the quagmire of other's people's business."* Max said.

She considered throwing a tantrum, it might feel good, but on the other hand she was exhausted. It was not only physical tiredness but an exhaustion rooted in trying to talk to him about her needs only to run into his walls of superior knowledge of her inferiority. In Max's universe whatever ailed her was her fault. He knew best about every aspect of life, even aspects he had never visited in person. Her desire to talk fled. Why did she even try? Perhaps the memory of a more tender and connected time inspired her. She knew better than to try to gain support from Max at this point. What was she thinking? She rolled over and went to sleep.

•••••

# 7

# A Sting in His Tail

The next morning, Tuesday, early, Crystal's Probation Officer was in Fremantle preparing for court. She dropped by Anna's office to say that Crystal had called in to advise that she was unable to report to her this week. The Probations Officer's approach was accusatory. Apparently Crystal said that the session she had with Anna had shattered her to the degree she could not do the urine test nor report as ordered. Crystal said that Anna had given her permission to *"take it easy"* so she would. Anna was sure Crystal had a big party to attend the weekend following their 'revelatory' session and she did not want her community based orders to interfere with her merriment. Anna had underestimated Crystal's street cunning. Anna was left with the distinct impression that her kind, well intentioned warning about self care had become a loop hole through which Crystal just drove a 16 wheel truck, and the Probation Officer was the cop writing Anna the infringement ticket.

This day had more than the usual quota of surprises. Sean O'Connor was on the telephone. He sounded distressed and said he needed an emergency session. This was a departure from his usual approach to therapy, especially as he had seen her yesterday. She hoped he did not want to review that session as she still could not recall it. Time was short and she only had her lunch hour to give him. She scheduled him at that time, more from guilt at being 'absent' from his prior session than from a real desire to see him.

*"I have not been entirely honest with you."*

A criminal of his level not being honest, where is the news in that?

*"I owed the bikies a lot of money for drugs, I mean a lot, and because of what I did to pay them I am now facing new charges."*

*"Have you been remanded?"*

*"Yes. The Adders were serious about 'offing' me if I did not pay them. I stole money. I gave it to them. I would rather be facing the courts and jail than the Death Adders. I had to pull a successful robbery. If I failed, and was caught and chucked in the slammer for attempted robbery, they would get me in jail. The walls are only barriers to the good guys. The Adders rule, either side."*

*"I do not know much about their culture* (she always found it best to plead ignorance when discussing patched up bikies), *but I would like to help you process your issues, what do you want to discuss?"*

*"How the hell did I get in this mess? Look at me; I am not the usual low life who skulks in here. If we learn from our mistakes I should be a freakin' genius"*. He paused, regrouped and continued, making sure she was listening, and on board with him. Satisfied that she had taken the bait he continued.

*"Shit, I've seen them doing drug deals here in the toilets right after the pee tests. They squirt clean, get high, leave the building with Elvis."*

*"Sean you are talking about others again. If you intend to get anything out of this you need to talk about who you are, not about others."*

*"I can't. I can't stay focused on anything, and you know that."*

*"Look you are amped, you have just been remanded for trial, you are still learning to relax and just for now, while you are in here, let the fear of the Death Adders go. They are not after you now, you paid the bill. Now you have the more predictable courts to deal with, let's stop, breath, take this a day at a time."* The rest of the session was on containment and anxiety de-escalation.

She did not know about the 'squirt clean, shoot up in the toilets, go home with Elvis' routine. Should she tell Charlotte? What was best practice here? She didn't know the protocol for dealing with confidential session-gained information. The Directorate tells you what not to do, for God's sake 'don't talk to the drug seeking, lying criminal's doctor', but what about this? Where were the rules for best practice? Her head ached.

She emailed Charlotte, she kept it low key, full of 'possible, or 'probable' or 'maybe', or 'you most likely are already aware'.

She typed the email. Anna sat staring at it, finger poised ready to press 'send' wondering if Sean was telling the truth. Was any of Crystal's tale of parental abuse and neglect true? Did she really use Anna's kindness as an excuse that would allow her to party hearty and excuse her failure to report and provide a urine sample? Who were these people? She sent the email.

Max was right on one thing; Anna's world view had changed. Her well educated intervention was supposed to bring change to the offender. Not one of her learned professors had warned her that the clients would resist change in multiple, unpredictable, unmanageable ways, and that she couldn't resist the change they would bring to her.

Back to reality. St. Benedict's called. They had room for Lachlan in his grade due to another boy's family having suffered a 'financial reversal.' Could he start next week? To facilitate his immediate attendance the school had arranged for their own store to assist. They had set aside the uniforms and books Lachie would need. Would she and Max like to attend a parent's orientation meeting on Friday? Whether they liked to or not they would. She called home, Lachie answered the phone. He squealed with delight when she gave him the news that he would be at school with Stu, he ended the call with.

*"I have to go pee."*

As the call ended her computerised calendar reminder pinged announcing that it was time for the weekly staff meeting. By the time she gathered her notes, closed down her office she was a few minutes late. Charlotte was on a roll as Anna entered, she was advising the appropriately awed staff that she had some highly sensitive information concerning drug activities in the toilets. Blah blah blah, what a hero! Shoulder height cameras would be installed. Anna was silent. She never mentioned the drugs in the toilets again. Charlotte never mentioned Dr. Tan again. Trade off. Hero making information deftly exchanged for a reprieve.

Charlotte launched into a loudly announced, full scale investigation to uncover the source of the toilet drugs. She would leave no stone unturned. She sounded more like a detective than a manager of a Centre. *"Role confusion was not usually a good base for action"* thought Anna. Ben, the officer Anna liked said he has heard that The Mob, a bikie gang were flush with drugs and might be involved. In direct opposition to Departmental established practice Charlotte directed all officers working with The Mob's members to turn in names and contact details to her personally for reviewing by the drug squad. Anna reluctantly turned in 'Warro's' details, noting on his file that she was given a specific directive to do so.

*"Anna, I need to see you in my office, now"* Charlotte almost whispered to Anna. She closed the door, this was not typical behaviour. Privacy? Charlotte meant it to signify the importance of the conversation. She meant her actions to 'say' *"this is our secret and you are my trusted one"*. Anna just felt trapped.

*"Anna there has been a dramatic spiked increase in the number of businesses being burgled. The break-ins are well orchestrated. The burglars hold nothing personal against the companies. This is a territorial dispute between two Security Companies. A new security company named 'Secure As' which is owned and operated by The Mob has sprouted. They are now involved in a full onslaught against Tony Trapone's Guardians".*

Anna was not sure how to handle this information. She was blindsided by Charlotte's approach. Charlotte had closed the door and with no introduction was deluging her with a crime update. Charlotte continued,

*"The Mob is out to prove that The Guardians cannot 'secure and protect' the client's property as well as Secure As can. To prove the point Secure As blitz burglarizes The Guardians' clients. They do it with finesse. They burgle 2 or 3 businesses or even homes at one end of the metropolitan area. When Tony's men, led by the ever faithful Gary respond with great show of force to the first crime site, Secure As then burgles businesses and homes at the other end of the metropolitan area, some 50 kilometres away. At the same time homes and business are burglarized to the east 30 kilometres away. There is no way The Guardians can respond to this three area onslaught. That means there is no Gary there to convince*

the second or third set of 'the burgled' that The Guardians are the good guys".

Charlotte stopped to make sure Anna was tracking her. Convinced Anna was she continued,

*"Secure As makes sure its men are there, sans Gary, clean cut and uniformed ready to help the distraught victims immediately. Clip boards and contracts in hand they assured them of their superior ability to 'secure and protect'. The police say that when the clients switch to Secure As the robberies cease, if they switch back, they are again burglarized. You gotta love these guys".* Anna was aghast but Charlotte wasn't done.

*"The Police believe your Warro is the CEO of the war between the security companies. He is only succeeding because he is hitting Tony Trapone while he is down. As you know Tony is 'otherwise' engaged with his ever burgeoning legal troubles. But it won't be long before he rallies and marshals his lieutenants to take care of this. And remember the killing fields for this war are the homes and businesses of Perth. If this isn't stopped all hell could break loose and we will get the blame for it as we are not managing our offenders. I do not need to remind you that both of these offenders are yours".*

Anna was too winded by this news to defend herself. She felt as though she was being identified as an accomplice before or during or after the fact. Somehow responsibility for Warro and Tony's behaviour was now 'hers'. If she had ever felt out of her depth with the criminality she had encountered so far, she was drowning today. Charlotte obviously enjoyed overwhelming this psychologist.

*"You can't ask Warro about this, if you do you will be viewed as interfering with an ongoing investigation. And his grandfather was*

*a war hero you know; in fact he just passed, I saw it in the funeral notices. If he knew about Warro's activities he'd roll over in his freshly dug grave. Warro is a lot heavier end criminal than any of us knew. He is the type that will rip out your children's throats while they sleep."*

*"Bloody hell Charlotte, that imagery is not what I need right now."*

*"Having it happen is what you need less, so keep your mouth shut."* Anna found it hard to believe that Charlotte cared about anyone enough to read the death notices in the paper. But right now Anna was complicit in Warro's criminality. She was being warned not to disclose confidential information about Police investigations, to a criminal. As if she would.  And somehow she was being held responsible for the future actions of two of Perth's most vicious criminals.

When Anna returned to her own office she sat staring at the rooves of the row houses visible from her window. As she stared unthinkingly it struck her 'Warro', Warren Leigh Conaughton was the grandson of Max's 'nasty bastard' Bernard Leigh Conaughton. Her thoughts screamed *"Charlotte, he wasn't buried he was cremated!  Not much rolling room in that urn."*

Anna did not know if Charlotte was being overly dramatic. Did she really know that the information she had just dumped on Anna was accurate or did she just enjoy scaring staff? She needed to talk to someone; Liz was in Broome doing pre-sentence reports so she called Max.

*"Max, I am going to be a bit late home, but I need to talk to you now, sorry I have to be vague on the details but the degree of criminality I see here is beyond my education, my ability and my*

*will to comprehend. I am drowning here. I am astounded at what these creeps do and I feel like I am being blamed their actions".* Max reassured her that she could handle it, and if she couldn't she would figure out what to do.

*"Come home babe, we will talk about it tonight,"* he added. And they did. With Max's support and by the light of morning the next day Charlotte's news didn't seem so threatening. It already felt like old news, something Anna almost knew, or should have known. She dared to wonder what positive effect the rotation of fresh faced Probation Officers and unarmed security guards with fruited tea bags, and her own rehabilitative intentions were against such resolute criminality. The first person she saw that morning was Charlotte. As they passed in the hall Charlotte examined her face quizzically, she seemed to be disappointed that Anna had regrouped so quickly. Anna heard her phone ringing and ran to answer it.

*"Hello, Anna Lennox"* she answered.

*"Bam has been arrested."* It was his Probation Officer. *"It was a cold case. But with the advances in DNA he has been identified as the home invader who broke into a home 2 years ago. The home owner came home, bad timing, or good, depending on who you barrack\* for. This startled Bam who threw his crow bar at the home owner. He said he did it out of shock more than malevolence. But the flying crow bar struck the home owner. It copped him a good one. This turned a home invasion into it an assault with a deadly weapon. Bam left some of his skin on the crow bar and long story short, his DNA calling card got him".*

Anna was more saddened by that news than she expected to be. This was the first time this over grown school boy had embarked on a meaningful (to him) exercise, attempting to do something 'normal' people do. His rehabilitative endeavours would come to a screaming halt by his having to pay the consequences for his prior nocturnal adventure. Again she checked herself, there was no guarantee he could or would follow through on his recent adventure into normalcy. And paying the consequences of anti social behaviour was really the point. Nevertheless she hoped they had writing courses in prison.

A few days later Charlotte sent a global email announcing her successful handling of 'the drugs in the toilets' case. She said that Police drug squad members had visited all of The Mob known to this department and who reported here, including offender 093547 (Warren Leigh Conaughton). Arrests had been made. Anna wondered how this would seduce 'Warro' away from crime and how Charlotte's actions flew with departmental policy. As far as she knew they would never co-operate with Police at that level and would not assist in such investigations. Anna concluded that years of rapport with bikies and others would be shredded. She'd be surprised if any reported to the Centre again. Charlotte had not let little things like departmental policy, role constraints or the need to protect carefully won rapport, rob her of the chance to excel. Actually it might result in an easier day for Anna if the offenders did not show, so why complain?

*"So how is Sean the Death Adder?"* asked Barbara the smallest of the smallest Probation Officers in the world. Barbara underwent a personality change every time she changed her hair colouring, which was often. Today she was red haired and vivacious, but still small. Tiny even, like a person in miniature. Anna noticed she wore a puffy gold heart around her neck. It looked like it had been attacked by something very small and sharp. Barbara became aware of

Anna's scrutiny of her jewellery and fiddled with it unconsciously, hiding it in her hand.

"Sean, a Death Adder, since when?" asked Anna.

"Since forever, didn't you read his file?" chipped Barbara.

"I read the file in your cabinet and there was not much there, nothing about him being a Death Adder" replied Anna.

"Which volume did you read?" demanded Barbara. Anna choked,

"Volume? How many damn volumes are there?"

"Three."

"Well I guess I read volume three" said Anna.

"He has been laying low, getting others to do his dirty work while he is on parole. When he comes to report to me he changes his appearance. No black clothes or piercings. But I know he is still 'a brother'. Of course the tatts are still there. I have not seen them in a while. He is not one for tank tops these days. At least, not when he reports to me, I think I have seen him kitted out when he sees you though. Anyhow do yourself a favour, read Volume Two. He is particularly angry at another bikie club. The Mob is moving in on 'his' territory, dealing drugs where Sean's club usually reigns supreme. He will do anything to stop them. Anything. He will use anybody to do it. Anybody."

Anna's heart stopped. She spun around so Barbara would not see the fear on her face. Sean set her up. Her misgivings about his story were founded. Why, in the name of anything sane did she fall for that? Why did she dismiss her own doubts? She called Max. She desperately wanted the Max of 3 years ago to answer. He did, they could always talk over the phone. She could not tell him the details but he sensed she needed reassurance and gave it.

Anna did not know what would come of this. She did not know how to handle it. She was not usually so naive; in fact her personal mantra was 'Don't believe the lying bastards'. She could not tell Charlotte what had happened, she emailed her own manager, Liz the Chief Forensic Psychologist. Liz was not available, she left a message.

Three minutes later the phone rang; PP announced that her manager was calling. Liz had great clinical and personal skills but was an incompetent manager. No requests for pay slips had been signed or submitted by her regularly since she had taken the position. It was beyond her ability to submit a pay or travel request on time. Administrative details like that completely eluded her. In fact one of the psychologists had not been paid for 3 months and was undergoing a subsequent financial crisis. Liz had overlooked submitting her new contract to HR. Anna needed Liz's clinical and personal support, at that moment whether her pay slip was filled in correctly and submitted in a timely fashion was her last concern.

*"You are supposing a lot here, you don't know that his emergency session was not genuine. You don't know how strong his present allegiance is to his bikie connections. You don't know that his rival gang was the one dealing in the toilet, or that he turned that particular rival in to you. Stay with what you know. Anna if you let the 'what ifs' plague you in this job, you will never sleep. Do you need me to come to your Centre?"* Liz offered.

Anna did not think she needed the company but Liz was right, she had been a great help. She felt grounded. Liz added

*"You need to bring this up with Charlotte, for an agenda item at the team meeting. Bikies should be clearly identified as such, especially when there are multiple volumes of files on an offender.*

*You can't be expected to track down and read volumes you don't even know exist on every criminal. Departmental policy mandates that Probation Officers do a hand over for every client. Especially when it is information the Probation Officers have so readily in their minds. How could you know he had a dual appearance presentation? Barbara is messing with you. She is the only one Charlotte never reprimands, might be a reason for that."*

Liz was now 'the agenda item manufacturer'. How ironic. She seldom remembered to even produce an agenda for the forensic psychologist's monthly meeting, but she was now dictating a point for Charlotte's agenda. Today was not the day for such administrative enterprise; Anna reached inside, but found no energy there for confronting Charlotte.

Anna noticed the time. She had arranged to have lunch with an American friend. Cindy was a clinical psychologist. They met some years ago, before the boys were born, in California when Anna worked there on a special project at the University of California in Fullerton. Cindy's husband was now employed by Woodside, a multinational conglomerate invested in mining in Western Australia. He was an engineer and a geologist. Anna and Cindy just recently rediscovered each other via facebook. They were equally delighted and surprised to learn they now lived in the same city, and within driving distance.

They met at the Villa Roma restaurant on High street. They greeted each other warmly. They chose the seating in the walled courtyard beneath the leafy vines. The most wonderful bread, warm and crunchy appeared in a basket on their table. They both enjoyed it. As soon as she sat back and took in the atmosphere and the music Anna felt the tension of the Department dissipate. This scene change was almost like a trip to the Mediterranean.

Cindy looked wonderful, she seemed settled. Cindy described her new life.

*"I have fallen in with a group of other expat wives. They are supportive and fun. Especially their Bunco nights. The children are enrolled in the American school to limit the disruption to their curriculum and education course. They seem to like it. Jarrod's work on the Northwest shelf is challenging. He is frequently away as he manages his project on the rigs, which is never easy. His work is subsea infrastructure replacement and he can't do it from home. It is important but demanding work. He gets very tired at times, and he misses out on a lot of the kids' development. But, Woodside is doing well, their sales revenues were up every quarter over the former, so how can I complain? Look, the kids are happy, the company is profitable; Jarrod is appreciated and his work adds integrity to the success of the project, so overall, we are all doing well".*

Despite the glowing summary of her Perth life, Anna wondered who she was trying to convince.

*"But how do you like Western Australia?"* she asked.

*"What is not to like?"* responded Cindy. Anna's brow furrowed.

*"Cindy that is the line your relocation specialist gave you. Everyone who works at Woodside or any of the other multinational companies gives that answer. Forget the talking point, tell me honestly, how do you like Western Australia?"*

Their conversation was interrupted as they ordered.

*"Well I am a bit mystified about some things"* Cindy confessed.

*"I am your personal demystifier, so shoot."*

*"Our cultures seem to be similar, Australians are so friendly."*

*"Are we?"* asked Anna, *"How many Australians have invited you into their homes for dinner?"*

*"Ummm none."*

*"You will find that generally speaking our friendliness is superficial."*

*"It may well be, I had not put that together, why doesn't that make me feel better? I do notice that I feel at ease with Australians, I think we are on the same page, we laugh, we joke, then I hit a cultural wall. It's like iron gates slam shut, I have done something, but I have no idea what I did to trigger it. I review it, I bounce it off Jarrod but I remain mystified."*

Their meal arrived. Cindy had a steaming pot of chili mussels, and Anna a chicken tortellini dish. The aroma was enticing. Cindy's meal required her full attention. Hers was not a twirl the fork and eat dish. Hers was a fish cut each mussel, hold the shell, scrape out the delicious centre, and discard the shell dish. They refocused. Food was centre stage.

Having eaten they returned to the subject at hand Anna said,

*"I am sorry I gave you something else to worry about with the meal invite thing, and I am sorry to disappoint you Cindy; I have no idea what you are experiencing. I will need more details. Next time it happens let me know exactly what is said."*

Cindy thought for a moment,

*"I think it has something to do with my congratulating them when they have done something well."*

*"Oh oh yes"* said Anna, *"The American habit of using recognition and praise comes across as disingenuous here. If you praise us we*

*think you are 'having us on' and we will close down".*

*"What is the remedy?"*

*"You have to insult us."* They both laughed, and it took several minutes to recover. Anna said,

*"I worked with an American private client in my private practice. He was the CEO of a multinational. He said when he praised the employees here, as he would typically do in the States, they shut down. He learned to say things like 'If you had half a brain you'd actually be worth your pay'."*

*"And that did it?"* asked Cindy.

*"Yup."*

*"Unbelievable. I will need to take the class, Aussie Insults 101."*

*"Come to dinner, we will draft the curriculum, bring Jarrod and the kids, how is next Saturday?"*

*"Oops can't we are going to Margaret River with some friends, I will take a rain check though."*

Returning to work Anna felt refreshed. She made a mental note to contact Cindy more frequently.

• • • • •

# 8

## Training Day

*W*ednesday was a day designated as a Training Day. Liz had not arranged any presenters to address her team. She knew that her squad of mainly new psychologists was wearing thin. They were being ground down by the relentlessness of the work. She wanted to provide them with an informal discussion forum on coping. The team never knew what to expect as they rolled up for their agendaless meetings, but today they were curious as Liz seemed to have something important to say.

They saw each other once a month at their monthly team meetings or on spasmodic training days. Each worked in different Centre and the Centres were many kilometres apart, spread throughout Perth's narrow, coast line hugging metropolitan area and beyond. The forensic psychologists basically functioned from their own vehicles and their 'offices on wheels' which they dragged over the curbs at their respective Centres.

This was Anna's second meeting and she was taken aback was her colleagues spewed venom and pain. Their language was spliced with foul words. Their humour was black. Their mood was overwhelmingly grumpy. She saw vicarious trauma in its rawest form. They reported feeling isolated by their centre allocation. Now that she thought about it, it was isolating.

After a mutual 'we work too hard in too difficult circumstances' catharsis Liz asked for discussion topics. Anna initiated the discussion with,

*"Liz I have been thinking about it a while. When you hired me you said that our Department was responsible to support the Centres in the rural areas. As far as I can see, and I admit I do not see 'all', it's not happening. Is there any way the team can be involved in consulting or supporting our colleagues in the remote areas?"* Liz informed her that the mandate was there sure enough, but it was an unfunded mandate. Until the budgetary office provided the funds they were unable to act on that mandate. Phyllis chimed in with,

*"So you want us to do even more than we do now, and for nothing?"* Anna ignored her; she expressed her disappointment and asked if she could offer another topic.

*"Well as the last one was a non starter, go ahead"* Liz said.

Anna was wary of Phyllis but she gathered courage to say,

*"I have noticed, and it is validated by the research, that the vast majority of crimes are committed by the vast minority of offenders. Most crimes are, from my perspective, crimes of passion, crimes of opportunity, crimes of stupidity, crimes of need, crimes of retribution, not real criminality. But those who are career criminals like Sean are the offenders of havoc. They run amuck, fast. The Department does its best to keep them in its sights. To do this the Department becomes its own con man, telling itself it is succeeding when it isn't, telling itself it isn't hurting its employees when it is. Telling itself it wants to keep doing what it is doing because it is working, when it isn't."* She did not look at Phyllis. Anna had what she thought might be a partial solution.

*"Why not test the offenders to weed out, as it were, the truly*

*psychopathic criminals, and treat the different categories of offenders differently? I know where we can procure the tests, we can all be trained, and it's not an arduous process."* It occurred to her that the programs and individual sessions offered to all offenders, as ordered by the Magistrates, at best, did nothing for the true psychopath. At worst, the carefully written and thoughtfully presented programs gave the psychopaths added skills. She added,

*"...and we largely ignore the traumatized. With all the new research indicating that the physiology of the brain is permanently altered with early trauma, we should adequately assess and then treat those who have been traumatised. If we don't, we won't really help them. Will we?"*

Phyllis had at least three chins. She had the largeness of head that sometimes comes with menopause. She had a frog like appearance. When she opened her eyes wide to illustrate a point her forehead creased into three symmetrical furrows. Her eyes were smaller than optimum. She was raging.

Anna was the last member to join the team, as Phyllis emphasized, so she did not know that she, Phyllis and Liz's predecessor had worked for months to educate the Magistrates that psychological intervention was viable. It was almost impossible to gain access to the Magistrates because of the 'judicial independence' concept. When their program was ready to launch the former principal forensic psychologist resigned. Liz then came on board. It was a steep learning curve for her. She had to take on someone else's vision. In their presentations Liz and Phyllis made sure they did not attempt to influence the Magistrate's decisions. They had to present their material in a 'take it or leave it' manner. To choreograph the wording and approach into one that was acceptable had taken the skill of a barrister, and neither of them were barristers. Phyllis advised Anna that the team had considered all the assessment and treatment options that were accessible and sustainable. *"Not exactly all"*, thought Anna. Liz's predecessor and a team of hand selected psychologists had painstakingly developed a research based, cutting edge program that worked. The emphasis was *"THAT WORKED"*.

Phyllis thanked Liz for carrying the vision forward and then demanded of Anna

*"After all that work would you now have us tell the Magistrates we got it wrong? That we need to make excuses for those who had shit childhoods? That we don't know what we are doing with psychopaths or the traumatized? So now we tell the Magistrates that these burglars, rapists, car thieves are to be pitied, they are* **victims!!!!!!**"

Anna did not have a short answer for her. The vehemence of the question temporarily derailed her 'come back' programme. She was not advocating social justice but best practice judicial intervention. Anna did not want anyone's criminal activity excused because of a traumatized past. She was proposing that the source of each offender's criminality be adequately assessed and treated. Crimes of passion, crimes of stupidity should not be judged by the same criterion as heavy end premeditated and violent crimes. How could she say that in one word? In the stunned and awkward silence that followed she shot a glance at Liz. Instead of the support she was seeking her dear protector and mentor agreed with Phyllis and the Directorate's present approach. The question ringing in Anna's head was *"where is the proof of concept?"* but she said nothing.

Anna's favourite male colleague filled in the silence with his own need to staff a particular case with the team. The team obligingly switched their attention to him, happy to remove themselves from the cross hairs of a Liz-Phyllis-'new girl Anna' standoff. He winked at Anna. He whispered to her,

*"Compromise. That means admitting she's right".* Anna laughed, Phyllis didn't.

Her male colleague said that the offender of note had arrived to report in a custom fitted Holden Monaro, this year's model, the one with the really sexy grill. Two door. Black. It was pee test day so the Centre was chockers*. As if on cue the male offenders all walked outside and stood in silent awe of the Monaro. They showed respect in the presence of excellence.

Not all were awed; when the driver prepared to leave he noticed a huge key scratch down the driver's side. He knew better than to acknowledge it. His psychologist noticed the damaged door when he bent the vertical plastic blinds at his office window to gain one last view of the Monaro. It sped by his window, scratch and all.

This offender was one of the most successful and dangerous criminals seen at the Centre. Yet there was nothing about his appearance to indicate that. He had to travel many kilometres into a neighbourhood far removed from his home to report to the department. Those who lived in his neighbourhood either did not offend or did not get caught. There were no departmental Centres there. The neighbourhood around the Centre made this well heeled offender nervous but he had no choice but to report there.

Scott initially offered a legitimate service for legitimate purposes. He was years ahead of the computer forensic security movement. He was one of the first to retrieve deleted and long lost 'to be forgotten' material from computers. Neither the 'delete' function on the computer nor the past were barriers to him.

He assisted companies to retrieve facts about their employee's on line behaviour. He retrieved information about any company they wished to purchase, or compete against. Commonly accountants prepare a 'for sale' version of the company they wished to off load, making it look much more lucrative than it was in reality. Through Scott the buyers could read the uncooked books as Scott reformatted the original accounting records. Scott's prowess earned him an international clientele. His wealthy clientele paid well for his services and his ability to protect them from buying unprofitable but beautifully packaged-for-sale companies.

Scott also manipulated the search engines so that non flattering information, be it true or otherwise, about his clients, could be hidden in obscure cyber corners, seldom accessed, or deeply embedded in positive information. He also presented what he called "OMMR - Opinion Making Market Research'. This aspect of his business assisted a competing company to release unflattering information, or suspicions about their competitor, without leaving a trace of the originator. Various PhD's and experts in a myriad of fields willingly sold their high sounding and well written opinions to Scott for this effort. Reality or truth in reporting was not a consideration, inflicting damage or doubt on a competitor was. Anna's male colleague understood how both these services could be invaluable in certain circles and circumstances. Fleetingly he wondered how much the offender would pay him to... he dare not finish that thought.

Scott did not use a crowbar or a vehicle to commit his crimes; he knew no home bakers. He would not dream of using drugs. He had no intention of impairing his cognitive abilities by snorting or smoking or injecting anything that would diminish them.

To protect his cerebral cortex he did not even drink alcohol. He attended one of Perth's most prestigious boys' only private schools. His childhood vacations were taken in Europe, most at the family 'gite'\* in Brittany. His parents' smiling photographs often appeared in the society sections of the newspapers as they attended one gala function after another. They were serious contributors to a number of local charities.

Accustomed to a favourable spotlight he easily handled his fame when his skills and his reputation increased. He learned how to buy and sell enormously valuable but invisible commodities. He was one of the first to use the extremely helpful commodities of bot-nets, Trojans, zombies and phishing attacks in the making. This mild mannered man, with the expensive suits and killer car developed malicious and dangerous software known as Spyware that could hit any computer anywhere. Through it he could link almost any computer with others, tens of thousands at a time, forming a bot-net. A huge International linked conglomerate of computers. This conglomerate, without the computer owner's awareness, or permission was sold to others. Those 'others' may be looking for money, they may be gathering targets for their spam or stockpiling information, stealing identities or may have been just plain malicious.

Scott learned earlier than most the value of aggregators. These data tracking systems quietly and unseen collate the maps showing where internet users travel on line. They provide an 'interests and assets' profile that can be sold and exploited by marketers of a variety of merchandise and services, legitimate and illegitimate, and potentially offer an opportunity for blackmail.

Scott's nefarious clients did not pick pockets. They picked entire family fortunes and futures. Instead of writing slanderous words on bathroom walls, they published their slander across the cyber net, in indelible ink. With Scott's assistance they tracked and brought down banks, international corporations, insurance companies, government departments, politicians and individuals. Carefully guarded secrets were unceremoniously launched into cyber space and with the precision of smart bombs they exploded through the lives and futures of those who formerly held them.

Scott described himself as magnanimous, he did not keep his talents to himself. Scott was the only client seen at that centre who could say, let alone spell the word 'magnanimous'. Scott readily taught others his skills. He charged a mere thousand dollar fee. He designed step by step software, complete with video instruction on how to do the more popular things he did. He initiated a real time chat room where master's degree level IT graduates supported those working with the program. Many of his IT clients were overseas. He made more money from those programs in a month than his father did in his medical practice in a year. Scott revelled in that Oedipal thought.

Phyllis demanded to know whether this male colleague was describing Scott's clinical presentation, or promoting him. The male psychologist did not follow his own advice and compromise with her; instead he ignored her and continued. The fact that an individual might not perform internet banking from his own computer, or give out his credit card on line, did not protect him from Scott or Scott's devotees. That information is recorded somewhere in cyber space, at a bank or an insurance company, and fire walls can only be built after the fact. Firewalls are always at least one pace behind cyber criminals.

Scott had historically excelled at all things mathematical. He was an arithmcmaniac, constantly counting, calculating, and devising mathematical games, formulating equations and mathematical solutions from early childhood. Early in his career he figured out how to bypass the firewalls of international corporations. He said they were cyber mathematical Rubik's cubes. When a secret assignment of the latest technology was to be delivered, to be released in a spectacular launching, Scott snuck down the dark alleys of the internet and around cyber corners, unseen. He easily cracked the protective code and let the competitor know 'the arrival date'. That competitor was thereby enabled to launch his rival's product a day or a week early, while the other goods were still enroute. This gave them preeminence over their market. The laws to protect companies from this behaviour had not been written when Scott took flight. Therefore there were no legal consequences for such behaviour. He honed his skills. His hard won ability and precisely exercised practice turned Scott Turner's computer into a globally sought formidable tool for business, for crime, destruction and indecent profit.

As Anna heard Scott's story she thought,

*"He was someone's 'Lachie' at one time".* Most of the forensic psychologists were enthralled with this client. They admired excellence. Even psychopathology, when it is intelligently performed with such flair and attention to detail is to be admired. They could respect the offender's abilities, his finesse, his success and his car. He may even have envied him. His psychologist said the scariest thing about Scott was his suit and legitimate appearance. He looked like a trustworthy businessman. Phyllis asked

*"So you want him to wear a sign do you?"* The mood she was

in nobody responded. Anna's colleague wanted to know how to treat Scott. Anna suggested that he be run through a battery of psychological tests by an experienced forensic psychiatrist. If he is a psychopath she would recommend he not progress through the usual programs. If he was, the Department would teach him how to improve his current people code cracking skill level. Anna stopped there but she wanted to explain that it would go viral through Scott, considering his approach to skill sharing; he would teach others his new Justice Department provided skills. He may well charge for that knowledge. She kept it to herself; one bombshell for the day was enough. She poured herself another cup of coffee.

Liz seized upon this situation. The majority of the psychologists present were really interested in this intriguing client. She asked the speaker to role play as the offender. She then instructed each psychologist, in turn, to 'treat' him for 3 minutes, when the 3 minutes was up the next psychologist took over. Anna was first; she announced that in this case capital punishment might work, especially if it was administered before his next crime spree. Only a couple of the psychologists laughed, the others were too intimidated by Phyllis to even smile. Then Anna got into it and acted out her intervention. They each had a number of turns. At the conclusion of the exercise the mood was lighter. Each psychologist had the opportunity to air his or her skill set. The psychologist said he had learned that even if Scott could out think him, he did get caught so he wasn't that clever.

*"He got caught!"* he repeated vehemently. Liz knew that revival of confidence was the variable he needed to provide a successful intervention for Scott.

Anna hurried home. She did not want to be late as that evening

Max and she were scheduled to meet Cindy and Jarrod in Perth, for dinner. They chose a restaurant in King's park overlooking the Swan River. There was nothing ordinary about the service, the food, the company or the view. The evening was warm and still. It was a perfect setting. She confided in Cindy that her that she and her colleagues were

*"Not sufficiently cynical to deal with the level of criminality we confront. None of us can comprehend let alone out think this level of criminality. We are too pedestrian! We walk while they fly, and they fly high!"* Cindy agreed, she was familiar with that same sense of incompetence despite her advanced clinical degree. She told Anna,

*"Remember the true psychopath is expert at making those they encounter doubt themselves and trust them. They suck us in so that we orbit around them, as the earth orbits the sun. You have to stay grounded in your truth and reality; you are not as incompetent as they would have you believe. If they can render you helpless to help them, they are free to move on to the next victim, stay confident in what you know. You cannot allow them to define you or your skills. You will need constant supervision to avoid that well laid deliberate trap. They may fly, but what goes up, has to come down."* Anna appreciated that insight.

Not wanting to spoil the ambience they postponed further shop talk. They also delayed Cindy's cultural emersion in Aussie Insults 101.

●●●●●

# 9

## *Ethel Grimshaw*

Thursday and Friday Anna drove her usual track, back and forth from Port Stirling. The seemingly endless halting parade of the bad, the brain damaged and the desperate came to her door and then left. She received a counter intuitive confirmation that Crystal had rescheduled her session today. Attendance was hardly rehabilitative, Crystal and these other clients were desperate not to be held accountable, desperate not to make changes, desperate to be anywhere but in prison or in the department's psychologist's office. It exhausted her professional enthusiasm at work and left Anna depleted at home.

Her first appointment at Port Stirling that day was a new one. Ethel Grimshaw, a 69 year old grandmother. Ethel was dressed in a crisp, most beautifully ironed floral print summer cotton dress. She wore a dainty cardigan with pearl buttons draped around her shoulders against the cool early late spring breeze. As the sinewy looking woman sat in front of her, her arthritically gnarled fingers fiddled with a neatly pressed embroidered (with a large script font E) handkerchief. Anna found it difficult to believe that this Ethel was the same Ethel who was a former trusted colleague of Tony Trapone.

Ethel had a hefty mortgage payment due each month; it came through no fault of her own. Her son had a little bit of a gambling habit. To pay off his debts, to help her boy she had remortgaged her home. His salary was factored into the lending deal. He was good boy. He had a good job in one of the factories in Kwinana. He said he would help her with the monthly payments as her pension could not possible cover them. She had not seen him since, neither had his employer, his wife or his three children. His abandoned wife worked full time so Ethel watched the kids in the afternoon, preparing dinner for them, overseeing their homework, each school day. Desperate not to lose her home and her ability to help her grand kids she had to get money. She had been intrigued by all the talk in the press and on the television about amphetamine use in Perth. Obviously there was a waiting market for it. She needed a product that would sell.

Ethel signed up for the Seniors Opportunities class. It was sponsored by the local Chamber of Commerce and held at the library, the big one by the new grocery store. There Ethel was encouraged by *"such a nice young man"* to learn how to use a computer. At first she was very nervous, she did not even know how to turn it on. That young man was a student from the local technical college and he coached her through the rudiments of computer use. This built her confidence. The college and the Chamber of Commerce had teamed together to bring the senior citizens in their community into the internet age. Her teachers, especially that young man, she wished she could remember his name, applauded her as she began to grasp how to execute each new task. Ethel was their most glorious success story. She had the certificate to prove it. She borrowed the money from family members and bought a computer, surfed the net and learned how to make methyl amphetamine.

She learned about Tony Trapone from her son. She telephoned

him at The Guardian corporate offices. She was surprised at how easy it was to reach him. He had such nice offices with an aquarium. Ethel thought you could judge a man's character by his love of living things, and Tony loved his fish. He had a pretty girl behind the front desk who made her tea. She said the pretty girl gave it to her in a pretty tea cup with a matching saucer, and one of those expensive biscuits*. She said Tony was ever so nice, not like the horrible creature the media makes him out to be. Once he sampled her ice he was hooked. He said she was his best baker.

Ethel knew of the dangers of toxic fumes and explosions. Consequently she used the 'Shake 'n Bake' method. She could only make smaller batches, but she had plenty of time. Most of the needed chemicals were easy to obtain. She had taught herself how to bake, she was very careful to do it precisely and safely, and apparently did a good job. When the over the counter medications procurement became difficult, even for a kindly crisp looking grandma Tony made sure she was well supplied.

Ethel said sometimes the effect of the drugs on the youngsters bothered her. But that thought did not stay with her for very long. She said that she had paid off her mortgage in 9 months and now was living *"quite comfortable"*. With this, she smiled.

Ethel said that she was ready to stop baking when the house was paid off but that Tony *"hisself"* had come to her home, and told her he had an incentive plan. She said,

*"Tony said I was his best baker, always reliable, I never mix a bad batch. I won the baking contest. I did not even know there was a contest. The prize was parked in my drive way. It was a brand new bright yellow PT Cruiser. Tony had had the seats covered with pale blue leather. He said he did that because he thought I would*

*like it. It was the most beautiful thing I had ever seen. How could I resign when Tony needed me?"*

How indeed? Anna thought Tony probably earned a better return on that car than most New York Wall Street investors did on their best trades. Tony's accountant kept very thorough records. Ethel was listed as a supplier of the Guardian uniforms. The special task force Police investigators investigated to see if she was registered with the taxation department as a viable business trading in uniforms. She was not registered. This naive grandmother whose only prior crime was to birth a stupid son was now officially under a fully fledged Police investigation.

When Tony was advised that Ethel was being investigated he sent the pretty girl from the office by to personally tell her how sorry he was. He said that if he knew she needed that paperwork he would certainly have had his people get it for her. He posted bail for her in cash so it could not be tracked back to him, of course.

When the Police searched her mortgage free home they did not find any uniforms on her premises but they did find her impressive laboratory/kitchen and her aprons. When they entered her heavily locked 'Kitchen' they found the ingredients separated, labelled and alphabetically stored. There were several sets of stainless steel measuring cups and spoons. Ethel was meticulous about the measurements and would only use stainless steel measuring devices. Her belief was that it kept her safer by minimizing explosions. The Police found a drawer labelled 'pinnies', it was full of neatly ironed, floral aprons. She had sewn them all herself.

Ethel was confused about something the Police said; it was something about 'asset confiscation'. What was that, can they confiscate her home, or her car? She still had not heard from her son, did Anna think she could help locate him?

As Ethel's trial was imminent no future appointment was made. If she was not imprisoned, or if she was, once she was released from prison they would see each other again. No, Anna couldn't visit her in jail, and probably could not save her house or find her son. If Ethel had known that Anna could not help her she said she would not have bothered with this appointment. She left and she was not smiling.

Anna's last appointment in Port Stirling was Crystal; she denied having used speed recently despite a recent positive drug result. She said,

*"The lab must have mixed up the specimens, they do that you know"*. Her face was picked and scabbed from her chin, up through to her hair line. These injuries were a dead giveaway that she was using speed.

Anna tried a cost/benefit analysis of drug abuse in an attempt to rouse within Crystal some awareness that there was a potential cost, to her, of her speed use. Crystal did not 'get it'. She could not track the point of the conversation. Her broken finger nails with their chipped polish flew over her face, brushing the scabs. It took all of her resolve not to pick at them. The nails skimmed over her face, up through her hair line and back down again. Over and over again her fingers jerked through a ridiculous haphazard pattern. She gave a urine sample, science would determine the integrity of her denials, or how efficient she was at clearing her urine quickly of any offending substance. Thirty minutes saw the end of her endurance to sit somewhat still, and that was a stretch for her. She made another appointment. She had to, in order not to be violated.

•••••

# 10

## Joseph Dorlani

*F*riday evening found Max and Anna in their finest clothing at a parent's evening at St. Benedict's. The school was imposing, it looked as if was impressed with its own grandeur. It was built with huge rough hewn lime stone blocks that looked as if they had originally supported an Egyptian pyramid. The flooring in the massive room was highly polished dark Australian Tasmanian oak. The wooden interior frames of the windows looked splendid in contrast against the limestone blocks. Linen table cloths with the school emblem embroidered in each corner graced the tables. Cups and saucers imprinted with the school shield, bright silver urn, cream in suitable jugs, and fresh flowers blazed. A CD'd orchestra played Mozart in the background. The parents spoke with the same semi reverent tones. They used the words of the educated and addressed polite subjects. It was a game that was played. Everyone knew the rules. No one was deluded.

Anna and Max had attended one of these functions when Stuart was first enrolled. However, they had not enjoyed the parental game so they had not returned. It did not seem to benefit Stuart's school experience if they engaged in chat with the other boys' parents at this level, so they didn't. But with both boys now in this school, they decided to engage with the parents and demonstrate their gratitude if not allegiance to the school.

Champagne in flutes, tea and coffee in cups with the emblem, refreshments a-la-grand. It was all so 'over the top'. Anna could think of a better use for her school fees. The President of the Parent's Group, Alison Cunningham approached. She looked like a Nicole Kidman wanna-be. What was it with Australian women that they thought they had to look like Nicole in order to be attractive? Anna noticed her clothes. They were obviously from the boutiques on Napoleon Street. She wore a unique, one-of-a-kind outfit and custom handmade shoes that could easily have cost her many hundreds of dollars. The style in that part of Australia was for natural fabric, such as silk or linen, asymmetrical pieces sewn together, with an Asian touch, black and white, or muted browns and olives, with a flash of red. Her outfit had it all.

She slipped her arm through Anna's and confided,

*"Anna as you know, my son is in the boarding school. I miss him terribly when he is not with me."* She further chirped,

*"St. Bennies is an exceptional school and we are all utterly delighted to welcome you and Max and Lachie. I heard about his 'trouble' at the other school. Such a shame".* She leaned in closer to Anna as if sharing another confidence,

*"I hope I can count on your increased involvement and support".* That was quite a mouthful, and an unusual level of intimacy at first meeting for those of her class. Was her warmth real? Was it necessary? Anna wished she could turn her mind off.

The mild murmuring of the room silenced. Abruptly, in the doorway appeared Joseph Dorlani. He was out of uniform, and he looked decidedly out of place. He was the only one oblivious to that fact. Instead of the indecently expensive suit, silk tie and polished $500.00 shoes he wore a track suit from a local football club and huge running shoes. He did not speak as they spoke. His accent was definitely from the 'other' suburbs, the ones where the mechanics and carpenters lived. His voice thundered above everyone else's, he did not know to lower it to within the polite and acceptable volume range. He unashamedly asked for a 'real' mug when offered the beautiful crest emblazoned tea cup and saucer. He moved too quickly as he barrelled toward Alison. He greeted her loudly with *"G'Day Alison"*. Being a tiler of repute he had retiled her 4 bathroom areas and he saw no reason to be other than familiar with her, even here.

Anna had often wondered how the boom for the tradespeople, who called themselves 'tradies'\* would affect society in Perth. The mining industries and housing boom had made instant millionaires out of many, and those 'many' wanted to live in mansions to proclaim their wealth. St. Bennie's was about to be shaken to its established core as the 'nouveau riche' abandon their allocated places in the state\* schools. They were now buying the places normally reserved for the children of the wealthy in the private school arena. Therein two divergent levels of society clashed. The fallout for both would be interesting. She chuckled at the thought.

Having extricated herself from Joe's grip the ever helpful Ms. Cunningham gave a short speech ensuring the parents of the school's support for their boys.

*"If your boys fail a term or a year you do not need to worry as the school will design a remediation term or year, especially for your child,"* she advised. Most parents murmured their approval. Joseph Dorlani called out.

*"He gets one shot at it from me with the prices you charge"*. No one laughed. Tradie humour was not funny here. Joseph Dorlani

noticed but did not understand how what he had said was the wrong thing to say. He was confused, that statement would have gotten a laugh at the work site. And it did the next day.

The night Max asked her what she thought of Joseph Dorlani. As Max was not one for gossip Anna was intrigued that he asked. She would not answer until he did.

*"I have been thinking about the rule that 'he who has the gold makes the rules'. With this building and mining boom the tradies are the ones with the money. Do you think it will change what is considered worthy in society? How many Joe Dorlani's can St. Bennie's assimilate without changing? How long before we are all drinking coffee from 'real' mugs rather than tea from cups and saucers? Even bigger how many Joe Dorlani's can the upper rungs of society tolerate without collapsing?"*

*"I can't believe you are saying that. I have been wondering about it too. How many of these tradies will be content to go to some pretentious restaurant with a name they can't pronounce. Eat food they can't fathom with menu items they can't read. You know the food that comes in minute portions, looking more like a miniature hat than a meal. And be charged for water, sparkling or still. Would Joe be content to still be hungry after paying $200 for his dinner?"* Anna asked. Max responded

*"Hang the tradies; I don't even want to eat at those places. And along those lines, I was in this upmarket furniture store getting some quotes for the reception area and board room at work. The furniture was low, so low you needed a home hoist to get into and out of it. And it was slippery as all get out. I wondered how many tradies would buy this uncomfortable leather crap. When I sat on it, it pushed me off onto the floor. Will the Joe's of the world buy it,*

*just because it is fashionable, made in Italy and Alison has it? You could tell at the meeting tonight he is not about to conform to what is considered 'proper', I think he and the rest of the millionaire Joe Dorlani's are going to redefine 'proper'."*

*"Crap, Max?"*

*"It's contagious".*

*"I don't know the answer to your, or to my questions, but it's going to be interesting as we find out. Night lovee".* It had been months since Anna called him 'lovee', it felt right. Thank you Joe Dorlani.

Monday morning Charlotte received an email from Anna about 'the agenda item' Liz recommended. She noted it. Anna ran into Bam's former Probation Officer. She wanted to ask where Bam was, or how he was doing, but she knew that could have misconstrued as her having untoward positive counter transference toward the ungainly Bamster. She merely greeted the Probation Officer, left Bam out of the exchange and proceeded with her coffee procurement.

By the time she arrived, coffee in hand, back at her post, the first offender was waiting. He flashed Anna his toothless grin. She sighed and invited him into her office.

Tuesday was a hard day. Anna was finding the work to be increasingly difficult. At times she had fleeting doubts that she might not want to continue to work with individuals whose language and body aroma were sour and foul. The majority of those scheduled to see her seemed to love to be loathed and loathsome. And then there was the Bamster, finally trying to embark upon something legitimate and his past snags him and drags him backwards. Anna muttered *"I can't win for losing".*

The stories were picking at her soul. They were all the same, the father left while the offender was yet unborn or at least very young. The mother was young, under educated, drug addicted, alcoholic or otherwise occupied, and the child was maltreated, abused and neglected on every level until his or her soul died. Often the child witnessed violence and crime which eventually spread to him/her. Children can't learn in school in the day if they are hungry and sleep deprived and awakened by adult violence through the night. The long tentacles of the childhood trauma reach into adulthood, strangling potential. The damage was all too evident and it appeared to be coupled with 'real criminality' in many offenders. Neglect and abuse spawned terrible consequences in the neglected. Few had life skills, it was as if they were born but not raised, left to grow alone and untended, like weeds. Weeds and crops can grow together; she seemed to recall a Biblical story about that. To the untrained eye initially they seem to be the same, but their value and end use differ greatly. Not much 'wheat' passed through her office, not on Tuesdays. That was pee day. The unwilling drug users and abusers came and donated their urine for testing.

From her end of the long table, at the staff meeting Charlotte raised the issue of alerting the psychologist to an offender's involvement in gangs or bikie clubs. All eyes turned to Anna even though her name had not been mentioned. Barbara noted that the former psychologist made it his business to ask about such things, and did his own research. Today she was blonde and asked in Marilyn tones if 'the rules' were now changing since they had a new psychologist.

Charlotte toyed with the idea of humiliating Anna with her response but she could see no one in the room had the patience for it after such a ragged day. She let the opportunity pass, for today. She instructed the Probation Officers to clearly identify bikie members when they were referred to the psychologist. She directed Anna to design a section on the referral form for such a designation. Anna was happy she was only stuck with an administrative task. She would make the changes to the form. After she submitted it to Charlotte, Charlotte would redesign it, taking no cues from Anna's version. Charlotte would then mandate that every one use her design. Anna could handle that.

•••••

# 11

## A Story in Ink

*S*natching the mail from the mail box that evening Anna found a gold embossed envelope. She was invited to the home of the St. Bennies Parent's Group President, Alison. It was an afternoon tea Saturday fortnight; it required a RSVP by email. She accepted.

Two days later, as she reviewed her diary, ensuring all the offenders had been duly logged in as attending she saw the doe eyed offender's name, Cory Henderson. She smiled. She had forgotten that the first sign you are dealing with a sociopath is that you feel altogether too pleased with yourself, or him. Not only are you his only saviour, the only therapist who ever made sense, he is yours. He saves you from the doldrums of monotonous defence mechanisms and from those who duck and dodge anything that could be therapeutic in their sessions. Anna should have reflected upon her positive response to this young offender, she should have reviewed how he made her feel about her own intervention. But she was not about to do either.

The next morning Anna trawled back through his recorded history. There were multiple drug charges, possession with intent to sell, but no record of his 'resisting arrest'. He was compliant and courteous when cornered. One transcript stated that the judge apologized to him for having to sentence him. Apologized? The judge apologized! She knew the Probation Officers would have been aghast at that, a judge apologizing to a multi faceted criminal, with a long history of offending, for sentencing him. She wondered what the arresting officer thought when he heard that at the trial.

Cory's family was chaotic with drunken rage-a-holic parents. His one sibling was institutionalised from early childhood due to his multiple disabilities which arose from an undefined source. There was no mystery in the fact his parents could not control or care for him. Few could. Cory had no emotional connection or allegiance to authority. The only rules he knew were based on rat street cunning. He was an expert at manipulation and other covert strategies. He did not fall into 'the cracks'. He carved out cracks and dove into them, using his invisibility as a cover. He had flown in under her radar and she was under attack. The nicest possible attack, of course.

Anna reminded herself that Cory was changing. He was demonstrating his desire to transfer his skills to legitimate purposes. Every one deserved a second chance, especially one who ran at it and grabbed it with both hands as Cory did.

At their next session she asked him,

*"Where will you be in 20 years"?* He gave her the standard

*"I want to be a better man, I will go to school, gain some skills like welding, probably still be a battler but I will have a small unit to live in".* She saw it this time,

*"No, really where will you be in 20 years?"*

*"I will be in jail for a long time."*

*"Really, why?"* asked Anna.

*"I have big dreams"* admitted Cory.

*"What kind of big dream comes with a long prison sentence?"* Anna quizzed.

*"You might know that there is a shortage of good drugs here in Port Stirling. To meet the demand I will get international connections from Vietnam or Thailand and form an Australian - Asian ring. I would get the gear shipped into Fremantle. I'd arrange to transport it down here. My local distribution line would kick in and in no time I'd be the king drug dealer. In fact my distribution boys would be couriers. They could travel up and down and all around and not raise anyone's interest as they deliver packages, mine and theirs. Hell, the courier companies would provide the vehicles and the gas, even pay them to work for me. Don't laugh, you don't know how much planning and thought I put into this. This would be a career, and a successful one."*

Anna had often contemplated how the drug lords, without MBA's, or advertising, no Better Business Bureau support, no carefully trained office staff and visible networks, no yellow page advertisements ran the most financially successful businesses in the State. Their business model maximized profits and minimized the chance of apprehension. Their secrets were protected by the silence of those who knew them. Their system of justice was swift and brutal. They took no prisoners, even amongst their own.

*"Yeah, you are right, a career, it is."* Then she asked, *"what is it about a life of crime career that really attracts you?'*

He responded *"It's the 'no's'".*

She did not understand. He explained and as he did his voice grabbed a melodic cadence similar to a rap song, with well practiced words,

*"No accountants, no rules, no taxes, no regrets. If the business does not legally exist there is no need for it to obey the law. It's the perfect con."*

The doe like black eyes hardened, he sat upright. Suddenly he was on full alert and totally engaged in the conversation. She asked him if the police would create any problem for him.

*"Yes they know everyone in town; they would spot me and stop me."* This statement rang hollow. Anna tested it by saying,

*"Aw but they are so stupid."*

Cory laughed a maniacal laugh until he rocked the chair, he was enjoying this.

*"Yeah they are, they are no problem. Sometimes we give them shit. Me and Sam."*

*"Sam?"*

*"Yeah my Rottie, he is 3. Every time he sees a cop and we are out at night he knows the race is on. He sticks his meat head out of the window, and anticipates where I am going to drive* (Cory laughed.) *The Samster leans left or right as he prepares for the fast turns. He knows when the turn is coming; if he does not know the road he watches the indicators. He pants, slobbers and smiles, which is his code to me for 'gun it boy' and this boy does. Have you ever seen a "Rottie smile"?*

Anna didn't think so.

*"He seems to know when I have a shit load of gear in the boot. With that stuff on board I don't want to get into conversation with the cops."* Anna was not really able to compute the depth or seriousness of his criminal intentions. She struggled to reconcile this 'drug lord' version of Cory with the Cory she knew. She looked at him. He seemed so pleasant, so charming, so 'boy next door-ish'. His shoes were so beautifully shined. Surely this drug lord version was an illusion, a harmless yet obscene fantasy. Surely it was a way to siphon off frustrations, a way to feel powerful when

disempowered by life, a way to feel important and recognised in the face of parental rejection. She knew he did not mean it, he could not mean it. That settled she asked:

*"Do you have any other ideas of an alternative outcome for yourself in 20 years?"*

*"Yes I want to be Prime Minister."* His response threw her. Anna had no idea where this Prime Minister version of Cory originated. Neither of these two versions of Cory seemed plausible. During their initial contact Cory gave no indication of grandiosity. In fact, Cory presented as a humble, 'I want help to change' boy, and then he switched to hankering after being a drug lord. Now he wants to rule Australia, was he for real? She dealt with the least noxious aspect of Cory's future fantasies,

*"What would you do as Prime Minister?"*

*"I'd tell the multinationals to go to hell"*. He was not really sure what a multinational was, or what the implications of booting them would be to Australia but he would do it anyway. He then waxed valiant on how he would not really have power, but the illusion of it as Prime Minister. However, as others were under the same illusion he would wield the pretend power with a vengeance and actually effect change.

Anna changed the subject. At her insistence he and Anna wrote a list of the dynamics necessary to be a drug king, then a parallel list of dynamics for Prime Minister. They were virtually identical. She was astounded by the list. Cory wasn't.

Despite her best intentions and her training she found herself lecturing:

*"There is nothing wrong with your dreams, you just need to make sure you choose a product that won't end you up in jail for a*

*long time, if avoiding jail for a long time is your goal."*

*"Well if I am to avoid jail I need to be elected Prime Minister in a hurry."*

*"That may take you more than a year to accomplish, so what will you do for that year?"* Anna quipped.

Cory had been harbouring the most amazing plan for using the artistic offenders he had met in prison to design and market prison tattoo designs. He planned to utilise the web for local, national and international exposure. He had a passion for tattoos; to him they were a secret code. He said,

*"Tattoos tell a story, a story that is written nowhere else. A story no one can take from you".* Little known facts and secrets that gather on the under belly of life seemed to crank his case. As he moved his hands while speaking she noticed a tattoo on the back of his left hand. Although she was reading it upside down she read, 'The Con'. She was slightly unnerved by this but said nothing.

He knew many artistic offenders he had met in prison and thought he could develop their ability to draw natural Australiana, bush flowers and creatures. He said these designs would sell at home and overseas. If blokes want to ink snakes, why not the Dugite or the Tiger Snake? If they want spiders, why not Red Backs? His favourite was a design of a frilled neck lizard. He was sure it would sell. He drew a representative sketch of it. Anna had never seen anything like it; a fully frilled laughing lizard sprang to life from the page.

Cory said,

*"You have to meet my mate, Mervyn. He is both Aboriginal and Japanese. He is into the kind of tattoos the Samurai's wore. Mervyn combines that Samurai shit with ancient Aboriginal body*

*marking. You know that the Samurai tattoos were so painful those who actually lived through the process did it to demonstrate that they could take enduring, excessive pain and not flinch.* " Anna did not know but she nodded anyway. Cory continued

*"They have had those tattoos in Japan for thousands of years. At first they were a mark of shame, a skin sign saying the wearer was a prisoner, a gangster or a prostitute, but it backfired. And soon they became symbols of courage. Even the edo firemen adopted the full body tattoo to protect them against danger. The more barbaric the general population thought the tattoo to be the more others wanted it.* " Anna wondered how Cory knew this; she wondered why he knew this, it seemed to be more 'under belly' stuff to her.

He described Mervyn's brightly covered tattoos. They reached down his legs to his ankles and were sleeves to his wrists. He said Mervyn was surprised at how well his combining tattoos from different culture worked. Mervyn's favourites were brilliantly and brightly coloured. Cory said

*"It might work so well for Mervyn as he only trusts the best artists. No amateurs are allowed near him with ink. He has 21 red back spiders hidden in various places in his body art. I have only seen 18 and I do not want to see the other 3.* " He spoke with a genuine passion and from a full fund of knowledge about tattoos. Anna's respect and admiration for him grew, over riding her original uneasiness.

Together he and Anna designed the necessary steps to formulate a business plan and network platform. His assignment from that session was to further develop these, and to put actual names to the contact base before his next session. Without his consent or knowledge Mervyn was locked into Cory's plan.

Anna worried over the lack of a link between the program and the ink artists in prison, paroled or on community based orders. She knew of a number of graffiti artists who could convert their art work to tattoos. They would need to gain permission to recruit the artists and enter into a contractual agreement with them. The designs had to be prepared in a specific format and payment disbursed. Setting that recruitment and payment plan up may be difficult. The Department was skittish over criminals being paid, and using any departmental program to contact each other. Cory assured Anna that he had the contacts. Later Anna thought she should have asked how he had that covered. She quickly dismissed the thought and the anxiety that oversight caused her. She had no idea how that would come back and bite her.

Anna consulted with Cory's Probation Officer. Cory had to report to the office on a weekly basis so they would organise his sessions with them both to be back to back. This would maximize his potential to attend and, disrupt his schedule as little as possible, providing him the opportunity to work on his tattoo business. His Probation Officer knew of a bank that was flush with cash and decided giving individuals with a dodgy* financial history 'Second Chance' loans. She knew the manager and would ask if he could help Cory.

In discussions with her supervisor Anna added,

*"I need to make sure I do not feel too pleased with myself over his progress, its early days with him".* What the clever forensic psychologist with the caustic tongue and dictionary of swear words did not know was that it was already too late to heed that self directed warning.

As Anna rode the train home her mobile telephone vibrated in her pocket. She answered it. It was a reporter from the major news-paper in the state. The reporter identified herself. Anna had seen her articles, mostly on crime. The reporter said that she and Ethel had had a meeting where Ethel told her she had met with Anna. Anna would not confirm or deny that and asked how the reporter found her private mobile number. The reporter said the call was not about telephone number procurement it was about a pensioner who was going to lose her home. An elderly pensioner who, in fact, was about to lose everything, even her car, did Anna know that? And while Ethel said that Anna had not been much help she did say she was nice and might be able to help now. Anna said *"this certainly is about how you got my private mobile number, and I cannot and if I could I will not give you any information. Goodbye"*. The other passengers looked at her with surprise. She was in no mood to care. She turned the phone off and worried for the rest of the journey that the boys or Max were trying to contact her.

The next day the morning newspapers and radio newscasts were full of the news that an elderly grandmother was being treated unfairly by the Department of Prisons and Corrections. The picture of her was priceless. She stood on the door step of her home, in her neat flowered dress and apron. Her youngest grandchild was on her hip, face discreetly away from the camera. You would almost swear it was posed. The copy declared that all this grandmother had ever wanted was to own her own home where she could help raise her grandchildren. The picture certainly seemed to validate that. There was no real criminal intent in her actions. She had been tricked and conned, forced into her situation by her son's debts and a social system that did not adequately support its senior citizens. All of this unfairness teetered on the fulcrum of a forensic psychologist who had refused to help an elderly woman or make supportive comments on her behalf. Mercifully not one newspaper printed Anna's name. Yet.

One reporter was pilloried in print when he dared to suggest the story was

*"Pre-packaged maudlin sentimentalism spurred on by social scientists"*. He further wrote that this approach deprived individuals of the right to take responsibility for their own actions. The controversy on this point was only beginning, and it was building.

Anna was glad not to be at Fremantle the following day. Charlotte always reacted intensely and punitively toward the staff if the Department was mentioned negatively in the press. She blamed staff if the Directorate was implicated in any way or if the offenders in one of her staffer's care re-offended. She made sure that staffer took it personally. Anna did not want to take this case personally neither did she want to face PP's questioning eyebrows.

●●●●●

# 12

## Mirror Mirror

As she drove back to Port Stirling, Anna was entranced by the clarity of the morning air and grateful that she could so easily clear her own mind from the news of the day. The sky was 'magic' blue. That's a phrase Anna used when there was no other description that applied. The 5 millimetres of rain that fell through the night had scrubbed the atmosphere clean. She quinted in the bright morning light. As she waited at the traffic lights on the slight hill she spotted the ribbon of emerald sea and Garden Island to the right. She had never noticed the island in such detail from that distance before.

The native trees by the roadside were olive and drab green, camouflage coloured, interspersed by the vibrantly red bottle brush blooms, the grass by comparison was neon lime green. The black and white of a huge magpie was accentuated against the brightness of the ground cover. The crude white wooden crosses that dotted the side of the roadway were decorated with mostly plastic flowers. One supported a young motor cycle rider's helmet, marking the spot of a fatal vehicle accident. In the piercing light they all took on an illumined appearance.

Port Stirling was 10 kilometres to the south of Rockingham, by the sea. It was an idyllic area of new Tuscan style homes, and planned parklands, children's playground, manmade 'lakes' and fountains. The beauty belied the fact that the area had been wrestled from the stark, barren egg yolk yellow sand and limestone. Today the sea was turquoise, emerald, and indigo. The air was like wine, heavily alcoholic wine.

She attended the early morning training on "Dealing with the Violent". The female facilitator was well known and respected in the Department. She had worked with violent offenders for 10 years. The information presented was excellent. The facilitator explained that her agenda was to describe the high end offenders, those who were less than 30% of their case load. They were a particular breed; they lived at the opposite end of the integrity spectrum to most people. She said that with the recent increase in bikie criminality she would focus her discussion on them and others in organised crime. She discussed the fear that stalks each bikie associate or member, and the fear each engenders in others. She said it was believed that fear of retribution within the gangs was as efficient as outright violence when it came to controlling both bikie members and their rivals. She said,

*"Violence is their first lesson of life. Often they learn it in the cradle. They learned early that if it comes their way they are to take it. They learned later if others deserve it, they dispensed it. It is their currency of life, at home and at work. It is the underpinning of their existence. Violence is the one seductress they really know".*

She described how prison continues their violence training. Prison is not punishment but graduation for the truly criminalised young offenders. The 'University of Crime' some call it. She said that the initiates are observed, recruited and vetted carefully in prison. Once selected the neophytes learn from their elder brothers the rules of the streets, a passion for crime and an understanding of its seductive soul. In the right setting and with the right recruiter prison can become a first class, government subsidized institute of higher learning. Tony Trapone was the best example she could name of the success of this type of education. He was first recruited and then a recruiter.

Without doing time in prison the initiates would remain free ranging amateurs with no connection to real crime or criminals. She said

*"Society screams for us to catch the criminals and lock them up. Because, that will teach them. They will learn to be good. And they do - good at crime."* It was a game that is played. Everyone knew the rules, no one was deluded.

While the information she shared was first class Anna recoiled from the speaker's brash attitude. The way she stood, the way she gesticulated, and the coarse language seemed 'offender like'. Her clothing had been worn too many times, and indicated a lack of care about her appearance. On her level 7 salary she had the means but lacked the desire to self groom. If it wasn't there in the first place, the attitude of the offenders had rubbed off and stuck to her. Suddenly Anna understood what Max had been saying. She was looking at herself.

Avoiding invites from her colleagues to meet Anna drove to Mandurah for lunch alone. She chose a vacant spot on a wrought iron and wooden seat by the shallow and calm bay. The turquoise bay was ploughed by mid week tourist boats. She watched the birds, especially George the local Pelican. The day was exquisite, it brought everything to life. Anna could hear children playing on the swings. She ached with missing the boys. She bought a peach ice cream cone. It was amazing, authentic down to the chocolate 'seed'. Even the guilt of eating ice cream without the boys could not quell the riotous pleasure her taste buds experienced.

Training over and paperwork mini avalanche cleared it was 3:00 pm before she saw the first offender for that day. She was a ballet dancer, a professional dance teacher. She had tried out for a place in the WA Ballet but had failed the final cut. That day, she who had never so much as jay walked before, walked into a jewellery store, tried on a ruby and diamond ring worth $2,600.00. The store clerk asked her if she wanted to take it. She did. She took it right out of the store, without paying for it. It seemed like a good idea at the time.

When Anna asked her why she had stolen jewellery she could obviously afford she dissolved into tears, her thin shoulders heaving. She meticulously wiped each and every tear away with her slender fingers. When she could support voice with breath she said

*"Something had to be easy"*. The ballerina poured out a tale of a life of extreme self discipline, insufficient food and too many hours at a ballet bar, since the age of 3. It had been hard. Too hard. When she was rejected by the WA Ballet Company she decided life was going to change. Something was going to come easy. She was surprised how easy it had been to walk right out of that store, ring on finger. The arresting Police officer had commented,

*"Not another ballerina"*. The ballerina's reaction was common, at least one that officer had seen several times before, especially around selection time.

Two offenders and an hour later than usual, Anna was driving home. She passed the huge area that was being cleared for the new mall. There were already two major malls and loads of strip malls in the Peel Region, many with vacant stores and offices. But an overseas corporation planned to build the 'Mall of Australia' there. The selling point was they would only use local products as building materials, and use local tradesmen as labour. What did they think everything else around here was built from and who did they think built it? The Australian slant seemed ridiculous to her but she hoped some of the offenders could be employed.

*"Max"*, she said his name with such urgency he stopped what he was doing and looked at her, *"I saw a mirror image of myself today and I did not like what I saw, really, I know it sounds lame, but I had no idea how offensive my language had become."*

*"Don't fail me now old boy, I need you to understand what I am saying"* she silently demanded of him.

Max was silent for a minute or two, he winked at her. Then he said,

*"Welcome home babe"*. When did he become so wonderful? She smiled and continued to serve their late dinner.

That evening Anna called Cindy and shared her new self knowledge with her. Cindy congratulated her on having the courage to accept what she had discovered, then, in harmony with their discussion at the Italian restaurant said,

*"If you had half a brain you would have known it months ago"*. They both laughed.

•••••

# 13

## Skills Transfer

The next morning, after parking at the highest point she started down the hill named Abernathy Street to the Fremantle office. She strolled by the mottled coloured solid cut limestone walls of the old jail. She was early so had time to look at them, and surprisingly she found them fascinating. The first prisoners had initially been forced to build their own prison. What would it be like for the convict builder to be shipped to Australia from the United Kingdom to build his own imprisoning stone box? She doubted that those imprisoned there, would have been similarly fascinated by the limestone, especially during the jail's darker periods of history. The empty guard box high on top of the wall wrapped in razor wire caught her attention. She stopped walking to view it more carefully. Climbing up and down those metal stairs multiple times a day would have been an arduous exercise, for the guard.

Anna had long been told strange stories of abuse by former prisoners. She remembered the story one schizophrenic offender told her about being raped in the jail on his first night, as an 18 year old. She had heard the same story from another offender, a veteran of a 20 year sentence in that jail. He told similar stories of rape and abuse against young offenders. No one had believed the schizophrenic. Yet others, perhaps more cognitively credible, had told exactly the same type of story. What if it was true? What if the ghosts who were reported to stalk the hallways were real? Perhaps they were the spirits of prisoner-on-prisoner or guard-on-prisoner pain and abuse? She'd talk it over with Liz, maybe. Did it matter now? The prison with its brutal history was now a must see museum, an art gallery, a cafe and a tourist stop.

It was a short walk down the hill which took her past row houses. These were turn of the century miniature dwellings with wrought iron trims and tiny gardens no larger than family grave plots. Judging by the amount of flora present it seemed as if every resident of these tiny places had a passion for gardening. Each mini garden bulged with plants and flowers. It struck her as strange that those with a passionate and uncontrollable need to garden would reside in a gnome's home with so little area for vegetation. Others with huge yards wouldn't know what seedlings were.

The row houses were intriguing, different enough to be identified apart from each other, similar enough to look like sisters. She wondered if she would have to bend her 5'10": frame to walk through the front door. Window openings and doorways had warped, paint was flaking. Some windows opened and closed, some did not, some were missing glass altogether. Fremantle had a brutal past. But Fremantle also had a heart, an ill shaped, out of alignment, time worn heart, but heart none the less, and she was looking at it.

As she considered a particular row house that caught her attention, a 7 year old boy fled out of the front door. A woman screamed at him in a broad Australian accent, *"You can't go out there without a jumpuh\*, look at yah. You stupid boy"*. That took the blush off that bloom.

Before she could begin her own day Charlotte summoned Anna to join her in her office. She had read the latest morning headlines about Granny Grimshaw to Anna, as if Anna could not read them for herself. Charlotte had yellow highlighted the line about the non cooperative forensic psychologist and asked her to identify that psychologist. Anna said one word *"me"*. Charlotte said *"well done, thank you"* she ushered Anna away from her presence with a wave of her royal hand. How does one acclimate to that kind of managerial insanity?

The first offender of the day called himself 'Greg the Burglar'. He was a labourer. He had rough hands, and zero fingerprints from handling the concrete pavers he laid every day. He said he wanted to 'go straight' and to somehow help the Police because he felt they had a lot to learn about the criminal mind. He was the man to teach them. After all it was only recently he realized laws were laws and not mere suggestions. He said sometimes he was so confused he could not remember if he was the good twin or the evil twin. He knew others felt this way too.

He had a broad Australian accent, not the easily recognised Crocodile Dundee accent but the middle of the word sort. The beginning and ending of words did not exist. He articulated only the centre of the word. You could not really call it 'English'. And he mispronounced the few words he did finish, for instance 'something' was 'sumfink'. At times Anna would have to contextually guess what he was saying. He had a riotous sense of humour. When she asked how she could help him he warned,

*"Do not disturb the already disturbed"*.

Toward the conclusion of the session she told him he was an extrovert. He was unfamiliar with that word, she explained its meaning. As he left the session he said,

*"After all I am an extrovert, I am surprised yah have neva'*

*thought of that, yah didn't did yah, I had to tell yah"*. She told him she was equally surprised by her grave omission; she stood reprimanded and would keep it in mind.

The substance of the session had been that he too had transferable skills; he was a burglar of some reputation. And he had no idea how to channel his new intentions. A theme was emerging. Dare she introduce Greg to Cory?

That night she talked her plan over with Max. She knew some of the brighter, motivated offenders had skills they could use for lawful purposes, she felt it. Together she and Max extrapolated a plan from their own business experience and from Max's MBA. They isolated 5 factors that were necessary for a successful business:

1. People Skills, developing both client base, suppliers, and recruiting staff
2. Attention to detail
3. Goal development and evolution, auditing periodically
4. Business plan development, self audit and re-development
5. Marketing

Anna used this frame work to develop a five Chapter plan for skills transference; she called it Justice Through Transferable Skills. She discussed it with her manager. Charlotte could see herself in a photo shoot, proclaiming to Australia that **her** Centre had developed and piloted this revolutionary program.

Anna emailed the draft proposal to the manager at Port Stirling. He was a kindly 50 year old man whose face bore testimony to more experience than one can usually cram into 50 years. His hair was white, as were his eye brows. He often fiddled with his eye brows which grew without being clipped. He joked that he was saving them. He said that when his hair fell out he planned to brush them back over his head. If Trump could brush his back head hair over his brows, he figured he could brush his brow hair back over his head.

He resembled George the Pelican by the bay. He was supportive and thoughtful and when approached he always gave his undivided attention. He was impressed with Anna's plan and a little awed by her enthusiasm. His wife and he ran her own business. The challenge of business enticed him. He proposed some changes to Anna's outline. He warned Anna against getting Cory and Greg in on the program together at this early stage. He said that the criminals find each other easily enough, without the department's help. He recommended they allocate one offender to a pilot program. They should shepherd it through to completion, thoroughly assessing it according to some preauthorised criterion before introducing convicted offenders to each other.

After some consideration the Port Stirling manager suggested she develop a screening process for other offenders, so they could be handpicked for the program at a later stage. He suggested she quarantine psychopaths from the program as,

*"One good psychopath could ruin our entire lives let alone sabotage the program"*. That made perfect sense to Anna, she was glad to have him as a mentor. Once Cory was through the program she would screen all those who followed him. The Port Stirling manager wanted to meet formally with Anna and Charlotte. *"Only if he chairs the meeting"* thought Anna. She booked the room and arranged the meeting, bought the biscuits*, made sure there was coffee, inviting him to be the chair.

The manager from Port Stirling agreed to chair the meeting. Anna had no idea Charlotte could purr, but purr she did. This was the first time Anna had seen Charlotte in a submissive role. It was entertaining. He wanted Anna's project to be titled a 'Mastermind Plan'. He offered to formulate the budget and oversight of the transfer of funds between the program and the artists, in accordance with departmental guidelines. He had set up a trust fund whereby the Department could receive donations for specific purposes. While it would be time consuming to set this up he did not think it would be a problem. He offered to have his assistant set up this funding process, rephrase some of the language in her proposal and review it again with Anna. They would need to add an exit strategy for Departmental oversight of the program. They had no mandate to actually 'own' a for profit business operated by criminals and must avoid all appearance of this. Perhaps a board could be established to manage the tattoo procurement and payment oversight. He would organise that. His assistant would also research the legislative support, if any, for such an endeavour. Charlotte agreed.

Anna emailed the 2$^{nd}$ draft of the proposal to Liz. Liz offered Anna her full support. Once she had the Port Stirling manager's 3rd draft Anna presented it to a number of officers within the department at each Centre. Some were totally confused. They had never thought about channelling the productive energy of the offenders as an independence maker, even a wealth creator for them. Some sent her timid supporting emails. Others offered more helpful advice; Anna was awash with moral support and advice, but no budgetary support. Then it came, the wrecking ball email that crashed through Anna's enthusiasm. Katherine Bourke a mid level manager one step above the Port Stirling manager wrote:

*"I am surprised this proposal has progressed as far as it has without it being submitted to me. It also surprises me that the staff and volunteers have already been preselected. There is nothing new in this proposal; everything proposed is covered within the community. We need to work with the community rather than, at great cost, reinvent their wheel? Competition with existing community resources is beyond our mandate. Budgetary cuts are coming and we can only fulfil our funded mandates."*

*"What wheel? And furthermore, who asked you?"* Anna asked her computer screen. She had never heard of Katherine Bourke and did not know she should have been consulted about anything. Anna had learned from her prior experience that there were no community resources to cover this aspect of offender re-entry to life after prison. Liz advised her early that Ms. Bourke may be able to either float or sink their tentative boat.

Anna researched the names and contact details of key government and nongovernmental organisations and approached them for help. While there were housing relocation, job finding, health care arranging, bus and train ticket giving organisations no one tackled the transference and adaptation of skills. And the governmental 'we have no money' line wore thin and became a cliff against which Anna's enthusiasm crashed. How could a State awash in mining billions not have the funds to adequately treat its offenders?

Anna tracked Katherine's email back and noted that one of the level 3 administration clerks at Port Stirling had forwarded the proposal to Katherine Bourke. At least now she knew who asked her. Liz educated Anna quickly about Katherine's existence and how important Katherine's support was. Anna was not so sure, she asked the Port Stirling manager

*"Is Miss Bourke's disapproval a terminal disease, or a passing virus?"* He was less intimidated by Ms. Bourke than Liz. He told Anna to ignore Katherine, they would go around her. Ignored she was. He also informed her he had arranged the funding side of the program. His assistant would oversee it.

For Wednesday, Thursday and Friday Anna drove to Port Stirling. She'd been so preoccupied with the politics brewing over her proposal for transferable skills that she had hardly noticed the long drive. She was glad she had an 'auto pilot'

●●●●●

# 14

## *Granny Gate*

$\mathcal{T}$he trial of the Department of Prisons and Corrections by the press over the Ethel Grimshaw saga roared. One columnist even called it *"Grim Grannygate"*. As Anna read that headline she thought, *"how 1970'ish"*. The one errant, already pilloried reporter wrote on behalf of the lives ruined by Granny's ice. He did not accept, as did other journalists writing on the issues, the convolution of the social justice aspect which blames society rather than the individual for the individual's crimes. Instead, he wrote that solid science had no way to prove that ice made by a grandmother, for the right reasons, without a history of criminality actually had less disastrous effects on those who used it than any other ice. How dare he mention that? How dare he call for personal responsibility? Did he not know her age? The armchair generals who supported or castigated him filled the Letters to the Editor columns with their opinions, for weeks. He was called 'Neanderthal' and largely dismissed as being unworthy of ridicule. The editor loved it; he had not sold so many papers since Princess Di's death.

The news leapt over the oceans and Australians watched analysis of their actions and their legal system on international broadcasts from the BBC, CNN and Fox News. News that was fair and balanced, and otherwise. There were the human interest stories as Ethel, her daughter in law and her grandchildren, a heart wrenching parade, all crying, were interviewed repeatedly. The national and international political uproar was effective.

Eventually the pressure from the media and the public on the Department crushed it into cowardice. To progress its Public Relations mop up Ethel was given a suspended sentence. Her property would be confiscated under the 'proceeds of crime' umbrella, after her death. Until then she would live in her mortgage free house, drive her gifted new car and live 'quite comfortable' on her pension. To maintain her world all she had to do was not contact Tony Trapone and give up her baking. As it was her first charged offence and her actions were judged to be crimes of desperation rather than to be truly criminogenic, she would not even be mandated to attend therapy.

When Ethel Grimshaw left the Court room that victorious day hundreds of well wishers stood on the steps and crowded on the city sidewalk. They gave her flowers, cards and small stuffed animals. The ever ungracious Ethel wanted to know what she was supposed to do with all that 'crap'. She left over half of it in the Court provided taxi once she arrived home. Anna decided not to join in the lunch room conversations about the case. Nothing she said there would change anything so why expend energy on it?

Anna was losing enthusiasm. In the prison program she had not worked in depth with individual prisoners past the assessment phase. As a senior officer in the programs she dealt with them as a group. They did not self disclose in front of each other. The one to one intervention required her to build resilience for the task and she was not there yet. Her days blurred into a parade of the remarkably ordinary, except for Tony Trapone.

Tony's words were as smooth as melted chocolate or a really

good Scotch. His studied much used smouldering look of 'I want you now' was to be avoided. Anna did not think she make any therapeutic progress with him. He lived outside the margins of those who had the potential to change. He was a true psychopath; she did not need the tests to know that. She had 2 more sessions with him before he violated his bail conditions and was re-incarcerated in the maximum security prison. The Courts were eager to isolate him from the war between the security companies. Anna wondered how many bikie nominees he would recruit while in there. He seemed to delight in every twist and turn of his life. He took whatever came at him as an opportunity to excel at what he did best. She wished the prison based psychologists well and hoped he was assigned to an obese, disinterested, ugly male psychologist, not knowing if one even existed.

She prepared her psychological reports in accordance with departmental protocol, including the final one for Tony. She overheard the Probation Officers talking. They were worried about an offender who had threatened to shoot the windows out of the Port Stirling office. She was unfamiliar with his case, but apparently he had psychotic episodes as a result of drug abuse. They did not know if he had the means or knowledge to put feet to his threat, but they remained concerned. Anna held an ad hoc debriefing session for them and contacted the manager at Port Stirling to relay concerns, and wait for his instructions. She emailed Liz and let her know the psychological mood of the Centre. The Police heightened security and implemented parking restrictions to prevent non staff cars parking within shooting distance of the Centre.

•••••

# 15

## The Birthday Boy

*F*riday was Stuart's birthday. Anna delighted in her mothering role. But now it was changing as Stuart turned 15. His voice had deepened, his legs were covered with thick 'fur', and he shaved his chin at least once every 3 days. There was an ever evolving manliness about him, a sense of adulthood in his eyes that caused her to back off as a parent. She was not ready to abdicate her parental role, yet something about him demanded she afford him the respect of an adult. She wanted to hold on to Stuart – the boy, yet he was gone.

That Friday Max and Lachie and Stuart and Harry their friend went to Time Zone in Fremantle, they chased each other through produced-for-consumers dark alleyways, tagging each other with lasers. Max and Anna sat out the second round.

Anna often said that mothering was not for wimps. She also knew that being born female did not mean she knew how to do it right. When Stu was born; he was full term but undersized. Her mother had asked her what she was going to do with him. Her smart mouthed response was,

*"What everyone else does, fly by the seat of my pants."* But Anna did want to do it right. She wanted to play with him; she wanted to feed him nutritious food. She dosed herself with guilt when she became frustrated at the ritualised way he played. She

never did understand why he took so long to set up the fort or farm or roadway only to abandon it and not play at all. She had to admit that sometimes she fed him fast food. And at times he went to bed after 10:00 pm.

Max would tell her to cut herself some slack and just enjoy the kids but wanting to do it right sometimes tripped up that good intention. She admired the way Max could stop the lawn mower to throw balls to Lachie leaving the lawn to mow itself, for up to a week.

Stu and Harry and Lachie ate at their favourite pizza parlour while Anna and Max grabbed a pub meal amongst a noisy energized crowd. They met up at the markets. Stu had wanted money for gifts, he got it. That night on the way home he asked if he could start work at the Beefy Burger Bar. He said he had already filled out an application, and had his uniform and if they agreed he would start the Saturday after the next. The two staggered parents needed time to think about this proposition. It was enough their first born had turned 15 without thinking about him entering the job market too.

•••••

# 16

# A Bikie's Wedding

$\mathcal{T}$he next day Sunday was the day of a wedding for one of Max's main contractors. Max's company was in the process of demolishing deteriorated homes in a 3 square block radius. The urban renewal plan was to replace the homes with smaller apartments, and offer them for sale at a minimal cost, to those who qualified. The main man for the demolition company was marrying his long time love. Max was invited, and by association so was Anna. Anna was edgy about it as she was not permitted to consort with known criminals and this demolition company was rumoured to be owned, organised, run and operated by criminals. Heavy end bikies, in fact.

However she knew what she knew by rumour, Anna had no specific information on any of them so she allowed herself to attend. It was a garden wedding. The bride had been wed before. No white dress and veil for her. She wore a pale green and black ball gown trimmed with black pearls. The bride had a child by her first husband and one by her groom. Both girls walked with their self conscious mother down the grassy aisle. The groom looked uncomfortable in his suit. He repeatedly stretched his neck as if to free it from its restricting collar and tie.

As the preacher requested to 'open the wedding in prayer' the guests walked around, chatted, open bottles and cans of alcohol in hand. When the preacher asked them to join in the "Our Father" prayer they refreshed their beverages and his was the only voice heard. It was obvious they did not know the prayer. But they did know their beverages.

The evening was warm and pleasant; unlike the participants. The reception was in a room decorated in the 70's, wearing all of the dust and nicotine it had accumulated since its first painting. It looked more like a beer hall than a place to celebrate a wedding. The light fixtures performed their lighting duties feebly as the light fought its way through the filth laced shades. The food was a smorgasbord of ethnic opinions. Anna was not hungry. The cake was homemade and asymmetrical. The baker-guest was recognised and loudly praised.

The guest seated behind her was one of the smallest men she had ever seen. He wore a 1970's mustard coloured suit. He said he had raised his 3 sons alone. His accent was Eastern European and Anna had to listen carefully to understand him. It was not so much the accent but the grammar and the idioms he used that confused her. She thought she was on safe ground when she complimented him on raising his boys alone. Mistake number one. He was offended to the point of being inflamed. He flared hostile over the idea that someone would thank him for raising his own children. It was not a lot of work, it was not something to even acknowledge, any father would do it.

Anna excused herself. She found the restroom. Mistake number two. In that restroom Anna encountered a group of the female wedding attendees. Their faces wore the mask of those who have been sworn at, spat at, hit, punched and abused. It is a hardness born of self protection. Anna wore no such mask; they immediately recognised she was not a "sistah". They ignored her greeting and attempts at conversation. Rather than feeling embarrassed she was pleased not to be counted among them.

She took the garden route back to her seat. Mistake number three. The best man and the matron of honour were having standing up sex against the rear wall. Her orgasmic scream startled Anna. The best man's wife watched. She did not dare protest or even indicate that she registered their fornicating actions.

Back in the reception hall a large male dominated. He was in his 50's, had long grey hair, a huge beer gut, tatts and a 'get out of my way swagger'. Anna pegged him as a bikie chieftain. He kept eyeing Max, wordlessly challenging him, reasserting himself as the chief mongrel, seeing if Max would challenge him for the position. There was no way Max would want to be chief dog of that pile. Outside of his 'at arm's length' business dealings he would not want to associate with, let alone rule them. Max lowered his eyes, refusing to engage in the eye to eye combat, thereby telling the mongrel chief that his kingdom was safe from any 'Max' threat.

Later, during the more formal part of the dinner the Matron of Honour, still flushed with her orgasmic glow thanked the bride for choosing such 'an excellent' partner for her. His wife sat silently, blankly, as if she had not heard. She was accustomed to this role. Then it was the bride's father's turn. Usually paternal wedding speeches are affectionate and respectful, perhaps tinged with a little sadness that the prized daughter is now another's wife. This wedding was anything but usual. The father who did not escort the bride down the aisle made drunken suggestive remarks in his speech about his daughter and slurred his way through her childhood and her promiscuous adolescence. His ramblings brought cheers from the males present; perhaps they knew first hand of her promiscuity. His finale involved a wish for the groom that this would be a Kentucky Fried Chicken marriage. He explained that meant *"lots of breast and stuffing"*. The most amazing thing, to Anna, about this father's rendition was that the bride joined in the merriment, unfazed by his disrespectful and deplorable presentation. She did not seem to know, or care that the crude joke was on her. Her mother was absent in person and word.

Anna asked Max if they could leave. After the obligatory 'business gendering goodbyes', leave they did. She concluded that if this is how her clients lived on their highest celebratory day no wonder their lives were in the toilet.

• • • • •

# 17

# High Tea with the President

The week sped by and Saturday saw Anna ready herself for the Parent Group tea. She could not compete with Madame President's clothes. But, Anna did have an elegant skirt she bought the last time the family was in California. At least no one would know what it had cost. She paired it with a simple beige silk top and high heeled strap sandals.

This section of the suburb was new to her. She was mystified how it had remained hidden from her daily life. Driving through leafy streets and past regal mansions, overlooking the Swan River she approached the destination house. She located it through ornate electronic gates and beyond elegantly manicured gardens. She was initially intrigued by her trespass into the brick and mortar opulence. However the novelty soon wore off and she became nonchalant toward it.

Madame President's front garden was divided into 4 equally sized unique areas. One was an orchard with a cacophony of beautifully behaved citrus trees surrounded by a perfectly clipped hedge. The second was a rose garden complete with a rose arbour; the new drought resistant burgundy iceberg rose had already bloomed. Anna had read about that hybrid rose in the local newspaper. Madame President has a rare collection of climbing and tea roses of brilliant colours and perfumes. The third section was a paved area around a water feature. She had never seen one like it. A gorgeously crafted bronze figure of Cleopatra was at least 4 meters tall. She stood with an urn high over her head pouring water onto monstrous bronze water lilies. There were growing water plants in the pool at her feet.

The gardener's voice startled her. She thought she was alone with Cleopatra. He said,

*"The missus likes Egyptology"*. Anna smiled and thanked him for his information. The sound of the running water refreshed her as the heat of the day increased. The fourth area was a large tiled swimming pool surrounded by teak tables and cushioned lounges. Remarkable. She walked up the short stair case to be greeted by a maid in a black dress with white apron and cap. She had no idea people still dressed like that other than as a joke on New Year's Eve or as paid for foreplay in a rented bedroom. She was offered savoury morsels in puffed pastry and champagne in a crystal flute.

A photographer mingled with the guests, unnoticed if not unseen, as he quietly recorded the event for posterity. The floors of the home were the popular highly polished black wooden boards from Tasmania. Huge furniture pieces, over sized chairs and majestic tables abounded. The piano would have filled a whole room in Anna's house but here it took up a mere corner. The wall hangings were massive. Even the smallest painting on display was 4 times larger than anything Anna and Max had. There were none of the usual knickknacks but there were life sized statues of Egyptian figures.

The other mothers were ingratiatingly polite. They were paid up members of the indecently wealthy club. Black was the colour to wear and the members knew that. Anna was delighted she had worn her multi coloured skirt. She thought *"How Joe Dorlani-esque, I'm out of uniform"*. Alison, the President greeted her, looking more like Nicole than before. Suddenly Anna realised the President's son was in the boarding school yet his home was two bus stops away from the school. Why was he boarding? She decided not to ask. Through the peripheral conversations she gathered that the President had married her husband, the provider of her life style 5 years ago, and her son was now 14.

The rented harp and harpist created incredible music. Anna listened to the cadence of the conversation; it ebbed and flowed with the music. She wondered if Mrs. Joseph Dorlani had been invited. If she was, she did not accept the summons. Anna nibbled at more savoury morsels, drank a cup of coffee, and left. Anna figured that to support the staff and the gardens and to clean and heat and maintain that mansion she would need the bald drug dealer's 50 grand a week, tax free. Or close to it. She did not know how Alison's husband made his money but it was quite 'a tea' his money had just bought her.

Anna had lived in this suburb for 10 years and this was the first time she realised that some of her neighbours lived like royalty. They not only lived on a different planet to her, but in a different galaxy, far far away from her mundane life. She had to admit she enjoyed the experience.

When she arrived home she looked for Stuart. She located him behind his locked bedroom door. She knocked on his door. He did not open it.

*"What are you doing son?"* she asked through the closed door.

*"Just sitting here in my uniform."*

Anna groaned. She had completely forgotten, it was that Saturday, Stu's first day at work. The world of Beefy Burger awaited him.

*"What time do you start?"*

*"An hour ago?"*

Anna called Beefy Burger and explained what had happened. The crew manager sounded as if he was around 12 years of age himself, he laughed and told her to

*"Bring the kid in".* He told her it was par for the course for almost every kid's first day. The parents almost always forgot - he overscheduled staff to compensate. Anna and Max had not decided Stu was even going to work but given the circumstances she brought 'the kid in'. Stu did not say one word during the 10 minute car ride to the fast food outlet. Anna knew it might be a while before he spoke to, or forgave her.

Max picked Stuart up 4 hours later. He did not speak to him either. His parents consoled themselves with the thought that their oldest was an equal opportunity brat. The next morning when Anna went to wake him to take a phone call from his school friend she found him still in his uniform fast asleep in bed. And that was where she left him with apologies to his mate. She had a sense an era was over, despite her spoken and silent protestations. She was not ready for it.

•••••

# 18

## A Show

Monday was a celebration of Queen Elizabeth's birthday. It was not really her birthday, but the official celebration day. Anna never did figure out why they were different. Normally Monday was spent in Fremantle with PP and offenders, this week she would spend it with her family. It was late September and the 110th anniversary of the state fair known as The Perth Royal Show, or 'The Show'. The weather arrived in its most splendid attire complete with a yawning blue sky, clear and fresh, not too hot. Arriving at the gates they joined the throngs of thousands of others with the same idea. The boys wandered off down to side show alley arranging to meet Anna and Max at the restaurant around noon. They were nowhere to be seen at the restaurant. Anna called them on their mobile phone.

*"We are stuck in the crowd, Mum, we can't even move. Honest, it is like trying to walk through neck high wet cement"* Stu claimed.

Apparently the theme of The Show that year was to celebrate all things Tuscan. The music reminded Anna of the chick flick 'Under the Tuscan Sun'. A line of well endowed young men in costumes, waving flags, danced, and threw their flags to the beat of a Tuscan drum. Great fun! It took a while for the boys to locate them, Max and Anna had a coffee. They met friends, and even had a chance meeting with their nephew and his new girlfriend. They later learned that a record 62,000 attended the show that day. No wonder the boys had to wade through a cement-like non moving river of 'others'.

Max and Anna had laughed and relaxed and gossiped. They drank too much coffee and petted one farm animal after another. The boys bought arm loads of show bags. These are plastic bags filled with whatever product a particular company is hawking, from stuffed animals, to chocolates, to comics, to a whoopee cushion. Kids all over Western Australia wrestled each other for the lift out magazine in the newspaper. This lift out describes all of the show bags available, listing their contents and their usual retail value. It takes hours to sort through them, some kids even plan all year which bags they wish to buy. There were always too many bags when the tally was finally counted at home.

Anna figured it would take the boys two weeks to work their way through the edible contents. As they were leaving they ran into Sean O'Connor. He was back in his bikie gear, showing his tatts, his muscles, his sweat, bald head, goatee, piercings, as he herded his three boys in front of him.

*"Hello mate"* he tossed at Anna through clenched teeth *"those yours?"*

Anna ignored his demand to identify her sons.

*"Hello Sean, how are you?"*

*"Fine, fine."*

When they had put a safe distance between them and the O'Connors, Max demanded

*"Who the hell was that?"*

*"Can't say"* Anna waited a moment; Max knew not to ask further.

*"No wonder you swear, if I worked with creeps like that I would be the foul mouth of the Galaxy"* was Max's only response.

It was Tuesday and Anna was in the Fremantle office. She didn't have the energy to walk to the train so she had driven to work and parked on the hill again. The day after the Show she just felt tired. Apparently the clients had not joined the throngs at the Show as they all attended for therapy, despite the rain. How could it be raining today after such perfect weather yesterday? How come the clients didn't melt in the rain today when usually they fear any contact with it and stay home? All seven clients showed, seven in a row with a short-gobble-your-lunch-down break. She tried to make early phone calls, but the clients in the reception area were too noisy. At 9:30 am 'the' family arrived, and amidst loud voices and clanging activities and took over the reception area. They were up and down the stairs, slamming the rest room doors, the front doors, swearing at PP. He defused their anger and rambunctious energy with politeness. He certainly knew his job.

It was raining. Thumping down rain. Face bruising rain. Traffic stopping rain. From her window Anna could see the roof tops across the street. These were metal steep inverted V shaped roof tops. The rain pelted down in one direction, it slammed into the slope of the roof, and bounced up forming a plume which curled over the apex of the V and blew to oblivion in the wind. It was fascinating. Not one of the clients was the slightest bit interested. Even PP refused to look as Anna described it.

Another of the noisy family members ran into the reception area and announced to Jason that he had seen hundreds of Rosellas, the noisy, bright coloured parrots which gather in multitudinous flocks, sheltering in one of the trees outside. They were disoriented by the bewildering force of the rain. They did not know whether to fly, or run, or dig, or leave, or stay, or squawk, or huddle in silence. They were soaked and totally confused. The down pour had stopped all road traffic, no one was driving anywhere in that blinding deluge. PP laughed and kept control over the whole group by engaging them in the topic.

As fast as it came, it left. The skies cleared before the pavement outside dried. It was one of those occasions where you see streams of water across the roadway but no clouds so you don't know how the water got there. It was like a drive-by water bombing blitz. Once the rowdy family had all reported to their Probation Officers, they left. Thankfully. Quiet returned and Anna could think again, but now there was no time left for phone calls.

Anna wondered what had happened to the Rosellas as she locked up her area for the day. She glanced back through the office and noticed a new security guard. He was tall, built like a building, shaved bald. He had a strange attitude about him, overly confident, like a 'go ahead, make my day' attitude. She had never seen him before. Maybe PP needed a substitute and went out to check on the Rosellas, or to check on any damage the noisy family may have done as they departed.

The Police called. One of the offenders, recently released, had been issuing threats against his Probation Officer. He was talking about it with his mates at the local pub, the one overlooking the Port itself. It was a favourite hangout for the local boys and frequently required Police intervention to restore the peace. The offender's name was Harry Browning. His name was often in the headlines with words like 'Perth's Mr.Big, or, WA's Most Notorious Criminal'.

He had a long standing grudge against the department. The department stripped him of his means to make a livelihood, decimated his client base, raided his house, and imprisoned him. His wife had left, taking his kids, and he had not seen them since. At night he obsessed over the way he had been caught, the words of the arresting officer, and the Judge. The Judge was Asian, a Malay, and Harry hated foreigners. He especially hated small, thin faced, posh foreigners with fat little hands who had control over his life. The fact he had a criminal record dating back to when he was 13 years of age, and the fact he was caught operating a nationwide bikie network that dealt with stolen goods and drugs was beside the point.

Harry was proud of his professional achievements and the luxury they brought him and his new missus and her two girls. They no longer lived in Mirrabooka, they had moved to Cottesloe. Cottesloe!!! Sometimes he and the missus could not believe they had a Cottesloe address. The neighbours found it difficult to believe too when he burned through the side streets on his huge motorbike. Children in that area did not run the streets bare foot, and mothers did not scream from the front porch for their marauding mob, but the Browning family did. His new missus would often summon her children home by roaring their names into the neighbourhood. Their business was exceptionally successful. Any one needed anything he could find it whether or not it was legal to possess the item. Crime was more than a profession for Harry, it was his identity. And his Probation Officer had the gall to insist he, Mr.Browning, remain crime free. He was beginning to hate her. Barbara.

The police found a security guard's uniform in Harry's car during a routine traffic stop. Charlotte circulated a photograph of the offender who was the focus of the present Police warning. Anna wished she had paid more attention to the bald, arrogant looking security guard. He certainly looked like the offender, or did he? She was afraid she would be judged to be paranoid or an alarmist if she mentioned it to Jason. Either one would be a highly undesirable trait in a psychologist. The tension between her and Charlotte had eased and she did not want to rekindle it. She felt fear when she tried to figure out why he would want to gain entrance to their secured building under cover of a security guard uniform. She swore at herself and wished she had taken more notice. She felt nauseous.

•••••

# 19

## Tattoos and Muffins

*I*t was Wednesday,

*"Port Stirling here I come"* she thought as she activated the cruise control for the hour and half drive. She bypassed the traffic lights in Rockingham by taking the cut off road at Ennis Avenue. Traffic itself was light, the sky was clear. The grasses suspended their seeds above their heads and threw them to ride the breeze. The effect was a purple/brown hazy cloud floating just above the ground cover. It was a Monet effect. The colours of the region were olives of many hues, beiges, ivory, and browns; if they were sown in velvet they'd make a great Australiana quilted gown.

Cory, the tattoo entrepreneur, was Anna's first client of the day. He was early. He had been working through his list and had identified contacts important to his tattoo business. He then refined the list in session to 4. He agreed that he would call or contact them. Two contacts were marketers, two were graphic designers and who could assist him present the designs on CDs and YouTube videos. He also knew the names of the artists who instructed prisoners on how to use various mediums, including inks or pencil drawing. He would contact them for more names of potential tattoo artists to add to his list.

Cory told Anna that he had already contacted one potential supporter, a professor at the local university. The professor was enthused by, and supportive of, Cory's idea. He had been thinking along these lines for years and would be pleased, no, obviously delighted to help. Cory said that the professor told him he had always believed that art could unlock hidden potential and become the medium of success even for those who did not succeed in other forums. He had written and published a thesis on the topic for his Master's Degree. He said the arts are like Miracle Grow for the brain. Cory didn't know that the excited professor repeated Cory's conversation to his own wife that night and that neither of them could sleep. She was delighted; finally her unacknowledged husband had found a meaning to the long class room hours. It seemed to make his life's efforts worthwhile.

Mervyn had asked to accompany Cory to his session that day. Cory wasn't sure what to do with him so told Mervyn to wait for him outside the office, but within earshot. Under Cory's direction Anna found Mervyn sitting on the wild grass leaning against the eucalyptus tree. Anna invited him in to the office.

Mervyn was quietly spoken. He was extremely attractive. Japanese and Aboriginal genetics combined most beautifully in this angular young man. He said he had some concerns at the speed that the business was progressing. He wanted to make sure Anna understood that the art he shared with the project had to be offered and accepted in the right spirit. It was not just about profit margins and marketing. He explained that all body decoration had deep spiritual significance for his peoples, both of them. He said

*"I do not believe that a man or a woman is free to change his or her appearance at will or recklessly, just because they want to, or just because it looks tough"*. He explained that it was a sacred thing to him. Mervyn said

*"I only use respected designs, mostly the designs of ancestors, so special care is needed. I design some myself and combine them with our scarring and permanent body painting. The scarification is an ancient Aboriginal art and has to be done respectfully with the right instruments, a shell or a rock. Ash or some other organic substance is rubbed into the wound until the desired kind of scar developed. I need to correct something, my designs are not really mine, they are a gift and I respect the gift and giver. Those who wear my designs must also be respectful of the gift. I work together a complex system of brandings, symbols and images that are spiritually based but that are at the same time client specific ornamentation for each client. See, while human beauty is skin deep, tattoos somehow reach all the way through to the sacred within. And the sacred has to be respected."*

Anna took him seriously. She noted each of his issues and goals. Once his concerns were stated Mervyn said he was leaving. He did not wait for her response. Anna was not sure whose presence she had just encountered, it looked like he bowed to her as he left. Did he?

Cory was unmoved by the content and depth of Mervyn's approach. He launched into his agenda. He did not need her help getting the tattoos; he had many mates who could provide them, and the prison art teachers would give him more names. He was not interested when she protested about his close associations with other criminals.

*"Look I have that covered, all I need is to know how not to get bored, I get bored and the Samster and me will be playing tag with bait the local police."* Was he serious? He spoke with a raw edged authority she had not seen before. He abruptly ended the

conversation before it had begun. It was like watching a switch flip from 'on' to 'outta here'. Sam was outside in the car. The rottie* started barking, Cory needed to leave. Sam would rip off the arm of anyone who touched the car and he did not need an extra arm this week. He was done anyway, he left, he'd return to reschedule with the receptionist.

Anna dropped by Franny's for a muffin. She asked her why she never baked apples into the muffins. Franny said she did not like cooked apple. Anna was astounded. Anna had a strongly held opinion about cooking apples and would repeat it whenever afforded the chance. Anna thought that apples were the one food product that died in cooking. She could not figure out why anyone would take a delicious apple, cook it, render it pale brown tasteless mush and call it 'good'. She had never found anyone else who held the same opinion. Franny had become a friend. They were bound together by their rejection of cooked apple.

After driving close to home she realised she needed to pick up some fresh bread for the boy's sandwiches tomorrow so she stopped at the local super market. She ran into Julie, a mother with a son attending St. Benedict's. Anna knew her well enough to comment and ask,

*"I was at the home of Alison, the President of the PG at St. Bennie's, what do you know about her?"*

*"You didn't go to her home for one of those teas did you?"*

*"'Fraid so"*said Anna.

*"I meant to warn you about those invites. I don't know much about her really. I do know that she married her boss. Of course he was married to someone else when they met. He is 15 years older than Alison, and he has four grown kids. She is his third wife.*

*He apparently takes good care of his ex wives and kids. And in a perverse way he is proud of that. He has a history of rotating through his secretaries, some are temporary trophies but I think this one intends to be 'a keeper'. She will not let herself age, or gain a kilo. If you watch her you will see she eats nothing at the functions, she drinks only warm water. He won't let her son live with them full time. To please him and keep their relationship in tact she dumped her boy in St. Bennie's boarding house. I overheard her telling one of the other mothers that she was doing it for her son. On her own she could not afford to buy him such a quality private education or send him on ski trips to Japan and New Zealand or for summer holidays in London. She figures her boy needs those more than he needs to live with her in a government subsidised flat. Maybe he does, they both have a lovely life that's for sure."*

"*And I thought her only deal was that she looks like Nicole Kidman*" Anna commented.

"*Oh my gosh you are right, I'd never have thought of that. I guess whatever it takes. With her lovely life style she has a British au pair – even though her son lives at the boarding school during the week and some weekends. The au pair is there to watch over him on the weekend and to keep him away from His Royal Highness. My son says he hates it, he feels like he has a 'baby sitter' but he too knows he must play the game to maintain his life style and keep his mum happy. Just watch what you say to Alison, she never met a secret she could keep, even her own.*"

That evening, after dinner and dishes and homework, Anna took a few moments to read the local newspaper. There on page 32 was a group of photographic renditions of Alison's afternoon 'tea' party. Anna's photo was front and centre, with her name and occupation printed below. She was talking to the gardener in the photograph as Cleopatra hovered in the background. She had been totally unaware that during the brief time it took to exchange those few words her picture had been taken. Its publication distressed her greatly and even frightened her. It provided a context to her private life, a location, information to those who might wish her or her family harm as it reported that she had children attending St. Benedict's College. It also gave some idea of where they lived. Julie was right she should not have attended that pretentious damn party. Max said she was over reacting.

•••••

# 20

## Two Stories

*S*aturday saw Stu rise at 7:00 am and sit in his uniform until it was time to go to work at 2:00 pm. Anna drove her wordless son to his scheduled shift. When he reached the door of the burger place he turned around and lifted his eyebrow at her. An eyebrow lift from PP aggravated her no end but an eye brow lift from Stuart caused her to feel a sense of well being. When Max brought him home at 6:30pm Stu smelled like cooking oil. Not surprising as he had stood, knees locked, directly above the fry cooker, putting them in, taking them out of boiling oil for 4 hours. Tonight he broke his vow of silence.

*"Mum what did one burger patty say to the other burger patty?"* How could Anna know that?

*"Oh look a cooking patty.' And the other one said 'oh look a talking patty'"*. She was so grateful to be spoken to she laughed. It was kind of funny. It was her introduction to burger humour.

Sunday was a day to relax. And Anna did it, splendidly, almost professionally. It included a raucous Sunday afternoon phone call from Cindy and Cindy's first lesson in Aussie Insults 101.

On Monday, the following morning, Anna was annoyed. She had arrived earlier than usual, so arrived alone. She was at the Fremantle office but could not get into the building. She had no access through the wrought iron gates that protected the Abernathy Street locked entrance. She could not locate her swipe (computerised key pad). She remembered putting it in her suede coat pocket. She had not worn that jacket for a week or two; the swipe must be there, in its pocket. She had not needed it recently as she had entered the office at the same time others did, so came in on their pass. She would retrieve it tonight, until then she had to wait for someone to let her in. Through the upstairs window PP noticed her standing outside. He gave no indication that he understood her dilemma. He went through his ritual of unlocking each internal door in accordance with his own routine at his own speed. He left her there, outside in the cool early spring air, until every internal door had been unlocked. When he did finally pass by the door that stood between her and the office, he did it only when it synthesized with his morning routine. He then gave her entrance. Anna thanked him for letting her in without further comment.

She had never seen her first client before. He was 55 but looked 75. He had foreign particles in his shaggy beard and he smelled sour. He was ill, physically and mentally. She was repulsed by the smell and trying too hard not to show it.

His throat was painfully sore and he was coughing uncontrollably. It was a dry cutting and painful sounding cough. Anna was pleased she had some throat soothers to give him. She offered him one; he readily took the entire packet. He was not accustomed to conversations longer than 2 – 3 words. He kept losing his train of thought as he stroked his beard. She offered him a cup of tea, he was most eager to have one. She returned him to the reception area, made him his cuppa*, and found two chocolate covered biscuits in the staff biscuit canister.

He was thankful to have a warm drink on that unusually cool

morning. She silently watched him slowly drink it. He dribbled and savoured each noisy sip and mouthful of biscuit, despite his sore throat. It took him 15 minutes to nibble and slurp his way through the offering. He said nothing but flashed Anna his toothless smile. They had connected. He wanted to come back in a week. She made the appointment for Alexander Lloyd. She sprayed the room with room deodorizer after he left.

Sean O'Connor was her next scheduled appointment. He was on time. He was back in 'the brother' gear, just as he had been at The Show. No more pretence.

*"Morning Sean."*

*"Whatever. Look I don't need to be here, in fact I am not the one with the problem. What about you Anna, you or your boys got any problems, why don't I see if I can solve them?"*

*"I appreciate the offer Sean, but this is about you not me."*

*"Don't get all psychological on me."*

She had to admit that traditional techniques would look ridiculous in this setting. She did not feel benevolent enough toward him to make him a cup of tea or coffee. She just sat wordlessly.

*"You are the expert here; you are supposed to ask me questions. You haven't asked me one valid question yet. Aren't you supposed to be in control here?"*

She said nothing. She was not going to take that bait. She waited. She knew the cycle, sweetness, if that failed, sarcasm and sow self doubt in others, if that failed - anger. Right on cue he slammed his open hand on her desk. His goal was to invade her space and to make the most noise he could; a closed fist would not do, so the open hand was employed. Anna forced herself not to react.

Still Anna said nothing. She was not going to reward this cycle.

Next she could expect silence and either he would huff out of the room swearing over his shoulder about how incompetent she was, or he'd return to the 'sweetness' segment. Sweetness it was.

*"I am sorry psych, you were such a help last time, and in fact you are the only psych I have ever met who made sense. By the way I saw your picture in the paper, I hear St. Benedict's is a great school, I even thought of sending my boys there."*

*"Why are you lot so bloody predictable?"* she thought but did not verbalise. She knew this was a clandestine threat, and that he was flaunting the fact he knew private identifying information about her. He could locate her and her precious boys at any time he chose. The tangential thought of Joe Dorlani's and Sean O'Connor's combined influence upon the pomposity of that school was to be savoured. She knowingly used it to mitigate the anxiety engendered by their exchange.

*"Cut the crap Sean, if you want to deal with real issues and end your offending cycle we can work on it. If you are going to engage in this theatre, then forget it."*

'Theatre' was the wrong word to use, or at least that is what Sean said. He swore and stormed out, somewhat out of sync with the cycle but it was inevitable. She caught Jason's eye, and Jason gave her 'the eyebrow' of disgust.

She felt like Heidi in the pristine mountain air offering the Lord of the Orgy and drunken feast a whole meal bread sandwich made with organically grown salads. Was it as ludicrous an exercise in futility as it appeared to be to her at that moment? Offering this hard end criminal the opportunity to live a law abiding life appeared to be pre-determined to meet with defeat. She sighed.

She told Liz later, in supervision, that she had permitted her own anger at him and fear of him to cloud her judgment. Surely Liz would understand. Sean could now locate her and her precious sons outside of the office. Liz was particularly non understanding. Anna needed to either deal with that or transfer him to another psychologist. He deserved the same chance given to all offenders, that of being treated in a professional manner. Her words bit Anna, more so because they were true. She had done nothing to ally with Sean; she had in fact set him up to storm out. She knew his cycles; if he left she could be rid of him for the day. She had blamed his sociopathy, when in fact it was her knowledge of how to trigger his sociopathy that was the problem. To assuage her guilt she had convinced herself it was a futile task anyway to try to engage him in a therapeutic encounter. Liz had called her on it. Outright.

The weekend came and went, this time the family schedule seemed to rotate around Beefy Burger. Stu took the manager's keys home by mistake. Stu asked her to drive him back to Beefy Burger at 5:00 am on Saturday to let the shift manager in with his own keys. Then Stu had a shift at 12:00 noon until 4:00, the next day, Sunday a mate asked him to cover for him from 10:00 am until 2:00 pm. With his own schedule he could not do the full 4 hour shift for his colleague, but he started at 10:00am for him. Lachie enjoyed the free family meals Beefy Burger provided but Anna and Max hoped this phase would soon pass.

When Anna collected Stu from the Beefy Burger he chatted on about how he had been allowed to answer the phone. His manager never let the new employees answer the phone, but he, Stu Lennox had been allowed to answer the phone. How magic was that? *"Way magic"* said Anna but she thought *"why is answering the phone at home not magic?"* However she left that question for another time in order to allow her first born to enjoy his Beefy Burger telephone success. The conversation was limited but it was conversation never the less.

That following Monday morning Anna could not find her suede jacket. She knew her swipe was in the pocket. If she could not find it she would have her swipe de-activated. Explaining her careless oversight of the swipe was sure to draw the usual tirade. She did not have the energy for it. She had to wait outside the building for another staffer to arrive and walk in with her.

The first client, Alex Lloyd was early for his appointment. Anna had his tea ready for him, milk and one sugar, and two more biscuits. To avoid upsetting the secretary she had brought these ones from home. It still took Alex 15 minutes to deal with the refreshments, even though his throat was improved. He told her he lived in the bush. She had to believe him but wondered where there was bush enough for him to live in undetected in that urbanised area. She did not challenge him. He told her how 3 or 4 mates gathered at 'the spot' towards evening. They rolled out their blankets, or tied up a piece of tarpaulin for shelter. No tents, he was scornful of tents, they are,

*"Too hot, keep the air and sky out"*. He liked living in the bush, he could not choose and did not always like his roommates but they went with the territory. In most instances companions diminished the dangers inherent in sleeping in isolation. He told her he had been charged with stealing money from an old girl in the park. He denied he had done it, and stated,

*"I was done like a dog's dinner"*. He did not know why he had been charged, but he had not been feeling well lately and wanted some protective housing until he felt better. Could she help?

Another appointment was made. Even though finding housing for clients was not within her job description Anna discussed Alex with his Probation Officer, and his Social Worker. The social worker spent her lunch hour contacting various agencies. It paid off, she found a half way house for him. The social worker made the arrangements, and provided a bus pass for him to travel there. Anna doubted Alex would stay long. She knew the house supervisors would accept his alcoholism or low standard of hygiene, but he did need protection. She hoped they had hot tea and chocolate biscuits.

Six days later Anna received an email from the social worker. Alexander Lloyd had been disinvited to remain at New-way, the half way house. He had stayed 5 days longer than she expected, but a lot less time than he needed. The other residents complained about his poor hygiene and invasive ways. Alex would be in to see them both tomorrow as scheduled. The social worker tried to locate another safe house for Alex. Perth functions like a large country town, if a client's behaviour was problematic in one situation his reputation would spread, even down confidential lines, and he'd be black-listed. A pungent, drunken, hairy man, with an exaggerated sense of 'ours' and without table manners could easily be blacklisted.

She checked her schedule. The stream of offenders had filed through her office and Sean O'Connor was next. He arrived, on time.

*"Sean I owe you an apology."*

*"Yeah, I know, well we don't need to hammer it to death do we?"* He was offering her mercy. In his full Death Adder regalia, bared arms to display his pythons and daggers, he offered her mercy. She thought that to be ironic.

*"What would you like to discuss today?"*

*"I don't know what this is supposed to do for me. I don't think I need counselling."*

*"Sean you know the deal, the Magistrate ordered you to attend, you might as well make any use of the experience that you can. Is there something you have done, some habitual way of dealing with life that you would like to process and change for your own advantage?"*

*"No I have no regrets. It's been a good life."*

*"Sean I counted 23 charges against you from driving without a valid driver's license to aggravated burglary and organised crime. You had a gun and a silencer in your car's boot. What were you doing, hunting 'roos with sensitive ears? Your court transcript states that you personally gave the orders for the abduction and vicious beating of one of your members as a disciplinary measure. They used spiked knuckle dusters on him. He was beaten to a pulp and he died because of the beating you ordered. And what did he do to deserve this? He did something you did not like in a money deal!!!!. The Magistrate called it the most appalling and violent attack he had ever encountered?"* She dare not look at him, she knew she was pushing it but kept going.

*"You were the master mind behind the equipment theft, from the diamond mines. You organised 6 other brothers to be employed as truck drivers, stay long enough to earn trust and learn the ropes, and then to haul that carefully calibrated equipment out of there. You then sold it back to them. You mean you don't regret any of that?"*

*"No. (pause) the only thing I regret is when I can't see my 3 boys. When I am inside it is very hard on them. But my life has*

*been a hell of a ride. I have made a lot of money, I have lots of friends. I can't walk down the street in Freo on a summer's evening without being mobbed by those who know me, like a friggin' rock star. Just being there I set the women off like friggin' fire alarms. It's overwhelming for my missus. I tell her, 'the only women I kiss are the old ones, I don't kiss no young women' that way she does not need to worry.*

*One day I am 'a nobody', the next I am 'The Source'. And do you know who made the difference to my life? Tony Trapone, that's 'Trap-o-nee'. It was a wizard transition and Tony was the high sorcerer. I owe him, and I enjoyed that transition. Now Superman comes to me for advice. Me!!!!!* (His laughter unravelled her sense of safety. As quickly as it came it left. But its impact remained)

*Anna, I have a question for you. Do you think me sitting here listening to your psycho babble will stop the tidal wave of crime, drugs and stolen goods in this town? Do you? Even stop one wave of it, one ripple?"*

Anna was shocked Sean spoke of Tony Trapone. That combined with his maniacal laughter rendered her unable to really register the question about crime. Her breathe caught in her throat and stayed there motionless over Sean's link with the bikie chieftain. It welded itself there with his laughter. She had not heard Tony's name since his sentencing and had no idea the Sean was part of that particular network. These details needed to be entered into a data bank somewhere. Their connection made Sean's quiet intrusion into her private life leap from annoying to ominous. She was temporarily derailed. To regain composure she wandered off on her own tangent. She tried to reconnect. What were they talking about? 'Regrets' that was it.

*"Would your parents think you need to have any regrets?"* She was pushing too hard on her issues, on anything, as she sought to refocus. As the words in that question hit her own ear drums they sounded absolutely ridiculous. Safe in her mind those words did seem quite logical, but spoken out loud they gained a ludicrous farcical nature. She was stunned by Sean's response. She had no idea that he would self disclose to this level.

*"Dad was a cop, we called him 'copzilla'. He could work himself up into a frothing, seething, spitting, swinging seizure in 0 to 20, and that's from standing still. When I got big enough not to be scared shitless I could admire the show for its pure entertainment value.*

*Mum was a dental assistant. Won't tell you what we called her. She had nothing on dad for entertainment value. They were good parents though. We lived mainly on the Kimberly. Mum used to travel a lot with her dentist, in a mobile dental surgery they set up in a caravan. The station owners and Aboriginal kids on the remote communities would have had no dental care without them. But - I had my own suspicions about her relationship with her boss. I think dad did too. He was always trying to be transferred to Perth so mum could 'stay home with the kids more'. It did happen, but late in his career. Mum could always get work in the country or the city, she said 'have career will travel' so it didn't matter to her, she said, where they were."* Sean laughed again. Anna asked him what he was thinking.

*"Mum and Dad are now Sundowners."*

*"Sundowners?"*

*"Yeah they are retired so they drive from station to station in the Pilbara or Kimberly. They arrive at the homestead at sundown*

*and ask if they can do some work for some feed."* He laughed again. *"That time of the day there is not much time for work but plenty for feeding. I guess they figure as many years as they worked in the area the food is part of their owed retirement plan."*

*Anyway, I am from a good home, they hung in there together. I even married my missus, been with her 12 years and we have 3 boys. I have a job, full time, trucking. I have a valid trucker's license now, I stop at red lights; I go on green, even on my bike. I am a solid man."*

Yeah solid all right, solidly entrenched in crime, a master mind and he enjoyed it all, the work, the excitement, the notoriety, the acclaim, negative and positive.

*"Sean you say it was a good life."*

*"No I didn't."*

*"No you didn't, that was my word to describe what you actually did say."*

*"Don't put words in my mouth."* She had to be careful to not activate his nasty reaction. So far this had been the most therapeutic like session they had had.

*"Right, you describe your life in positive terms but there are 3 little boys who need you on a daily basis who have had to go without you for extended periods. The woman you married and obviously love has to do a two person job, alone. So while you do what you do, and enjoy every aspect of it, they suffer."*

*"What do you want me to do? Leave the Adders?"*

*"I was talking about your family, not the Adders."*

*"The Adders are my family."* Anna sat silent. Sean was not going to offer any more.

*"See yah."*

*"Yep."*

Perhaps Liz was right; maybe she did need to transfer him. She emailed Liz. Liz declined the offer to reallocate him, *"Just because it is hard does not mean it is wrong for you to continue to treat him. You now understand your feelings and are aware of them. He will be good for you, and with any luck you will be good for him. Stick it out for a month or two and we will staff it then. With his self disclosures it seems you are getting him to engage. Also Anna if you don't think what you have to offer him is valid; he sure as hell won't either."* Anna wondered how a woman who could not submit pay slips or contracts on time, lost the travel allowance requests, and forgot every week where the psychologists and social workers are on which days, could be so bright?

She found herself thinking about Sean. If he was telling the truth his father was harsh and unpredictable and virtually ineffective as a father, husband, and home protector. His mother was absent much of the time Sean filled in the parental power gap. Sean installed himself as the shadow cabinet at home, and was maintaining that role now. He was in charge, but illegitimately so. The law was the government, representing his father, and he was the shadow government as he led the Death Adders. Valid or not, this explanation made sense to her and gave her a way to understand him, or at least tolerate him. It did not excuse him but if what he said was true, and if typical psychological interpretation was to be trusted Anna thought it just might define him. Whatever, the reality of the dynamics of his family of origin Sean had failed at attempts at counselling in the past. Those dynamics may explain his poor counselling outcomes. The last Magistrate he appeared before warned him that if he failed again he would be sent back to prison. His case was coming up for review. It was imperative for Anna to produce a positive report about their time together, citing his engagement with the process and positive outcomes. Without that his boys would be without their dad again.

Anna could not say she actually had anything effective to offer him and besides she did not know how to effectively engage with him. How did Liz know she doubted herself and the efficacy of therapy in Sean's case? Was it that Sean failed, or was it that their psychological offerings were impotent to help him?

Barbara caught up with her in the hallway. She needed to talk to Anna about Sean and the positive report he needed from her. Barbara reminded her that due to his counselling failures in the past he was out of chances. Her report needed to be positive if he was to stay out of prison. Sensing Anna was not with her Barbara asked her

*"Is there really anything to be gained from putting him back in prison?'*

*"Barbara, with all due respect, if you are trying to influence me – don't! Sean and Sean alone is responsible for the report, not me. He will get the report he has earned. Whether or not he goes to prison is the judge's decision and Sean's responsibility, not mine."*

*"Think about his boys Anna."*

*"Does Sean know how important this report is?"*

*"Of course, and I told him you were the one reporting on him, he knows his future is in your hands. And Charlotte knows it too."*

As furious as Anna was she did not respond to that comment. There is no way to unscramble scrambled eggs. Once Sean knows it he can't 'un-know' it. Anna would report Barbara's blatantly unethical behaviour, on two counts, but not to Charlotte. Firstly, seeking to influence the outcome of a psychological report and secondly endangering Anna by discussing it with the offender in the way she did. Anna told herself that she did not have time to make that complaint today but she would on Monday.

Stuart's Saturday 4 hours at work routine was becoming just that, routine. Even his answering the Beefy Burger phone was ordinary business now. At least this hum drum phase was easier than the misplaced keys, and fill-in-for-a-mate chaos. Anna and Max were working at adjusting to the fact that their first born had taken his initial fledgling step toward self reliance. They were not always happy about it. To add to their aggravation they were adjusting to it at different rates and at different times.

Sunday morning the Lennox household was torn from sleep by the sound of 20 vociferous motorbikes sputtering out a guttural *"potato potato"*. They slowed, one at a time, for the corner right outside the bedroom windows. The bikies sat astride their Harley Davidson's with flag patches on their backs. It was chilling. It sounded like the low ominous extended, unending roar of a male lion just before the females pounced. Anna leapt out of bed to watch them through her bathroom window. Standing on her toes, in her pajamas she understood the threat this morning's motor bike ride implied.

On Monday Anna did not report Barbara's two infractions; perhaps Sean rode by Barbara's bedroom window too.

The following Tuesday in Freo Alexander Lloyd showed for his session to discuss how his housing placement failed. He said he was not well again, he dreaded going back to his 'bedroom' in the bush. He had not done anything wrong; he did not take anything that wasn't his. He showered once in the few days he was there. He was not drunk. He cut down to 4 glasses of wine a day instead of 2 litres. Every day he prayed that the Lord would keep him honest. So what was the problem? He had not even been charged again for *"public intoxism"*. He did not even complain about the room inspections even though he found them to be *"evasive"*.

He was totally confused; he did not know why his best behaviour was not good enough. He had no idea that he was under socialised. He had no sense of 'mine' so had no concept of 'yours', all he knew was 'ours'. He was willing to share, either way, from others or with others. He said he missed his mother. Anna waited a few minutes to acknowledge his grief then asked him about his mum.

*"Me mum led a tragical life"*. There was not a flicker of an expression to indicate that Anna had caught let alone acknowledged his word error and she certainly did not intend to correct him.

*"She married young as she was preggers\* with me. Me dad left before I was born an' she got tied up with his brother. He was pure bastard and all I can remember is his hitting and belting her. From then on there was no relaxating. When I was 8 I hit him with a shovel, he kicked me and mum out. We was close, me and mum."*

*"Where is she now?"*

*"She died when I was 24, cancer. I wish she was here now, I would love to show me mates how pretty me mum was. She made every day good - like magication."* That was it, he had no more words. He coughed as he ambled away toward his bush bedroom. His social worker was on the phone trying to convince the administrative officer at another half way house to at least give him a chance. Anna was afraid his bush environment would eventually kill him.

Jack Williams was scheduled for an appointment. He did not

show and offered no reason for his non attendance. Anna checked with his Probation Officer. She said *"Jack has been arrested"*. Drug related charges, possession with intent to supply and sell. He had moved up from purse snatching to the big league. He could not make bail so was in jail awaiting trial. Anna wanted to blame Dr. Tan but even as she tried she knew the blame was misplaced.

Sean O'Connor however did show. Anna did not know whether to ask him about the Sunday morning show of colours outside her bedroom window or not. If he did not know where she lived Anna would be telling him. If he did know and was threatening her Anna, by acknowledging her fear, may encourage further demonstrations or a rerun. As it could hardly be a coincidence she decided he did know where she lived, and he was threatening her, so she asked

*"You and the brothers out for a ride Sunday morning Sean?"*

*"What, where?"*

*"Don't be coy Sean you know what I mean?"* she demanded.

*"Yeah it was just a brotherhood building exercise. Eh we are not like the other clubs you know, we have nominees and patched up members but we are just a group of motor bike loving mates who support each other's love of the road. Whatever criminal activity I may or may not have done has nothing to do with being an Adder. If a brother gets in trouble with the Police he is on his own,"* reported Sean.

Anna knew he had just deflected the question about his morning ride by her window. Also his story about his gang was an utter falsity. It was the party line. Bikies always distanced themselves from the organised crime side of their membership. It was a particularly successful tack to take as no bikie gang had ever been successfully charged with drug production and distribution in

Australia even though individual members had. To protect the gang each arrested member claimed sole responsibility for any crimes. It was impressive that never had a bikie betrayed his club regardless of the plea bargain offered. Anna knew she could not crack Sean's code of silence and gang loyalty. He had already told her too much by declaring his connection to Tony Trapone. Any disclosure of the club's liaisons may endanger him and expose him to being disciplined for such an indiscretion. From now on he would be sealed over, locked down and stapled shut.

Despite her fear of Sean, her knowledge of his criminality she still stated,

*"Sean I know that you know your report is due. If you continue to refuse to genuinely engage in therapy and threaten me, you will not receive the report you need from me. I don't care how many times you and your hoons ride by my house."* Sean gave no indication that he understood how unacceptable his current behaviour and dealings with Anna were. He looked her full in the eyes, held the gaze then asked

*"Are you sure?"* He got up and left.

Anna reported his activity and his clandestine threat to Liz, leaving out Barbara's and Charlotte's collusion with Sean's cause. She resigned from his case without staffing it with Liz. She declined to discuss it with Liz and further declined to submit a report for or against his progress. She simply listed the dates and times of the sessions he attended. She deleted the portion of the form that asked for outcomes. This created a dilemma for her; she knew that ethically she should advise the Directorate of his non-compliance and his threatening behaviour toward her. She also knew she should report Barbara's complicity. But now hers equaled Barbara's.

Anna tried to convince herself that prison did not rehabilitate Sean, all his imprisonment did was place hardships on his family, especially his children. Keeping him out of prison might even save some other offender from being recruited into hard crime. She did not know how long she would buy this rationale but she did know she was becoming increasingly frightened. Ironically she did not know that Sean O'Connor was literally the least of her worries. Not knowing that she worried anyway. She called Max and told him to let her know any time he saw Sean the bikie from The Show or anyone who looked like him near him or the boys ever, at any time. Did Max understand that? He did. This time he did not minimize her fear.

•••••

# 21

## *Fruited Tea*

*L*iz called an emergency meeting for the psychologists and social workers. Anna took the express train during the getting-to-work-rush-hour. That way she avoided the rigors of city traffic and parking.

Anna was more tired than she should be at this time of the morning. She felt irritable. She leaned her head back against the train's window and listened to the conversations around her.

*"Stop me if you have heard this before".*

*"Stop her!!!"* Anna's thought voice screamed, I have heard it before, so has every one on this train. And I don't ride this train very often. But the speaker's travelling companion obviously wasn't listening the first 24 times the story was told, or perhaps she knew there was no stopping her. So the story went on again about the daughter in law and the grandson Cody (everyone has a grandson named Cody, or Kody, or Kodie) and the day the bully at school broke his first front tooth. The story teller's voice droned on.

Mercifully it was a short train ride. Soon Anna was in the crowds disgorged simultaneously as multiple trains delivered them to the underground train station in Perth. Irritation aside she enjoyed her breezy jaunt down St. George's Terrace. The clean wide pavements, the trees, enlivened her stroll between the glass canyons of high rise office buildings.

She sauntered up London Court, the open arcade between Hay Street and St. George's Terrace. It was built in 1937 to replicate Tudor – Elizabethan England. While it was out of place in modern 'wide brown land', it was a favourite with locals and tourists alike.

Anna checked the time on the clock at the end of the Court where St. George perpetually sought to slay the dragon. She had a few minutes to spare. She bought herself a coffee and feeling lucky, a lotto ticket from the Indonesian woman at the newsagency under the clock. Liz had also walked to The Terrace. As was her daily work day habit she took the London Court route. She always looked for the statues of Dick Whittington and his cat at the northern end and Sir Walter Raleigh at the southern end. The latter looks bewildered at finding himself in high on a wall in a time a place foreign to him. The expression carved into his stone his face certainly is open to interpretation.

Her re-acquaintance with the statuesque Sir Walter complete Liz arrived at the central office early. She started the coffee and chose a seat at the long table. She greeted those who came in after her and settled in for a long discussion. Liz had an announcement. I.T. had developed a new computer program. The offenders' data would be computer analysed and stored. Perth will be the first location in Australia to trial this process. Liz said that her team would be compiling the most significant technological catalogue and analysis of offender data anywhere in the country. Anna saw its application if she could research the updated whereabouts of offenders like Jack Williams. They all appreciated the need for a centralised data bank of accurate criminal activity, gang liaison and updated arrest information. They each had one unspoken concern.

*"Who is going to enter the data?"* asked her ever practical male colleague. Anna had always liked him. He seemed to be deliberately irreverent, in dress, approach and speech. The offenders loved him. His simple question so obviously needed to be asked but he was the only one to ask it.

*"The admin staff is going to scan it in, starting first with the archived files, moving up to the current ones. For your current and future clients you will each have to go to the shared drive and download the appropriate forms, the initial session, ongoing and closure forms. They are all there. As you type your usual file notes they will be automatically filed into the system and statistically analysed."* Liz said that there was a level 3 who had been employed simply to check their entries to ensure standardization of data entry.

There was a phone call for Anna. She left the meeting to take it. The social worker at Fremantle was on the phone. She had located a halfway house for Alex, it was not deluxe accommodation, but he would be safe there. She had reserved a room on the ground floor for him, no stairs, no room inspections. The other residents were similar to him. No one would fuss over his drinking or aroma. The Probation Officer would tell him about his new address. He would have counselling there so his future sessions with Anna were cancelled. Anna was pleased to have an extra hour in her schedule that afternoon for a new referral but she was sorry she wouldn't see the toothless man who loved his pretty mother. The social worker offered to call a wait listed client and arrange for him to be there at Alex's usual time.

As the meeting closed Liz said nothing about Anna's emails resigning from treating Sean O'Connor. Anna took her lead and left the subject unaddressed. Her male colleague was driving through Fremantle so he gave Anna a ride back to that Centre. Anna asked him how he was doing with Scott the computer expert. He laughed and said

*"You mean The Teflon Man who rules the blogosphere?"*

*"I guess",* she replied, *"Why do you call him that?"*

*"Well, I threw all the approaches at him that we tried during the training day, and none of them stuck, none, nada. He did not even take any of the suggestions under advisement. He catapulted them all into oblivion with such a pleasant smile. He is impervious to intervention. Totally. I think the gains of his life style outweigh any of the potential down sides. He is just too happy being big and bad and rich. He is 'The Man', he drives better wheels than me and he is a lot smarter than me."*

*"He drives better wheels than all of us and he is smarter than all of us – put together. From your description, even Bill Gates should go to him for answers,"* quipped Anna.

There was nothing left to say. Anna had her own Teflon men and women ruling various spheres. To fill the silence her colleague cranked his new CD. Anna closed her eyes and freed her mind to roam with the music Teflon coated offenders notwithstanding.

Anna found starting half way through the day to be somewhat disorienting. At the appointed time when Alex had been scheduled then cancelled, the new client showed, but so did Alex.

*"I came to come say 'good bye' to you doc, and I wouldn't mind another cup of tea."* She exchanged well wishes with him, told him his mum would be proud of him. She left him in the reception area, sipping his tea with three chocolate covered staff biscuits. She just hoped the secretary wouldn't notice that she was using food bought

with staff tea money on clients. The secretary could be somewhat territorial about tea fund money.

The secretary did notice but said nothing. She was too observant not to know what was happening to the cookies and biscuits under her sole jurisdiction. But she felt as if she knew Alex. She had seen him, morning after morning sitting on the nearby park bench as she walked past him to work. On cold mornings she bought him a large hot coffee from the local Koffee Kart. If he was still in the park at night when she left work late, she bought him a cup of hot soup in the winter or a cold drink in the summer. She was Level 2 admin staff, She did not earn a great wage, but she had enough to share and could always buy a cold old drunk a warm cup of something. Anna could give him as many biscuits as he needed.

Many in the town of Fremantle took a protective stance toward Alex. One March he was gratuitously beaten by a group of youth and found lying in his own faeces and urine, deranged but basically unhurt. A local business man half carried him to his office. He allowed Alex to shower on premises and sent the receptionist out to buy Alex 'new' clothes and shoes from the Salvos. He made a generous donation to a local men's shelter thereby secured 3 nights' accommodation for Alex. That Alex-directed benevolence was by no means an isolated case.

Due to the summer weather and warm dry days alfresco dining was common almost throughout the year. The sidewalk diners left uneaten portions of their meal for Alex. Alex knew the diners with sharing potential. He never even considered the overweight ones who ordered chips and fried food. Experience taught him that they ate every bite, even finger licking the plate. But the slim diners usually shared. He said

*"The Asians are best, most giving, or most leaving; they get the good sushi and never eat it all"*. Anna smiled over Alex's well defined palette and culinary preferences. An unshowered bush sleeper with a penchant for sushi, who knew? In defiance of the restaurant owners' or managers' direct orders, and contrary to food handling laws, some table staff sliced the bitten portion away from the uneaten pies, pasties, sandwiches, wraps, pizza or steaks, and saved the rest for Alex. The bosses all said it was akin to feeding seagulls. You feed them and they crap all over you. But the wait staff and table clearers did it anyway. Alex was their 'little battler mate'.

Anna asked Alex why he ate this way. He told her that the food left on tables was *"too good to chuck"*. He got lots of variety, and had learned about all kinds of food he could never afford to buy. He thanked his mother for making him eat everything on his plate *"because of the starvation of kids in India"*. And the best part, because he rarely bought his own tucker* and slept in the bush he spent little. He sent half of his meagre monthly welfare check to an organisation that fed hungry children in orphanages in India. He said sharing-eating and bush sleeping allowed him to sleep easy. At least he knew 'kiddies' on the other side of the world were fed before going to bed because of him. He said,

*"I cannot sleep, not a wink if I think one of them kiddies is hungry."*

The new client did not care if Anna used some of his time for Alex but he saw the empty tea cup, realised the last bloke had some and wanted some tea too. Anna asked PP if he would get some for him. He wouldn't. Neither would the new admin girl. Consequently the second offender went time shorted and tea-less. Anna did not want to spend more time making and fetching refreshments for him. With later reflection she regretted that decision. She thought it might have been the most therapeutic thing she could have done for him. It was for Alex.

One client stood out in her day. She was a young mother who had been caught repeatedly driving without a driver's license. The judge actually raised his voice to a shout when he sentenced her. His tirade against her was printed word for word in the local newspaper. She did not know how she would live through that embarrassment. She had been imprisoned for 12 months, but was out early on parole. During her imprisonment her children were raised separately by different family members. She rarely saw them as the women's prison was a train ride and two bus connections away from their relocated homes. She was sobbing, something was different. The kids did not play together as they used to, sometimes they would cry to go to their 'other homes'. They did not seek comfort from her as they used to. She said she felt as if her heart was breaking. After making that statement she sat silently, her face frozen in grief.

Anna knew the children's attachment to her and to each other had been disrupted. Anna did not know if it could be repaired. She did not understand why such minor offenders were imprisoned for lengthy sentences. Did the judges not know how families were torn apart? This mother had lost her HomesWest home as a result and was now bunking in with her sister awaiting another home. The waitlist was 2 years long. Could Anna write a letter for her to request she advance early in the queue? Anna could. Anna would. Anna knew all things were not hers to understand but this one absolutely outdid her. She saw this situation too frequently.

The afternoon ground on until the time of the afterhours staff meeting. This felt like a long day. Charlotte was on leave so the second in charge, Sophie chaired the meeting. There was laughter, and pleasant banter. The Probation Officers worked through their piles of tattered, closed and re-opened offender files. Anna gave her views on the clients assigned to her, making suggestions to their Probation Officers. Barbara asked her to share some of the training she received on dealing with the Violent Offenders. She gave a brief sketch of the discourse and offered a more comprehensive overview if they wanted it. They did. It was put on the agenda for the next meeting. There was a brief admonition to keep the ever watchful eye out for Harry Browning, the criminal at large. His prison photo was recirculated to each staffer. New cases were allocated. The meeting concluded in rapid time. Staff left with their moods elevated.

As Anna exited the building the secretary ran after her with a muddied cloth. It was Anna's suede coat. The secretary found it behind the park bench, it obviously was rained on, and they both hoped, nothing else has 'rained' on it. It smelled like mud, Anna took it and gingerly searched the pockets for her swipe, it was not there. Odd. She dropped the coat in the nearest rubbish bin.

It was morning already. Tuesday. Anna roused both boys. Lachlan was no longer at the neighbourhood school. She was pleased not to be sending him back to Ms. Hopkins. She drove both boys to St. Bennies as Lachie asked

*"Mum who is anonymous? He sure wrote and said a lot of stuff? How could know all that stuff" How could he live that long?"*
Neither Anna nor Stu knew.

As she walked through her office door PP handed Anna a tea

bag of a fruited tea with,

*"I thought you might enjoy this"*. It was his 'welcome to the team, at last' gesture. Anna took it gratefully, made a cup of tea, giving him profuse praise.

Four out of the five scheduled offenders arrived and stayed at least 45 minutes each, no disapproving eye brow from PP this day. They were learning to trust and respect each other. The Police contacted Charlotte again. Harry Browning, the offender with the security guard uniform in his car had been talking in the local pub. He repeated that he had a plan to teach the department a lesson. He boasted that he had access to the building. A Police informant passed that information along. Charlotte was back, she emailed every one with the news. Laughter in the office became too brittle, voices too forced, everyone was scared.

Charlotte had prepared an agenda for the 2nd team meeting for the week. Having missed yesterday's meeting she scheduled another one that she would chair, properly. Anna's summary from her training on "Working with the Violent" offenders was not included on the agenda despite the staff asking for it to be there. Anna did not mention it, neither did anyone else. A deliberate collusion of silence. Charlotte discussed the evacuation routes and procedures, providing procedures for all the staff. Charlotte explained that she did not think anything would come of a drunken offender boastings in a bar but suggested they be alert and stay more safe than sorry. The team had already chewed through the pile of files and redistributed or discussed urgent issues concerning the clients at yesterday's meeting. Tuesday's meeting closed early.

Despite wanting to avoid a dramatic episode Anna decided to tell Charlotte of her fears of the 'security guard with attitude', and her missing security swipe. She couched her conversation in tentative terms. Charlotte took it seriously, within minutes two uniformed officers were knocking on the door marked 'Staff Psychologist'. The officers took down the fragments that Anna had registered. She told them she had lost or misplaced her coat; complete with the entry swipe but that the coat had been found, muddied, without the entry swipe. There was no way she dropped that coat where it was found.

The Police Officer gave her more information about Harry. He was a heavy end criminal with suspected connections to the Death Adders and other career criminals. His arms of crime circled the globe with his international connections, especially in Asia. He knew that to gain true international respect he needed to broaden his influence to include the Americas, both the USA, and South America. That was his next goal. His crimes were planned, unnecessarily violent and usually successful. He had stolen more money from armoured cars carrying cash than any other criminal in Western Australian history. In some quarters that made him a hero. He had a Police truncheon he had stolen and used in every crime. His gang partners had guns. He prided himself that his truncheon had a distinct advantage against any gun, and he had proven it to be so. During his last robbery a security guard was beaten so severely he was permanently disabled. None of this information added to Anna's sense of security.

•••••

# 22

# The Parents' Party

There was to be a sun downer cocktail party for the parents of students at Stuart and Lachlan's school. It was hosted in a Tuscan mansion owned by a school board member in Mt. Goldsworthy. The party began at 6:00 pm. Stuart had soccer practice until 5:30. Time was of the essence. Anna left work a little early. She swung by to collect the boys. Waiting for them she parked under the massive awning provided by heritage listed trees at the school. A river of spotless new cars swept down the road and around her, each car picked up one or more blazer wearing, pressed white shirt, perfectly tied tie boys. The parent chatted as the boys sat silent and sullen.

*"It must be a boy thing"* she thought. Stuart ran toward the car, turtle boy Lachie dragged his feet. In another place and time she would have shouted for Lachie to keep up, but such behaviour was not accepted here. Mothers' voices were never raised in these quarters. It was a rule, it must not be done. She waited quietly.

The boys showered quickly, 'turn around trips' she called them. They would meet Max at the mansion. The drive up to the board member's home was impressive, decorative but sturdy metal gates swung wide as she inched the vehicle forward. A security guard checked her ID and officiously motioned for her to park to the left. She had a brief internal dialogue about parking to the right, but she followed instructions. The professional painted signs and arrows directed them towards the back garden. As they walked close to the home, Anna peered in through the lead light glass windows. She saw glorious furniture and draperies. It looked like a museum to opulence.

No one was admitted inside the home. No one. The carpets were all vacuumed in a manner that left a pattern. Either by accident or design this pattern, if disturbed, would inform the home owner if anyone had set foot in those hallowed areas. The guests were directed away from the upper garden, with its night blooming Jasmine and roses. They were herded into the lesser area. While there were no flowers here the grassed areas seemed to be manicured by an obsessive compulsive.

Anna stood on a paved area, under cover, backed up against a bar-be-que. She hoped it was thoroughly clean as she did not fancy a reminder from last week's steak on her dress. The mosquitoes were plentiful and in 'war' mode. The crowd of parents was so closely packed together she could not even bend down to swat at the annoying flying biting insects when they attacked her ankles. She rubbed her right foot over her left ankle and her left foot over her right ankle in a vain attempt to mute their attack. The boys located their friends and took off for the beached area. The boys were then conscripted into a beach sand football game under the guidance of the gym teacher.

One of the first parent greeters was an intense woman, short of stature with frank watery blue eyes and bobbed blonde hair. That hair style was worn by most of the wealthy women in the area. It declared 'we have arrived'. The greeter told Anna how she had grown up in Mt. Goldsworthy. Her parents were born and bred there, as were her grandparents. There was a message in that for Anne, 'respect for me I am obviously old money'. To emphasize her Mt. Goldsworthy roots the woman told her,

*"I moved once, to Cottesloe* (5 kilometres away) *and I could not stand it, I had to come home so moved back to Mt. Goldsworthy".* Anna asked her where she lived now, *"down the street"* said the greeter.

*"Where 'down the street?'"*

*"Down the street"* asserted the woman with the authority the rich use to instruct underlings as they assert their obviously superior opinions. Anna decided one of two things about her greeter. She may have lived in a mansion, and did not want to reveal the location of her immense wealth for fear Anna would nick it, or she lived in a Homeswest apartment and did not want to reveal that. Anna responded

*"I don't know what it feels like to have emotional ties to a place, I was born here, and educated here but we moved frequently when I was a child and I have lived in three different countries. I really don't have a sense of 'home', in fact home is where I am not. If I am in England 'home' is Australia, if I am in Australia 'home' is England, or America. When I hear people make the sort of statements you just did about roots I feel like a hungry kid outside the candy store, looking in through the window watching you eat."*

The woman demanded,

*"Where did you spend your childhood?"* There was no way Anna was going to tell her that. She was born and spent her primary school years in a working class area, Maylands, on the other side of Perth. Anna knew that would not rise to the splendour of the woman's own roots.

*"It doesn't matter where I was raised; I have no felt connection to it as 'home'"*. The woman demanded to know again, this time her tone was slightly more insistent. She launched into a discourse on how Anna must feel like that was 'home'. While she answered no direct personal questions herself she was clearly unaccustomed to others daring to deflect her personal probes. Anna repeated that it did not matter as she had no connection there. The greeter had reached her tolerance for frustration level, although she was far too cultured and refined to mention it. She moved on. Anna assumed that everything she had she had gained either when someone else died and gave it to her, or she married it.

Such hierarchical attitudes made Anna pine for California. She had lived there for 3 years, before she married, working in one of the universities, and had been swept away by the sense that heritage and roots are not as important as the individual's own input and self development. If an individual earned his or her way by effort, or creativity, or even luck, it was acclaimed and respected, not diminished in the presence of inherited wealth. Anna could not understand how wealth and status was only valued if someone else earned it and died leaving it to you. That understanding had to be baked into you from birth; it could no more be added to the understanding upon adulthood than a baker could add yeast to flat bread after its baked in an effort to have it rise. Anna couldn't compute that information in her Maylands data bank.

She saw a colleague from her prison based days. And right behind her, Max. She was pleased to see them both. The colleague was a neighbour, they did not live in Mt. Goldsworthy but edged on to it. The colleague had earned her own place in life. No one died and willed it to her. She earned a doctorate and used it in her clinical practice. The colleague was bright and articulate. She was 50 yet the sun had carved and quilted its presence into her face more deeply than one would expect for a 50 year old. However her face hinted at the former glory and beauty that was hers. She loved to tell the story of how her 6 year old grandson suggested she 'iron' her face. Besides her honesty, she was a pleasant person with a killer sense of dress. The olive silk she was wearing was splendid. When Anna remarked on it her colleague whispered she had borrowed it from her sister in law. That news was a welcomed and refreshing touch of reality. Borrowed clothes brought an irreverent wink to a world where home owners had homes too splendid to share, paid servants and security guards. They chatted and giggled; Max found a colleague and excused himself from the ladies. He squeezed through the crowd over to Jack, an American who managed one of the international oil companies located in Perth.

Anna was sure they were to be soon inside the home, or be allowed to use the facilities and escape the mosquitoes. The owners had no such intentions. The board member had rented a line of outdoor portable toilets. They were too nasty to use, Anna would wait, the boys couldn't. Over her colleague's head she noticed an elderly woman's hair. The hair was swept up and threaded through with ribbons, pearls and tiny fabric flowers. The design was asymmetrical, yet quite lovely. Anna wondered if arthritis and aged related immobility demanded she had hired help to fashion it. As if the woman was aware of someone noticing her she turned her head and smiled at Anna, her bright blue eyes twinkling. She reminded Anna of her own very young grandmother. Anna smiled back. They gave each other the gentle, gracious sideways nod that women often exchange indicating mutual respect.

The food was impressive in variety and quality. The squillionaires who owned the home did not provide it; it came from a rostered committee of parents. The crowd was finally directed toward the linen covered tables and excessively polite staff. The guests had to move in unison in order not to stall the crushing lines. Max and the two sand covered boys joined her and they decided it was time to leave. She left her place in the food line and blew a goodbye kiss to her friend. They drove home as they had arrived. Lachie rode with her, Stuart with Max. Both cars pulled up at Beefy Burger as the boys were 'starving'. With appropriate flourish Stu used his employee card.

The next day the local newspaper editor blasted the board member for hiring security guards to monitor the behaviour of the parents of children from an elite private school. 'The family' stated it had employed them to protect the invited guests from gate crashers. Anna did not believe that for a minute. The only guarding they did was to guard the home and inside toilets from the invited guests. She was incensed to think that the board member had to protect his precious belongings and home plan from her. She determined not to attend such functions again. Max thought she was overstating the facts but he was not impressed with having had to stand for 4 hours after a hard day's work and did not much fancy going again either. Anna was relieved.

●●●●●

# 23

## The Fairer Sex

*M*ax needed the family car for work the next day. Anna took the train. She looked at the male passenger in front of her; she thought she recognised him as a Fremantle client. She had the last available seat and did not want to stand and move away from him. The likelihood of getting another seat was slim. She turned side on and tried not to look like herself. As they left the train he moved behind her and said,

*"Good morning Ms. Lennox"*. She remembered the voice, he was, Jack Williams, the toothless methadone abuser, Dr. Tan's patient. What a difference being drug free and wearing dentures makes. She responded,

*"Good morning Jack"* in deference to his request to use his first name. They both smiled.

Anna's first client was a slender Aboriginal woman with dusty coloured skin and green eyes. She was 30 years old. Her most recently charged offence had been a stabbing. She had stabbed two of her former partners, one she was charged over and went to jail, one she was not. The Magistrate ordered her to include her partners in therapy as part of her non re-offence plan. His instruction was that she learn to deal with frustration in a relationship without violence. She had been dismissed by her partner of 2 years and today was bringing in her new mate. She was 30 and he was 27.

She was not particularly pretty but she was striking and there was a quiet seduction about her.

Anna's client spoke of the two near murders in flattened tones. No emotion, no guilt, no sorrow, no insight into why they happened. She was almost robotic. Anna wondered if she was as empty as she appeared to be. The young woman spoke of her near murders as 'them accidents'. She said,

*"I accidently picked up the knives, accidentally stood too close to the blokes\*, I accidentally pushed the knives into their chests".* Accidents? Anna thought this member of the so called 'fairer sex' could easily have her murderous urges unfairly overlooked. You would have overlooked them too if you saw her. There was nothing about her that warned any one of her homicidal abilities.

The young woman introduced Anna to her partner in a rudimentary manner, more with a nod than words, and they both sat politely in front of her. Anna took time to carefully observe her petite client. She was astounded at how different she seemed today. Anna had seen her with three men now. She had known her for years, before and after her imprisonment when Anna worked in other aspects of the Department. Each time she had a new partner; it appeared to Anna that she took on a completely new character. A new man equalled a new woman, remade, totally.

Anna stopped focusing on the content of the session and observed the process. Was the stabbing the ending of a chapter? Was it the closing of a portion of her book leaving opportunity for the writing of a new plot? When Anna worked in the United States she had heard Dick Morris on American news say that Bill Clinton was 'a headlight reflector'. Dick said you shine your lights on to him and think he shines back. You swear he's illuminated but what you see is only the reflection of your own light. That was her client! Anna wondered why she had remembered Dick's comments; perhaps she was just waiting to find a place to park them. Now she had.

This young offender answered any and all of her questions with as few words as possible. She left a silence at the beginning and the end of her response. The silence induced such discomfort in the listener that it begged either an introduction or a conclusion from the questioner. The only way to quiet that discomfort was to answer for her. Her demeanour induced sympathy and a sense of wanting to take care of her in the questioner. Those two, discomfort and an invitation to rescue her caused the questioner to fill in the blanks. The questioner actually created the response he or she thought the young offender wanted to render. This woman allowed the questioner to create her as the questioner needed her to be. These were the psychological traps she set for others. The carefully placed 'take care of me' laced silence became a void the questioner filled. The illusion created became a buffer between the questioner and the real person, if there was a real person.

She did not fight against her situation, or take on the responsibility for everyone else's feelings. Instead she made those present feel responsible for her and carry her through life. If life was a vehicle she was a non driving passenger. She didn't even hold the map for the driver.

Anna knew if she told her how concerned she was about these dynamics she would say,

*"I am worried too".* She knew that if she challenged her, she would say how she was challenging herself on that same issue. There was no way to really bring change to this woman. Anna

wanted to tell Liz that to keep throwing resources at this woman was like shouting into a cave. The only outcome would be an echo. Anna and Liz often discussed the concept that some offenders were not reachable. Liz did not agree with that contention, especially if the offender was Aboriginal. Her reasons were more political than clinical. It could be misread as racism if the Department was seen to be withholding services from Aboriginals. It was difficult to get an Aboriginal to engage in the totally alien white scheduled talking way to heal. Any Aboriginal client who would engage became part of the statistics that demonstrated the Department was including the indigenous in its programming. Since the Gordon Inquiry this statistic had to be preserved at all cost. Anna thought that not dealing with her honestly in a way that she could actually utilise was a perverted form of racism. But the question remained, was there a way to work with her so that she could take responsibility for her own actions and empower herself to change? Would Anna find an answer to that question?

Anna's next client, Albert Dixon infuriated and frightened her. Anna telephoned Liz to tell her that the parole board should never have released him.

*"Liz his release endangers the lives and well being of every person within the system that he now encounters. The security offices, his Probation Officer, the administrative staff and me, were all less safe for having known him. The community at large is endangered",* Anna said. She recounted his history to Liz. As a last year plumbing apprentice he had taken a sexual liking to a young woman. She repelled his advances so he beat the 15 year old female to death with his plumber's wrench. He then pursued her terrified 17 year old boyfriend and murdered him by drowning him.

The Coroner had assessed the unfortunate youth's unusually high number of defensive wounds. He said that they indicated that the youth fought long for his life. The Coroner concluded that Albert had relished and prolonged his victim's brutal death experience.

He was incorrigible. For the entirety of his imprisonment he refused to discuss his crimes with the prison based psychologists. He adamantly refused to attend any of the classes thought to be rehabilitative. He had been released 8 years earlier. Upon release he had savagely beaten a bus driver who refused to allow him to ride the bus without paying fare. The driver survived. Albert had received a 10 year sentence but was released last week, early. During his last incarceration he had still not talked to psychologists, still not attended any of the allegedly rehabilitative courses. Anna wondered if his non engagement was his kindest action, without it he should not have been released, without release he would not harm another. But that attempt, if that is what it was, at quarantining society from his murderous impulses was sabotaged by a generous parole board.

Anna told Liz she had telephoned his prison based psychologist, an experienced criminologist with an earned doctorate in clinical forensic psychology. She had interviewed Albert years ago but she remembered him vividly. He was a tall, freckled, ordinary but pleasant enough looking fellow. There was no outward indicator of his murderous potential. The psychologist said initially she was completely disarmed by his 'normal' appearance but within moments she had become absolutely terrified. At their one meeting they sat in a small prison based interview room together. His crimes mandated that he had a Prison Officer handcuffed to each arm. Albert appeared not to notice his human appendages. He said nothing but suddenly he had an electric aura of violence about him. He looked at her then looked through her, as if he was reading her mind, her motives, her life history. The psychologist was exhausted by the encounter. Without explanation he refused to see her again. She admitted to Anna that his opposition to attending treatment did not dismay her in the slightest.

Anna valued her relationship with Liz, politically and personally. And she knew her well enough to know that hysterics did not work with her so she would be wise to rein it in. Nevertheless she found herself shouting down the telephone that this offender was a true criminal, he was a psychopath. He was a remorseless narcissist. She requested permission to test him to determine his level of psychopathy. Liz denied that request.

*"Anna, get a grip. Neither your hunches about the client, nor the prison based psychologist's observations and fear of him are legally testable. They simply will not stand up to the rigors of the Court room. There is no money in the budget to procure the necessary licenses and psychometric tests that you would need to adequately assess him. And if you did indeed determine, with standardized instruments that Mr. Dixon is a psychopath and could prove it in Court the parole board would not reverse its decision. The Department will not re-imprison him because the parole board made a mistake, if mistake it was. Besides there are no community based programs, no prison based programs in place for those identified as psychopaths. There is not even a standard-ized and accepted protocol in place to direct you as a clinician on how to identify them within the offender population. Albert is out until he murders again"* Liz said. *"As much as I might want to, there is nothing I can do about any of this."*

Anna tasted vomit; she had a sense of foreboding. She did not know if the alarm she felt was real or a combined figment of her colleague's fear and her own impressions of Albert.

•••••

# 24

## The Wedding

$S$he arrived home in an Albert induced whirl of emotions, including remnants of the foreboding. She opened the mail. There was an oversized, overstuffed ivory envelope of great importance. Max and her names and address had been individually done in hand calligraphy on the envelope. The stamp was custom printed with a photograph of the loving couple within intertwined wedding rings. She had seen these stamps in the Post Office but she had never actually received one nor known anyone who paid the extra for such luxury. The cover of the invitation had coloured pearls on the right hand edge, arranged in descending degrees of colour intensity toward the left hand fold. The names of the bride and groom were embroidered on the outer paper flap under the pearls. It was tied with luscious ivory satin ribbon in a perfect bow.

She and Max the boys were invited, nay summoned to the wedding of Harry's older brother. Harry had come to Stuart's 15th birthday party and was his new 'best friend' at St. Bennies. Anna and Max formerly met the family at a school function but could not say they knew them. The wedding service was in the prestigious chapel at St. Bennie's, such privilege being reserved only for students or graduates. The reception was at the Royal Lord Forrest Yacht Club in Mt. Goldsworthy. Max estimated it would cost $100 per head and wondered why Harry's family would pay $400 for the privilege of their presence.

Stuart later informed her that Harry was going to be alone through the event as his family would be otherwise engaged. Harry sensed boredom coming on and had begged for Stuart to attend. The parents were afraid of what that boredom might inspire and being well bred, extended the invitation not only to Stuart who would occupy Harry's time but to his entire family. In their salary range $400 would be a cheap fee, and money well spent if it bought Harry's contentment during the evening. Max was willing to attend, so was Lachie. They would go.

The couple had registered their preferred gift choices at a local mall in Karrinyup. Anna downloaded and printed the list at home. They had been very thoughtful. There were items from $30.00 to $3,000 on the list, accommodating the finances of all comers. Anna bought them a coffee machine that made lattes, cappuccinos, and other forms of inventive coffees. In selecting the model the couple wanted she learned more than she ever wanted to know about the machines from the sales clerk. It was $350 being reduced by 50%. It was an expensive gift for strangers but the gift was worth less than the $400 dinner tag for their wedding dinner. The sales assistant gift wrapped the box, tied it with an elegant store imprinted ribbon.

The weather on the day of the wedding was grey, unusual for early December in Perth. The skies threatened to rain. The rain did not materialise but sent a cold wind in its absence. As they walked toward the lime stone steeple of the chapel in their finest the bells called others to the event. The attendees scrubbed up well. Hats. Elegant gowns. Black suits. Even the boys were in their maroon school blazers, grey pressed pants, white shirts and maroon and yellow striped ties. The couple's Scottish ancestors were honoured with kilts and tartan shawls by the attendees. The bows on the pews were a subtle tartan ribbon and the usual flowers were replaced with heather sprigs.

The bridal march was titled, 'Amazing Grace' and played by the Western Australian Police Pipe and Drums band. It was an amazing CD version, beginning with kettle drums. As the congregation stood, goose bumps trawled up and down their spines, dispersing through the skin on their limbs, to their fingers and toes. Some cried and the bride had not even appeared yet. A flower girl in The Flower of Scotland tartan led the procession as she distributed a single heather sprig to every one sitting on the aisle. Knowing this would not impress Lachie, their aisle sitter, Anna told him to accept it from A GIRL without fuss. He did. However, Anna had failed to tell him what to do with it after that. He proceeded to force Stuart to take it, with fuss.

Anna was not as proficient as her own mother at 'the look', however the optical withering she passed to him through her eyes worked, and Lachie resentfully settled. It was bad enough he had to wear his school clothes, and be on school property on a Saturday, he now had to behave himself. This was not shaping up to be a very good day.

The service was well organised, the priest was elegant in his ironed robe and satin sash. Anna always noticed if the robes were ironed or not. She hated the crumpled I-have-rushed-here-and-was-too-busy-doing-important-things-to-prepare-for-this-minor-marriage-event approach of some priests. The candles, the gentle homily where he cautioned them against selfishness and toward tending each other's needs, the personally written vows, the music, the flowers were in apparent harmony with each other and became a symphony of joy to this couple's union.

Anna noticed the woman beside her crying politely, she hoped for the couple's sake it was with joy. After the service Max commented with a relieved sigh,

*"That was not too bad".*

Anna good naturedly added,

*"Not as far as weddings go anyway".*

The crying woman stated,

*"The priest is my husband and the bride's uncle".*

Max groaned and hit his head with his right fist and apologised. She smiled and enjoyed the joke on him. She had obviously heard it before.

The reception at the yacht club was not for 2 hours. As is common with weddings the couple were driven to the University of Western Australia. They both graduated from this university. Their photo shoot would be taken amongst the columns, arches and gardens. The guests went home or to nearby motels to change into even finer clothing. The men donned their dinner jackets, pleated tuxedo shirts, bow ties and the women their longer gowns with fur, or other wraps. Jewellery was meticulously chosen and changed from outfit to outfit. Hats were removed and hair re-coiffured.

Entrance to the yacht club was gained through oversized metal gates that security guards opened for each properly identified guest. The wide sweeping driveway was bordered by illumined oversized peppermint gum trees. There were huge, gnarled, lofty silent sentries, hovering above lush manicured lawns, paying homage to all who passed. The view was glorious, over the mouth of the river, to the pretty city beyond. The sky was darkening with night. The eerie neon glow that appears prior to darkness flashed across the scene. The weather had cleared and was pleasantly warm. Bejewelled and gorgeously clad guests were greeted by champagne bearing, beautifully groomed young staff. Each guest's personal beverage choice was memorized and the staff followed each around with their chosen liquid refreshment. The boys were already bored.

Seating was not left to chance. Each guest had been handpicked to sit by another. The attendant at the table map announced each attendee as he escorted him/her/them to their selected seating. Anna and Max were placed in a pleasant situation. Anna guessed it paid for them to have a son chosen to be Harry's friend. Harry was to sit by his family. He did for ten minutes, but then as happens at such events the youngsters drifted toward the same area. The adults formerly entrapped by the sprinkling of the youthful amongst them, now freed, slipped into the spots their absence had left for them amongst other adults. With the guest directed reshuffle they were now seated beside a physician seeking to retire, his wife, an author of children's' books, a solicitor who was a partner in a prestigious firm in Perth, the superintendent of education from the Northern regions of the state and a French couple who had flown in for the event. A business man and his wife and a huge Italian man with his daughter completed the set. The Italian did not move his face or body but his eyes assessed the entire room repeatedly. He was a retired detective, retired due to illness; but never off duty. His wife was ill so his daughter, a home decorator and event manager in her own right, accompanied him so as not to waste $100 on an empty chair. Anna appreciated that attitude. Had it been her $100 she would not have wanted it wasted either.

The food was stunning, it was eye candy. As they entered they were given a choice of beef, chicken or fish, or a combo plater. The staff found the correct person for the order placed and soon the guests were savouring a succulent meal, decorated with the flair of a Melbourne Cup Hat Maker. Anna's fish had long skewers protruding – threaded with curled wisps of carrot and leeks. She wondered who would have time or inclination for such frivolity. However it did help set the mood. Max's combo plate was equally decorative. Petite slices of rock melon wrapped in smoked ham and cheese 'sailed' above the skin of a slice of rock melon, each designed to look like a sail boat. Anna enjoyed being treated like royalty. Between dinner and dessert and the cheese platter came the speeches. This was truly a loved couple who had gained a significant reputation for their own achievements. She looked serene wrapped in a cloud of ivory satin, lit by candle light and he handsome and happy in his white tailed tuxedo. Anna wished she knew them better.

This was a Scottish mob so there would be no toast to the Queen of England as was the custom at non Jacobite functions. Strange how the Scots carried a grudge for centuries, sometimes forgetting the reason for the grudge, only knowing that it must be carried and passed on even in far flung lands. The likelihood that the Bonnie Prince would re-appear here and lead Scotland, from Australia, to a glorious future had long since faded. However Elizabeth from the House of Windsor would find no one drinking to her health at this wedding, despite the name of the groom's brother.

The bride's father's voice faltered at the appropriate place in his speech, as he led the toast to the bride. His love and respect for her was evident. His wife, the bride's mother quietly stood beside him. This was a departure from normal protocol but signified to their daughter 'we are in this toast together babe; it is from both of us'. The groom responded by beginning his speech with the obligatory

*"On behalf of my wife and I..."* which brought the usual jeers and cheers from the crowd as it did at every wedding. When he lapsed into sentimentality his 2 brothers booed and told him to *"get real"*. He quickly changed his approach. It was obvious that this crowd loved this couple.

Harry and Stuart and Lachie and some other St. Bennie's boys drifted toward the doorway. The security guards noticed and shooed them back to their seats. What was it with guards and this socio economic level? They seemed to be indispensable. The guards would not permit the boys to be out 'there' enjoying themselves by running around like children in those secured grounds. They may even have fun. No, they must stay and suffer inside by being with the adults, and they would sit still.

The music had obviously been chosen by the Bride's father. The band shamelessly impersonated the Rolling Stones. The parents took over the postage stamp sized dance floor and sang and moved to Mick Jaeger's inability to get satisfaction. The younger brigade was disgusted.

The teenagers were the rightful holders of the knowledge of what was cool and what was not. Their own parents, knowing the words to songs, laughing, singing, dancing and having a good time was not cool. They knew that the youth are the ones, and the only ones to be catered for at such events. They knew that all music, to be of worth, must be from their generation's genre. They knew that they and they alone had the right to get on a dance floor and make fools of themselves. When youth do it, it is 'cool', when parents do it is 'disgusting'. The parents were breaking the rules and must be punished. The punishment came in the guise of attitude known as "'tude". To express 'tude they sat slumped, sullen and silent, with disapproving toxin oozing from their eyes onto the dance floor. An adult dancer must be singled out and visually fastened upon, and optical scorn and ridicule sent their way. Anna said

*"The boys don't seem to be having much fun."* Max was. He said

*"Stuff 'em".*

*"Well done old boy"*, thought Anna and they danced away from the youthful purveyors of disapproval to a part of the dance floor where they could wriggle, jerk, twist, jive and do whatever else they wanted to do without silent offspring disapproval. They danced the jive together with the familiarity reserved for long time partnerships where each move and reaction to the music was pre-scripted and anticipated. Obviously they were having too much fun.

The bride's grandmother was a white haired woman with the arthritically moulded hands. She and her kilted, tubby, bald (without a razor) husband held each other, eyes closed, moving in unison. They were not so much dancing as remembering how they once danced. Singing every word to every song into each other's ears, rotund bellies and sagged cheeks touching, remembering how it used to be, imagining they were still doing what they used to do. Some things are better in imagination anyway.

The author, the doctor, the business man and his wife, the retired detective and the French couple knew what the youth did not, they knew that though their knees creaked, and their skin and guts paunched and sagged, they were really rock and rollers on the inside where it counted. Nothing as insignificant as age changed that. Parents shouted and flailed as they lyrically ordered each other to get off of 'My Cloud'. It was all too much, Lachie and Harry had smuggled in their game boy hand helds and as the older boys seethed and the old farts danced, he and Harry chased creatures across their mini screens alternately destroying or restoring the earth.

By midnight there was no sign that the bride was going to throw her bouquet or leave and return in her 'going away' outfit. The couple had no intention of going anywhere so the Lennox family decide to leave. Genteel goodbyes, air kisses near the cheeks of strangers, handshakes, and they were soon driving back down the sweeping driveway under the approval of the multi coloured flood lit peppermint gum trees.

*"I thought you would never leave"* growled Stuart, Anna and Max did not answer, they were snuggled and enjoying the warmth The Stones had rekindled. Warmth retrieved from their own youth, their own wedding, and their own hearts. That night Max and Anna did what they knew the bride and groom were doing. But unlike the newly married, it had been a while.

•••••

# 25

## A Therapist's Judas

*M*onday saw Anna at Fremantle again. She had trudged down the steep pathway, dragging her office behind her in the wheeled brief case. This parking situation was fast becoming 'old'. Anna had a new client first up. She was a convicted embezzler. She was formerly the office manager for a psychological corporation and had embezzled huge sums of money from her employer. She asked the psychologist to sign blank requests for insurance payments. The embezzler filled in the details for billing as they were submitted. Her employer travelled from office to office over thousands of kilometres to the remote regions of Western Australia. There she screened clients and prepared reports. She especially enjoyed going north to Broome. The heat, the humidity, she felt like she was breathing in moisture. When others were exhausted by it she found it strangely refreshing. And the relaxed lifestyle, she loved sitting crossed legged on grassed areas yarning* with her Aboriginal clients as she assessed them in an environment familiar to them. Being spry the up and down physically of that was no bother.

In her absence she needed strong administrative support. It seemed sensible to have a stack of blank but signed insurance forms on hand for a trusted employee to complete in a timely fashion. The trusted employee was of slim build, with tiny thin hands. She appeared in a business suit, unusual attire for Anna's clientele. Straight on her face took on the expected symmetry. The profile provided a startling contrast. It looked as if an artist's imagination had morphed her face downwards, stretching, sharpening, distorting the proportions. Unseen face on, the forehead sloped back sharply and abruptly from the eyebrow, the eye protruded, the nose was thin and sharp and pointed downwards. The upper lip was the usual proportion but the lower lip bulged furthering the 'pulled down' look. The chin was abrupt, sharp and short. Anna was mesmerised by the lack of synchronisation between the two presentations.

The fact two faces were on the same neck was amplified when the nervous, twitching female flipped her face, front, side, front, side. This action emphasized the lack of synthesis. Anna watched as this 45 year old woman sucked her thumb, and moved her head side to front, front to side. She was unaware of the age inappropriateness of the thumb sucking action or the social impropriety of face flicking. Perhaps that habit created some of the facial distortion. When she wasn't sucking her thumb she was trying not to. Either way sucking or not sucking it she was thumb focused. It provided a diversion for her, away from her crime, and it was a 100% efficient. The charges against her revealed that she had submitted insurance claims for inflated prices and for sessions and psychological testing that never actually occurred. She was careful to keep amended copies of the claims on the file so when her employer checked, everything was 'in order'. She had set up a series of bank accounts with similar names. She then filtered the money received from MediCare and the private insurance companies into those accounts. Then she siphoned off the excess and returned the expected amount to her employer's account.

She had professionally implicated the ethical but unknowing psychologist in massive insurance fraud. The psychologist was charged as it was her signature on the original claim forms. The charges were dismissed but her license to practice in Western Australia was revoked. For not keeping a closer eye on the billing practices of her staff a noted psychologist suffered professional and financial ruin, and now the fraudster sat, expecting another psychologist to assist her. This required added supervision. Anna already felt resentment toward the frail looking, thumb sucking Judas of psychologists.

The client was sad. Nervous and sad,

*"No I do not want to discuss my offending behaviour; I do not want to discuss my family history. That is personal. My mother had nothing to do with this. I do not want to say how much I had embezzled. It is not important why I needed the money"* she said. She did not own nor discuss any regrets. She had no goals for counselling. Anna sat silent, the client sucked her thumb. After 15 minutes of silence, save for a sucking sound, the client excused herself. She did not want to reschedule. In such cases Anna had to report it to the Probation Officer, and it was up to that officer to decide what to do. Counselling for this client was not court mandated; there were no legal grounds, based only on her failure to engage in therapy, to violate her.

As Anna made her way to the lunch room Charlotte accosted her in the hall. In unusually subdued tones she said.

*"The Police found a stash of weapons and explosives in the basement of this building, in a janitor's closet. Forensics is testing the security guard uniform they found in Harry Browning's vehicle*

*and will get back to me later with the results. I hope he has not graduated from a truncheon to bombs".*

There was no beginning and no end and no context to the conversation. Anna did not know who else knew the information newly spat at her in the hallway. She stood in the hall watching Charlotte swish away after her information drop. How does someone that slender 'swish'? Swishing is really the domain of the plump. Then a violent pang of fear riveted her to the spot. What if her swipe gave Browning entry to this secure building?

Anna needed to be distracted. As she had a 'no show' she used the time to edit a 14 page proposal for the "Transference of Skills: Mastermind Project" she had written. It included a proposed budget, alliances with the community, goals, time lines, legislative support for the project, an organisational chart, clinical back up and Cory's testimonial. His tattoo business was up and running, the first month he had the advertising CD's made and distributed and a web page on line. A private company in Vietnam was eager to buy his designs. While his court orders restricted him from leaving the country the Vietnamese merchant travelled to Perth to negotiate sole rights to some of the prison designs. Cory was consulting with a solicitor. Anna smiled at the thought of Cory dealing elegantly with the solicitors. She was sure Cory's shoes were more highly polished than theirs.

Typing and reading the sheer volume of words was soothing, a pedantic task, she felt herself deescalate. The secretary offered to retype the proposal, adding her expertise and knowledge. She made sure it was bound with a spiral bound spine and plastic cover sheets. It would be impressive. It would be forwarded by Charlotte to the next level of management. She was getting the hang of this line management process, despite her contempt for it.

There was a competition for entrepreneurial expertise from within the pool of government employees. Unbeknown to Anna, Charlotte had forwarded the proposal to the judges of the competition.

•••••

# 26

## Visitors

*A*fter working on her proposal Anna's eyes were blurred, she stepped out of her office and was greeted by a strange sight. Aliens had overtaken the waiting room. Charlotte sidled up to her, and whispered,

*"The explosives on the uniform match the explosives in the basement"*. Anna tried to think who she was talking about and what it meant. The Police told Charlotte they had reason to believe that when Harry came to report to Barbara that day he planned to bring weapons. Most of the offenders knew, and they assumed Harry did too that when the duress buttons were pressed at that Centre the Police responded immediately. They were located across the street, beside the row houses. Their orders were 'respond first, ask questions later'.

The Police believed Harry's plan was to shoot Barbara first. He would then take out as many employees and responding Police Officers as time permitted. His survival was not the point. His would be a legendary death by cop. This was an often repeated fantasy. Many small time thieves, who felt they had missed their true criminal potential, lived with this compensatory finale as their final Chapter. Even heavy end criminals harboured that fantasy. The beginning and middle they could not control but the end was theirs to rewrite. They would insert the memory of their death into the cultural psyche. The Police needed to apprehend Harry and asked special permission to do it at the Centre. The Centres were mandated not to cooperate with the Police in that manner. Never before had a Centre used its reporting routine to entrap a criminal, even a nationally acclaimed criminal like Mr. Harry Browning. The Directorate begrudgingly gave permission.

The watchers. The wino who sat on 'his' bench in the park, the Aboriginal rolled in a blanket, sleeping under a tree near him, the women who kept them both company from time to time. The street dwellers. They knew the hum, the throb, the rhythm of the town. They knew when the couriers came, when the security doors were unlatched, the clothing styles, the work schedule of each worker. They did not know they knew, but know they did. It was a knowledge born of watching. And when even one note in this watched symphony of life was dissonant, they knew it.

The police had arrived one at a time so as not to create a disturbance. They were dressed in civilian clothes and sat in the waiting room outside Anna's door, in front of Jason, trying to act as if they were offenders there to report. They had neat salon haircuts versus the amateurish kitchen-friend cuts sported by offenders. Their casual clothes were fresh, colour co-ordinated and new; their shoes had been worn only by them, and were in perfect condition. They had mobile phones. Not the second hand, often bought and resold, originally stolen ones. They owned the new ones that came out of a box for the first time not so long ago, with individual paid-for ring tones. They had clean hands and neatly trimmed nails. The watchers knew the music of life was 'off'. These alien strangers did not belong, in the day to day Centre symphony of motion. So one told someone, told someone, who told someone and the Department wondered why no one showed up to report, or for programs, or therapy, or to pee that day.

Unseen Harry Browning, in his vehicle, observed the activity from the parking lot at the top of the hill. He scoffed as the Police arrive in unmarked cars. He laughed as one then another piled out of a non descript car and walked casually to the door, pretending they had not arrived together. Browning swore an oath. Believing Barbara his Probation Officer had turned him in to the cops, his hatred of the department raged. Within 2 hours he had fuelled up, driven north, as he and his weapons passed through Northam and headed to the top end.

Every staff member was evacuated, one at a time, by different doors. No one knew what to do once they were outside. The seniors had omitted to give the staff directions. No identified meeting place was arranged. Some met at a local coffee shop where they occasionally met after a difficult day. This day qualified as difficult. The watchers knew that was strange. Never before had so many of the workers looked so confused as they met for coffee in one place at this time of day. Other staff, totally baffled and annoyed by the exercise simply went home. Each one of these differences in the usual routine became dissonant notes that registered loud and clear with the watchers. Never before had the watchers seen the employees of the Department exit from different doors, take their brief cases, lap tops and purses with them at this time in the afternoon, meander around, meet, not meet and walk to their cars and leave. Cops in, staff out, something was 'up'. The watchers of the town recognised it immediately. Everyone who watched, or listened to the watchers knew it. The good people of town were oblivious to the quiet drama.

One naive offender, unaware of the usual harmony of the office actually reported as required. He leaned against the counter as Jason logged him in. He noticed a female Police Officer lying on the floor behind Jason. Her coat was askew revealing a weapon. He pretended not to notice. Jason pretended she was not there. The Police officer pretended not to be there. Jason further pretended that the Probation Officer was out of the office on a house call and the offender was ordered to re-report tomorrow. The offender knew this to be bollocks but rightly decided bollocks was the order of the day.

As the offender looked at the Police Officer he didn't see, lying there which she wasn't, with a weapon that she didn't have, he perpetuated the illusion, without knowing why. He politely thanked Jason and left. Quickly. What no one had realised was that Anna was in her office to the side. She had not been notified of the impending evacuation, or that Browning was expected. It suddenly struck her that the office was whisper quiet, she opened her door. The female Police officer on the floor drew her weapon, so did one of the clean shaven male officers in the waiting area. Anna screamed

*"Don't fire, I am staff"*. The last thing she needed was to be hit by the so called 'friendly fire'. By the time Anna opened her door Harry was long gone. He was on his way north to his family's camp on a remote community at Fitzroy Crossing. The fact he had lived there as a child was not in his record. He deliberately omitted it in case he needed to retreat there someday. Now he needed it. Though not Aboriginal his half siblings were and he was as welcome as they on that top end community.

Stu and Lachie first thought it was 'cool' to have their mum involved in a Police sting. But as they thought it through they demanded that Anna quit her job, now. They were almost hysterical as they demanded that she take whatever steps it took to live and not be killed by some 'stinking criminal'. She had to admit she was rattled. At 1:00 am she was still awake watching the digital clock change, one minute at a time. 1:15, 1:16, 1:17.

•••••

# 27

# Harry Heads North

After a sleepless night Anna forced herself out of bed, and drove back in Port Stirling on Wednesday. Her mind swirled over the events of the previous day. She could not concentrate. She emailed the Fremantle office to find out what was happening there. Charlotte emailed back that the offenders were still not showing up to report or for any other reason. The office was quiet almost silent, and empty. Jason had time to read the newspaper. He was doing the crossword. If it was a virus Port Stirling had caught it, Crystal was Anna's first appointment. The early appointments did not usually work for her as her nights were so long; it took her until at least noon to recover. Crystal did not show. Anna advised her Probation Officer, her last urine analysis was positive for amphetamine, just as suspected.

Anna still could not focus, she telephoned Liz. She told her she was shaken by yesterday's debacle. Anna was distressed that she had been overlooked in the evacuation effort and was left alone to face the drawn guns of officers. For a professional Police operation it was an amateur show. Liz knew better than to interrupt at this point. Anna told her that Harry Browning was a psychopath. She said that the Directorate had to get serious about assessing and treating psychopaths effectively. The cost of the testing instruments and the licenses be damned, what did that dog and pony show cost yesterday? And it did nothing but stop the honest offenders from reporting. Liz bit her lip, she wanted to tell Anna,

*"You are upset, sleep on it, tomorrow is another day, we all work within limitations, you will see that more reasonably tomorrow"* but as she was forming the words Anna shouted,

*"And don't patronize me"*. Liz asked if she needed her. Anna whispered

*"No"* and hung up.

Anna was trembling; she closed her door and tried to sob. She was too angry and instead of tears she produced expletives. She had a growing sense of misgiving that bordered on a dark foreboding. She asked PP to arrange for the appointments of her later clients to be cancelled. She, dragged her wheeled brief case over soft yellow sand, chucked it in the boot of her vehicle and drove home on auto pilot.

Bald made way for long and scruffy hair. Harry grew a beard, unkempt. His time in the sun tanned him. He changed his clothing style from smart casual to bogan. Instead of pressed fitting shirts he wore loose tartan shirts and track suit pants. His shoes were non-descript, and he gained 20 kilos. He recalled that international spies who wanted to alter their gait to avoid discovery placed a pebble in a shoe. The pebbles made him limp consistently, ensuring he did not forget to limp. The gait change dramatically changed his presentation. Even his mother would not have recognized him.

Harry's dream of a fantastic exit, that killed as many Police as possible was so close to becoming a reality now he could taste it. He took weeks to prepare and gather the necessary equipment to make his weapon, a car bomb. He freely moved between the remote community and the red earthed town some 23 kilometres away. To get there he had to drive down a rugged and unyielding road, baked hard in the dry season and a quagmire of sucking red mud in the wet. He ate, drank, laughed, lent a hand to one of his mob when his car engine seized. He helped a brother build a shed, played bush football at night in the dark with the kids. It was too hot to play in the sun in the day time hours, and there was no money for lights for the night field. Harry told everyone in the local bar that he was sure this night footy gave Aboriginal footballers the edge when they reached the professional level. They sensed the ball. They did not need to see it to fly high and mark it. Throughout this social time he gave absolutely no indication of his murderous determinism. He transitioned from dreaming and gathering to often rehearsing what he needed to do to pull off a successful mission.

•••••

# 28

## *Cory's Really Bad Day*

The next day Anna pushed herself to rally. She drove to Port Stirling early and decided that obsessing over Harry Browning was futile. Sulking about the lack of cooperation between her Centre and the local publicly funded psychiatrists and other mental health professionals was equally futile. She should take proactive action. She could do little about Browning so she telephoned the local mental health clinic. She arranged to drive there and meet the psychiatrists and duty doctors in person. The office was disorganised, it bordered on being a total mess. Papers were strewn everywhere, files were stacked two meters high in disorganized columns from floor level. The carpet was soiled. The seats in the waiting room wore ground in dirt and what looked like urine stains. The walls and doors were dirty. Plastic cups littered the floor around the water fountain. Anna was surprised to learn the office was only two years old. It had been abused.

The staff members were pleasant. She was pleased to meet each member, and each seemed pleased to meet her, even the duty doctor. They directed her to the least chaotic corner of the office behind the door 'Staff Only' where the chairs were still clean. They were members of the same team, fighting the same enemy, with similar tools. And they all felt it. Anna hoped they could retain this spirit of collegial co-operation. By the time she returned to the office Cory the tattoo entrepreneur had been waiting for 5 minutes. He was surly and depressed. He barely spoke. She asked him what his story was. He told her he had called his dad and asked if they could meet soon. He wanted to tell him about the tattoo deal. His dad usually went to the Returned Servicemen's League Hall on Wednesdays for lunch with his other Vietnam War mates. The hall was across the street from Cory's house. His dad promised to drop by this next Wednesday. Cory had cleaned his apartment, and even bought his dad's special beer. Cory was a wine drinker, so it was a departure for him to get the beer. Cory had sat in his surprisingly neat apartment with the cold beer and waited, and waited, and waited. Alone.

Like every Little Aussie's footy match, every school assembly, every parent teacher night his frickin' father DID NOT SHOW!!!!!!

Cory cried then stopped himself from crying. Anna ached to think of Stuart or Lachie having gone to such remarkable effort only to be disappointed by Max. Cory scolded himself, told himself not to be such a

*"drongo\*, pansy\*, poofter\* prick"*. That took care of that. Conversation over. No he did not want to talk tattoos, he didn't give 'a shit' about anything. He said

*"I will see you next week"*. Sam barked. Cory left.

Anna was not having an exactly successful or satisfying week. The sadness she felt for Cory lasted for days. She did not understand the dereliction to sacred duty by his parents. They had neglected and abandoned him since birth. But, this recent vignette of appalling parenting demonstrated the father's total lack of connection to his son. It seemed especially sad now that Cory was trying so hard to rehabilitate.

Anna received an email titled 'Suicide'. She struggled to recall who the client was. Then she remembered. She was the woman who embezzled the funds and reputation of a prominent therapist. The email stated simply that she had suicided yesterday. Her death was a fitting end to a catastrophic week. Anna felt empty; she wanted to feel sad. This one had slipped through her fingers. After all she had requested counselling of her own volition. No one ordered her to attend. Liz assured her

*"Anna they can't all be saved, some suicides do schedule therapy. It was on her 'bucket list' and was the last item she ticked off the list before she found and kicked the bucket - the last thing she tried that did not work. She knew it wouldn't. Therapy's pre-ordained failure somehow legitimized in her own mind, the act of suicide, for it proved she had no option. Perhaps the client could not accept the help of a therapist, after all look who she embezzled money from, and what it cost her employing psychologist."*

Anna could have written that platitude herself. It did not help. Anna knew that she had the client there in the office and let her own anger at the misshapen little thumb sucker stop her from working harder to form an alliance with her. Anna made sure her notes about her were in order ready to surrender them to the manager, Charlotte. No room for psychologist error or neglect in a suicide and departmental audit.

●●●●●

# 29

# Cory's Good Day

*F*riday morning Max needed the car again so Anna rode the train south to Port Stirling. It was a longer journey than when she went to Fremantle or Perth. Being a psychologist she took particular interest in those who rode with her. Many of Anna's fellow riders had the appendages that hang from their ears that were connected to ever smaller 'what nots'. Sometimes the ear pieces fit badly and allow the rasping beat of a drum to escape, that's about all that filters through. Pppsssh Pppsssh pppsssh!. One of her companion riders, a fresh faced young man with wide blue eyes listened to his 'what not' and looked at the rest of the riders with an expression that says,

*"You would be surprised if you could hear what I hear!!!"* What musical secret does this boy hide in his transistorised digitalised 'what not'? She would never know. His expression amused her.

A passenger Anna recognised sat opposite her. As passengers usually sat in the same area in the same carriage many had heard her conversations over some weeks about how she and her sister had decided to get pregnant together (Anna wondered how literally 'together' is taken). No one mentioned how the husbands felt about the dual pregnancies. Anna knew all of their names. Anna was formulating theories about their relationships when the passenger Anna recognised was told, in a matronly tone, to sit by her friend.

Obviously she had won the race to conception. No bump, but sitting down is a sure sign. Many in the carriage smiled.

It was a short walk to the Centre from the train. The weather was splendid, yawning blue skies and early summer cool breeze. She hardly noticed she was dragging her 'office on wheels'. As she went through her appointment diary, making sure all the offenders had been logged in she saw the tattoo entrepreneur's name, Cory Henderson. She smiled. Then her observing ego caught up with her, it had been chasing her for weeks. She hadn't sat still long enough, even on the train, for it to 'speak'. It was warning her that she was altogether too happy to see him and altogether too happy with her impact upon his life and his progress. She soon shut that voice down. Anna and Cory's Probation Officer worked together to authorize and allocate the funding from the tattoos already sold for Mervyn to travel to Vietnam and Thailand on Cory's behalf. This was not easy as the Directorate had already reallocated those funds into the general fund. De-merging money from the central account was a tedious and difficult undertaking. It needed the accountant in charge of the funding to believe in Anna's cause and to have some money left over in the budget. If he did not retrieve and allocate those funds to an item this year they might not be available next year. He could really need the funds then. In order to get it next year he had to demonstrate that he needed it now. This motivated him to assist Anna.

Cory said he knew others, who had international contacts ready to buy the Australian tattoos, find qualified skin artists and procure traditional Japanese tattoos for the data bank. But he could not leave Australia. Anna did not think to ask how he had those contacts, or why. Mervyn had only travelled locally over

Australian desserts and oceans in smaller planes with external propellers. Those planes were so small the passengers are carefully allocated seats in order to balance the weight. Flying internationally in passenger jets without visible external propellers was a new adventure. The acquisition of Mervyn's birth certificate, passport and luggage seemed to be a daunting task.

Anna contacted a group called Successful Out Comes. This group of volunteers assisted those being released from jail. While Mervyn did not exactly meet their acceptance criterion they were enthused by the task, adjusted their criterion and assisted him. The Directorate had difficulty understanding that this program could be cost neutral. One of the managers even confided in Anna that he was having trouble getting his head around the whole idea. He had been a government employee so long he had lost sight of the fact that the rest of the world was mandated to focus on and pander to the bottom line. He had never had to balance a budget or consider the real cost of anything other than 'was there money for it?' Where that money came from, how much was left, the intrinsic value of the item bought were never considerations.

The tattoo designs were selling well locally and internationally, on line and were now fully funding the costs of the Mastermind Plan through the trust fund. Anna was grateful that at least the manager at Port Stirling understood business and assisted others to deal with such revolutionary concepts as a profitable bottom line.

Mervyn was overseas for 10 days. He sent cryptic but daily emails to Cory and Anna to advise them of his travels and successes. The international artists he discovered were genuinely excited about acting as consultants to Australian skin artists. They were willing to share their knowledge on the inks and methodologies to use for best effect. The Vietnamese business man with Australian ties was an invaluable asset. He had a carefully cultivated a Vietnamese network of artists and producers of inks and equipment to work with the Mastermind Plan. It was reciprocal, many of the skin artists Mervyn met were eager to learn the ancient Aboriginal scarification techniques. Mervyn's feet barely touched the tarmac at the Perth airport before Cory had a potential employee for him to interview. She was a well known tattoo artist with a solid reputation. She had recently been released from Boronia, the Women's Prison. They needed her as the business was booming and the two skin artists they had employed could not handle the volume of the customer demand.

During their initial stage of the interview Mervyn was impressed with her passion for the skin arts. Her tee shirt read,

*"A man without tattoos is invisible to the gods"*. She said *"it was an Iban proverb, whatever that means"*. Mervyn thought those shirts would sell in the salon. So far so good, however an unexpected problem arose. This artist, Jody, did not 'do' tattoos she did not like. She did not like Japanese designs. Her work was unique; it was a collision of glowing colours and designs. Her portfolio of work, though shabby and tattered, displayed a collection of impressive art. Her inked Celtic art was fuelled by exaggeration and largesse that enhanced, without distorting, the original concept. She was not constrained by conservatism in any shade. The colours were electric and jumped off the skin, bold to a fault. She had a way of combining the harsher lines and brilliant colours with the soft stippled inking effect.

A true professional, the aftercare protocol she used was impeccable. She applied a newly released topical medication made from tea tree oils. Mervyn was not familiar with that medication specifically but he knew of the healing properties of tea tree oil and was eager to try that product line. His mob had learned from the Bundjalung mob from upcountry New South Wales, to treat coughs and colds by inhaling the oils from the crushed leaves. They also applied crushed leaves to open wounds with amazing results. He was annoyed he had not thought of using these leaves in tattoo after care before.

Another point in her favour was that she understood the self harmers. There had always been a subset who wanted tattoos, which 'jonesed' for pain. In addition to tattoos some burned and used needles to scar and razors to cut their own skin.

Instead of classing self harm as a 'symptom' of mental illness that required modification, she celebrated it. She said markings on the skin wrote a coded journal. Every entry was equally valid, those she applied with ink and those the skin owner applied with razor or cigarette should become an orchestrated self tale. Mervyn was familiar with self harm. His thighs told that story. So was Jody. Mervyn noticed the designs on her inner forearms were built around horizontal, self applied scars and scarified words he could not read from that angle.

As intriguing as her overall presentation was, she refused to 'do' Japanese designs. Since his trip overseas Mervyn had become increasingly 'financial' about the business. He knew that the money was in the Japanese. As she remained resolute that she was 'not into' Japanese, he was 'not into her'. He could not tolerate the salon losing money as she waited around for a request for a non Japanese design to walk through the door. He told her,

*"We are not asking you to do sleeves but we want you to do Japanese".*

*"Forget you mate, no one tells me what to do. I am an artist and art cannot be controlled. No one tells me what to do. All matter in the universe is made up of protons, neutrons, and electrons, except for you, you are composed entirely of morons."* With that she turned on her heels and left.

Jody was a single mother with two children 4 and under to feed. With her prison history her occupation opportunities had diminished. Three days later she was back at the salon with a Japanese dragon design she had modified, traced and further worked over. The dragon lifted off the paper and looked right at Mervyn. Sold. She perched on a stool, changed the radio channel, turned up the volume. There she stayed and there she worked. Mervyn never said another word about it. Neither did she. And she never called him a 'moron' again either. Not to his face anyway.

The customers loved Jody's 'in your face attitude' and her own tatts and piercings. She especially charmed the hairy and the scary clients. The music of Guns and Roses blasted whenever she was on duty. She sang as she worked, patrons sang and bumped and ground with her. Some days her hair was Goth black, other times bleached yellow, other days it was shaved in part or the whole. She wore rings, several of them on every finger and toe. When she showed her naval she hung a mini chandelier from the pin therein.

Cory didn't care what she sang or what she looked like, what jiggled or flashed as long as the cash rolled in. Jody did not accept the limitations of the needle. Mervyn yelled at her,

*"Be careful with that, that ink comes with commitment but it does not come with an eraser"*. Her response began and ended with expletives. The more expletives the more the customers loved her. When challenged about her language Jody responded,

*"What do you expect? I live and work in a testosterone world; these freakin' words get me respect. From what I see the world is divided into two tribes, those who have tatts and those who are afraid of those who have them. And you know which tribe is mine. And I intend to make sure our tribe keeps growing."* That was met by cat calls and whistles from the crowd in the shop. That crowd paid the bills so Mervyn left silently.

Soon Mervyn and Cory bought one of the store fronts quite close to Franny's Muffin Parlour. It was a brick building, salmon in colour, and had a two bedroom apartment in back. They renamed the company 'Con Artists' to emphasize the prison tattoos, they said. There was a huge parking lot that circled around the building, offering free parking for all. Sam guarded the store at night. Either Mervyn or Cory was always on site. It worked well. With its accessibility and free private parking especially at the rear of the building, patrons came and went - scores of them.

Monday at Fremantle was unremarkable. Anna's clients were beginning to trust that all was well again. The watchers felt the usual vibrations and were at peace. Anna was in Port Stirling on a Tuesday. This was usually her Fremantle day. However, as she had an urgent report to submit to the Court she was further south than usual for a Tuesday. She literally bumped into Cory's Probation Officer in the narrow hall. They had become quite friendly since the setting up of the Mastermind program in that Centre.

The breathless Probation Officer informed Anna,

*"There was a drug bust. A huge haul. The largest in the Shire. The names have not yet been released. It seems it might have National and International connections".* Anna hoped none of her clients were involved in it. She ran through her list, she could

not see it being the ballerina, the bad, the bald or the minimally brain damaged. She had not heard that there had been an increase in the drug supply in the area, but obviously there had been. She completed the urgent report. Liz emailed her

*"Where are you? Call me."* Liz was such a ditz; she never remembered where any members of her team were. Anna had told her she would be in Port Stirling on Tuesday even though it was usually her Fremantle day. Obviously it didn't register; she emailed her that information again. Liz called her.

*"Anna I have some good news for you, your Mastermind Program won the 'Enterprising Government Employee Award' for the year. There is going to be a grand dinner. Max will also be invited, and the Premier will award you. It puts our department on the map and gives you incredible visibility within the department. Also you will receive a $5,000 bonus. Not much by free enterprise standards, but a huge leap forward for the State Government. Congratulations."*

Anna couldn't think. She never imagined such an outcome. She called Max. He was proud of her. He asked to take her for lunch and a drink to celebrate. All she wanted was a sugar encrusted muffin, raspberry and something at Franny's. He'd be there in 30 minutes. He was developing an appetite for those muffins too.

Max and Anna enjoyed their coffee and muffins, savouring the warmth of the café against the cool late spring day, making plans to spend the $5,000 award. Anna noticed Franny had a new muffin. It was rhubarb and apple. Apple? After Franny's declaration that she did not cook apples, Anna was puzzled. Franny sat with them,

*"Anna I have to tell you something, a confession really. The secret ingredient in all of my muffins is stewed apple; I add a little*

*apple to every batch for consistency and moisture."*

Anna was stunned; they had a 'no cooked apple' pact. But she said

*"Well a lot of things are not as they appear, eh?"* As she and Max walked back to the Centre her mobile telephone rang. A little boy said

*"'Gratulations mummy."*

*"Lachie, how did you know lovee?"*

*"Harry's dad came to school today to talk to us about his work, and he works for the gov'ement and he knows everything, he told me."*

*"Thank you lovee, I will see you tonight."*

*"Hats off to you mummy."*

*"Love you."*

Did life get any better? Max kissed her goodbye and she opened the door to the Centre. Crystal was in the well worn reception area waiting for her session when Anna returned. This was Crystal's last session as her orders were completed in two days. As she was so close to completing her orders she was not violated for her 2 latest dirty pee tests. She was still prostituting and Anna feared for her safety. Anna's inability to connect with Crystal was becoming legendary in her own mind. She had been remarkably unsuccessful with this woman-child. Anna did not know how to reach this gorgeous china doll. She was recently spending her time with a wealthy 55 year old Indonesian business man. He was the one developing the new mall in the area. He paid $1,000 a night for her 'companionship'. For a single mother who had to hock her DVD player to buy cigarettes, this was the high life. She told Anna she had to get drunk or on the gear to not care or know how the evening progressed. She often woke up not knowing how she had arrived in that particular bed, or who or how many she had been with. There was always a car outside waiting to take her back to her unit. That income stream was too vital to forgo. The warnings about her daughter's safety, her own health and risks fell on deaf ears. The china doll left no better than she had arrived at the first session.

*"If I got paid for outcomes I'd be paying the Department for this one, for life"* Anna thought.

The ballerina showed again. Anna had not seen the petite dancer for some time. This client understood the reasons for her theft. She had insight and self examined. She demonstrated resilience and she said she understood the steps she needed to take to avoid re-offending. She had family support which was usually the key to ending the offending behaviour. She thanked Anna for her help as she walked out of the office, for the last time.

•••••

# 30

# An Out of Perth Experience

"*The situation has multifarious ramifications not available to the un-assisted optic. This immature zygote holds it to the ultimate desideratum to consort with the dominant aborigine of the trifurcate variety. Through a judicious use of benign mendacity, exhibit A performs as a surrogate, in spirit, if not in letter.*"

Anna had not met this Fremantle client before. He was small, his long hair was silver, and he flaked. Flakes fell from his scalp, his face and his clothes. He looked to be 45 years of age. Even sitting still he flaked. His crime was exhibitionism. He had a taste for picking young girls who were not yet in school. These children were 4 or 5, and were independent enough to walk away from their parent in a store. They were dependent enough on their parents to predictably be taken along with their parent. These small girls were too old to strap into a stroller, but were too young to leave at home, alone. This meant that if he could locate a young parent, a child would be nearby.

He lived in a lower socio economic area. One block from his home was a tall block of HomesWest apartments. Many young women, with small children lived there, alone, or with any one of a list of transient non protective males. In the centre of Coolbellup was an aging strip mall, and across the road was a huge Salvation Army recycled clothing store. The young mothers patronized the store, looking for bargains. They stopped by on a weekly basis and knew the staff by name. Monday was picking up the discarded items day, Tuesday was sorting day and Wednesday was 'hanging the new clothing on the hangers' day.

Wednesday was the day the exhibitionist went shopping. Wednesday was the day the mothers trekked to the store, child or children in tow. Once settled in the store, he wandered around carrying an item or two as if he was looking to buy. Then he chose a child and watched her mother. As soon as the 19 or 20 year old mother was engrossed in a conversation or selecting clothing he sidled up to the child and flashed his penis. Some children did not know what he was doing but moved closer to mother. Some children knew what he was doing but remained silent, or quickly burrowed their head in mother's legs or their own hands. Others, and these were the ones he dreaded, would scream, or cry or tell him *"no"*. Some even punched at the air as if to punch him away. If that happened he scurried away. He would mutter complaints about 'children today' to the clerks, and buy the paltry item he had been carrying. He then disappeared. The mother usually turned on the child, yelling at her to be quiet, scolding her for her causing a scene. Some of the mothers did want to hear what distressed the child had to say. It often took several minutes to settle her down to be able to understand what she was saying through sobs. The exhibitionist was long gone before he could be accosted. Those stores were not equipped with surveillance cameras.

The game was won when he could flash the same child more than once and not get the scream reaction. He took this to mean she enjoyed it. That made perfect sense to him.

*"Does what you just said make sense to you?"* asked Anna.

*"Yes,"* he replied.

*"What is it?"* asked Anna.

*"Something from a book I read and memorized, can't remember what,"* he said.

*"Why did you think it appropriate to begin our first session with that announcement?"* asked Anna.

*"Because everyone in this building thinks I am stupid, I am showing you I am not,"* he protested.

*"How can I help you?"* asked Anna.

*"You cannot."* That two word declaration of her impotence was issued with a tone that was almost threatening. Anna sensed the second half of that sentence was *"so don't even try"*.

*"We have 6 initial sessions, these are mandated, you are required to attend. Failure to attend even one session is counted as a violation,"* stated Anna.

*"I know."* He seemed less interested in that than he did in his own finger nails. It was obvious he was not going to engage in meaningful dialogue so Anna administered the Rampant A7. He scored high in every category that indicated he was actively intent and planning to continue his crime. His intent to commit crime was high, his impulse control was low, his ability to feel empathy for others had flat lined, he had actual plans to continue, he had access to non relative victims, he had multiple victims and no inhibiting factors were identified. This client was a high risk to re-offend.

Anna relayed this information back to him, in accordance with the protocol. She advised him that she needed to report the outcome to his Probation Officer. He was well aware of the ramifications of her report to the Probation Officer. He appeared to be unfazed.

*"Whatever your test says I am not going to be engaging in my hobby again."*

*"Hobby. How could he call scaring the hell out of vulnerable little girls and their mothers a hobby?"* Anna thought this but did not verbalise it.

*"Have you decided what will stop you?"* she asked.

*"Mobile telephones with cameras. The last two times I was nabbed it was because both of the mothers had a mobile telephone with a camera, I was photographed."*

Anna doubted he could keep to that commitment. She was equally sure that he would find another location, perhaps at a local beach. If a mother and her child, at the beach were separated from their telephone by a few feet of yellow sand towels might provide him with initial covering, and then quick access to his anatomy.

It took Anna approximately an hour to draft and finalize the report for his Probation Officer. Although he was a small man he cast a long cold shadow over her day. She did not look forward to his next session. Writing the report she became even more alarmed. Each and every of the danger scales indicating he was likely to reoffend and soon, were elevated. Perhaps she had misinterpreted his responses. She needed supervision on these results. She called Liz and was surprised to reach her on the first ring. Anna ran through the responses and her interpretation of his scores to ensure their accuracy. She read her report to Liz and made the suggested minor changes. In a perverse way she was not happy to know she had scored him correctly. She preferred to have made a scoring error and to have the female children of the area be safe from this predator.

She had to get out of that room, she decided to walk. Seldom did she meet such raw criminal intent head on, resistant to change, non retractable criminal intent. She left the office. It was warmer outside than she realised, so she walked across the leafy park, enjoying the coolness loaned by the trees. The solitude of the park evaporated in the busy street. She slipped into a café and ordered a coffee. She glanced through the local newspaper; she began to make notes on how to formulate his care. How could she draw any goals of integrity from a habituated criminal? Could he possibly identify problem behaviours to be remediated? His paradigm for life was decidedly warped. Perhaps he was intellectually impaired? What was that introductory speech about? Perhaps she should have written it down verbatim. Maybe it contained the key to his thinking or rehabilitation. She wondered if he could repeat it. Somehow she had to motivate him. If he did not buy into the process, no intervention would work. Was it likely that mobile telephones could continue to protect the little girls of Coolbellup from this freak? Her only comfort was that he was on strict community based orders, any violation would result in his being imprisoned, locked away from little girls.

As she re-entered the building, PP saw her. He could tell this was no day for sarcasm; she looked as if she needed support and he would give it.

*"Tea, Anna? I have some of my fruited tea?"* Her look said it all; he was actually offering her a tea bag, as before, so she could make her own tea. He could tell from her expression she was expecting a hot steaming cup of tea. The receiving room was quiet; no one else was scheduled as it was still the lunch hour. He got her some tea in the best mug he could find. Alone in her room, door locked, Anna sipped the tea and began to sob. She could not explain it, she did not know who she was crying for, but it helped to sob. Perhaps PP's kindness was the catalyst.

The next morning Liz sent her an email inquiring if she was open to a week's teaching stint in Kalgoorlie. Liz knew Anna has an interest in supporting the rural areas. She sensed Anna needed a change of routine  She asked her to present the newly adopted core curriculum training to new Probation Officers. The scheduled speaker had been injured in a car accident and was hospitalised. Anna was intrigued by the offer. She would discuss it with Max.

Max and the boys were mildly supportive but not entirely enthusiastic about the idea of her being gone for a week. They left the decision up to her. So she packed her bag. The secretary cancelled her scheduled clients. Anna left the house noiselessly when the taxi came at 4:00 am. The driver was playing music in Farsi. It sounded like a war dance. Anna recognized the music style from her visit to the Middle East. Whilst there on vacation she had heard young Muslim men singing war songs against Israel. She asked him why he had migrated to Australia.

*"It's a large land, large enough for a good man to live…"* Anna remained silent.

*"Or a bad man to hide."*

Anna did not ask which he was but she did ask him to lower the volume on his radio. She texted his personnel identification to Max, with the note "in case anything happens to me". She then reprimanded herself; hanging out with those with criminal intentions was obviously getting to her. She must relax. When the taxi pulled up at the Perth airport, she paid the driver with her government voucher, minus the usual tip. If he was the bad man hiding she did not want to finance that endeavour.

Her plane was scheduled to leave early, 6:15am. An early summer thunderstorm was thrashing Kalgoorlie with winds too fierce to land. Why leave if you cannot land? Their flight was delayed. She opened her book and settled in for the wait. Thankfully this storm was short lived so within 2 hours they were in flight. It was a small plane. It was crowded, every seat was taken. Her companion travellers were mostly young, mostly male, mostly wore huge working man boots. The smell of stale beer and sweat hung heavy in the air. The men either side of her were clean and neat but that wretched odour-de-human was embroidered into the cloth fabric on the seats. She had to take the middle seat with such a late booking. Neither companion wanted to talk, this was their work commute. They were part of the fly in fly out mob. 1 week on one week off, two weeks on one week off, three weeks on one week off, it depended on the company. There was no novelty to this morning's commute. She was glad she had her book.

The food served was scones, jam and cream and hot tea. That hit the spot for afternoon tea, but not breakfast. She declined. The flight was anything but smooth. That small plane rocked and rolled. Her companions slept, and she tried to read her way through the aerial gymnastics. By the time they landed she felt quite ill. Taxis were in such a high demand she had to share one. It operated more like a bus, dropping off and picking up passengers at the requested spots. The short trip took her longer than she had factored. She was last to leave as her hotel was the one furtherest from the airport. The secretary said she had booked this hotel for her as it was allegedly an international hotel and had a pool. It looked impressive from the exterior, probably because in this flat land with most buildings being only 2 floors high it was a high rise, perhaps 8 or so floors. She passed a tour bus in the parking lot. The driver and tour host was scrubbing the wet mud resulting from the storm and suicidal insects off his bus as he readied it for the day's trip.

Anna pushed the glass doors open and stepped into the air conditioned lobby. The first thing that caught her attention was the art. It was Aboriginal in origin. Although the art was indigenous Australian the staff was Asian. Her room was adequate but basic. She did not know if she imagined it or not but it felt like ground in dirt inhabited the carpet, the bed covers, even the drapes. Perhaps it was just because she rode the elevator with three miners, and they were indeed grimy.

Once she unpacked and settled into the room she ventured down to the dining room. It had shining polished wooden floors; the napkins were real linen, folded most beautifully. The waitress welcomed her to "brekkie". The food was served in silver tureens. Services began at 4:00 am to accommodate the miners. However the tables were refreshed frequently and there was food aplenty. She chose her table, picked some of the more edible foods offered, fruit, yogurt and eggs. She hoped it would settle her stomach. She recognised her elevator companions. They now wore fresh shirts and shorts, clean socks but the same dirt encrusted boots they wore in the elevator. They were trying to remove their warmed rolls from their linen softened bed of silver with tongs so small they could more appropriately have been called 'tweezers'. The louder one amongst them gave up and just grabbed his crusty fresh rolls with his hands. His cobbas* knocked into him, called him various unflattering names, and did the same. They looked to be at least 19 years of age. They probably cleared more money a week than she did in a month.

The breakfast buffet table was decorated with an ornate creation carved from fresh fruit, melons, kiwis, strawberries, grapes, pineapple, oranges - obviously trucked in. No one dare disturb its symmetry by taking anything it offered. As Anna arranged for the obscenely priced breakfast to be paid for by her department she spoke to the petite Asian petal about the boys in the dining room. LeiMing told her in whispered tones that indicated she was sharing a secret,

*"This hotel is paid big bucks to pamper these boy workers. The mines said that replacing staff was expensive. The hotel is most excellent in helping them retain their staff by looking after these dirty boys. They were told they did well when the boys had a full stomach at breakfast, and reeked of stale beer and sweat as they fell into their turned down bed at shift end."* She advised Anna not to use the pool. Point taken.

Anna was not scheduled to present her topic "Trauma: A Criminogenic Variable" until 1:00 pm. She felt better so she decided to take in some local colour. She knew about the super pit and decided it was time to see it. The taxi driver was pleased to transport and wait for her. The pit was just at the end of Burt Street. This was his slow time anyway. He seemed to enjoy regaling her with stories of the antics of his drunken fares. The super pit was so massive Anna could not photograph it in one shot. Its size seemed ludicrous. She decided that one of the postcards showing it from the air would show its dimensions to the boys more than her rim shot would. From the top of the yawning abyss she looked at the trucks. Those monsters looked like tiny toys. To prove how large they were to the boys she asked the taxi driver to photograph her standing in one of the truck's bucket scoops at the rim of the mine. Despite being tall she reached only half way up that scoop. The trucks were relentless in their pursuit of gold as the super pit runs

24 hours a day every day of the year.

Sensing her interest, the taxi driver demonstrated his knowledge of things local.

*"Missus did you know the pit was designed by our Alan Bond in 1980?"*

She did know that, yes, thank you.

*"Did you know Bondie decided that one big open pit was the cheaper way to mine gold? He bought up the individual leases along the golden mile. And bugga me he never got to see it done under his oversight but in 1989 all those involved got their ducks in a row and the pit was born under KCGM."*

He said that as if he expected her to know who and what Kalgoorlie Consolidate Mines was and how it administered the massive project. She did not, and she had had enough local colour for one day. Everyone knew of the flamboyant Alan Bond and his 'America's Cup' win and his subsequent criminal history. She did not need more information but her driver was not yet done.

*"Bondie was a pom\* yanno, he came here at age 12 I think, with his pommie parents. He ran into a mess of trouble. I think 1992 was his first prison sentence, and again in 1997 he could have gotten 45 years. But things being what they are he got 7 years in prison. Course he did not serve them all. Rumour has it he was ordered to hand over the family jewels and other treasures. Seems he could not recall where he had put them. Anyway, he was able to save enough of what he had nicked from others to start again. I read he worked or lived, I can't remember which, near Buckingham Palace that figures eh?"* His laughter was infectious.

It did seem appropriate to Anna that a convicted criminal was the one to think outside of the lines and envision an open rather than the time worn and dangerous tunnel pits to mine gold. His skills were transferable, legal, illegal, and back to legal. Or so the story went. They returned to the hotel where she tipped her driver, paid for this fare herself and decided to walk to the Department of Justice. Walking around Kalgoorlie was easy. The skies were still resplendent with swirling towering clouds of black through to white. The streets were unnecessarily wide, and to add insult to this excessive width injury in the middle of the roads were concrete islands. She had read that the streets were this width because of the camel trains of yesteryear. She was informed that it took a lot of room to turn a camel train around. Being summer and December it was predicted to be 40 degrees Celsius. At 11:00 am it was already too hot for her to walk far, she was glad it was a short trek.

•••••

# 31

# A Class Alone

Thirty prospective Probation Officers for both adults and juveniles were present for the training. Some had earned degrees, some had not. Recruiting qualified staff in this area was often a challenge. Sometimes the hiring criterion had to be massaged in order to meet staff quotas. The director introduced Anna and publicly thanked her for agreeing to teach the class at short notice. She commended her for lending her support to their staff member who was transferred first to Fremantle then to Port Stirling. Anna had forgotten about her. It was nice to be acknowledged, even for kindnesses forgotten.

Her presentation was well received until she came to the section on intergenerational trauma. One woman took umbrage at Anna's thesis that trauma focused families can have adverse effects upon the adjustment levels of their offspring and set them up for crime. The attendee was not going to be mollified, she made sweeping statements. She punctuated her protestations with tears and upped the volume to the yelling decibel range. Her defence of the insane, her unwillingness to review statistical data, her inability to regroup and assimilate incoming information set off warnings for Anna. Anna closed the discussion with her favourite

*"This topic does not allow for such a broad discussion we need to progress to the next step".* With that the attendee fled the room.

Three others fled with her, ostensibly to comfort her. The fact that a professional needed such an overlay of comfort when confronted by statistically supported concepts amazed Anna. She had little patience for it.

At the conclusion of the session Anna informed the Director of her concerns. She was advised that the attendee was part Aboriginal; she was a rare find for the department. She had an earned degree in psychology and was slated to be installed in a lead role over a team of Aboriginal liaison officers. Anna was advised to find her and discuss the issues with her, bringing the discussion to a satisfactory conclusion. This was defined as calming her and convincing her to return. She had to be present to pass the course. Failure was not an option. That night while another thunderstorm punished the inhabitants of the area and turned the dirt roads back to sucking mud, Anna emailed Max:

*"A long time ago in a galaxy far, far, away...well Kalgoorlie actually, the inmates ran the asylum...I love you, kiss the boys for me."*

Despite her own misgivings and to allow time to defuse the angst Anna arranged to meet the woman for breakfast in the hotel, tomorrow. This new employee looked younger than her stated 30 years of age. She was slightly overweight, lightly tanned, with the more typical almost Polynesian features of the mob which lived in that area. At breakfast she informed Anna she was actually from Albany and was way 'out of country'. She was missing her mother and sisters and was not settling well in Kalgoorlie. She explained that she thought Anna had been attacking her. It was difficult to convince her of the facts of the case. Anna did show her the research, revealed her sources, and explained how it related to her point. While she did not understand Anna's point she did sense her genuine respect for her and accepted that Anna was not attacking her or her culture. Professional objectivity had no place in her thinking today. She was still too escalated and distressed. By the time they parted she appeared to at least settle.

Anna's elevator companions were there again, and appeared to be extremely interested in Anna's discussion. One of the young men brushed by her in the reception area and told her his mum was a most excellent psychologist too. They wished each other a 'g'day'. Anna still had the morning free so she strolled around the town. It was slightly cooler today. Last night's storm has brought some relief, it was not always the case she had been told. There was a pub on almost every corner. The pubs ranged from magnificent domed and turreted mansions to the plain understated brick or wooden buildings. Some had their establishment dates set in cement on building facades and were 1895, 1898, or 1908. She decided her favourite building was the Exchange Hotel with its distinctively Australian/British design. It combined Tudor like slats, wide verandas, with corrugated iron roof and green railings. Many pubs of the town advertised, on chalk boards, that they hire "skimpies". She knew enough to avoid these establishments on "skimpie" night. "Skimpies" are scantily clad, nearly naked females. They were in fact topless and wore only "g" strings. She had heard they were instructed to bend over frequently. She was not interested in finding out if it was true.

Anna was over heated by the time she arrived at the seminar room. She peeked inside while another presenter was engaged in persuasive arguments over aspects of anger managerment. She noticed that the attendee who fled yesterday was present and smiling, obviously enjoying the topic at hand. Before Anna began her discussion she acknowledged her breakfast companion by name. She set up her topic by explaining it was based on research. She basically gave a frame for the material, the same frame she had given her breakfast companion. Her presentation went well, the attendees enthusiastically joined in when she assigned group tasks. The information they shared indicated they did indeed understand her position, and could apply what they had learned. Obviously the framing worked, she must remember that for her next seminar.

The director asked for a brief moment in private, after her presentation. They slipped into an empty conference room. The director thanked Anna for her intervention with her new employee. Anna assured her she was welcome but repeated her concerns that she had baggage that required treatment before she was given a position of leadership. If the Department failed to act in this regard they would be setting her up for failure and themselves up for a disaster. This information was not welcomed by the director but she did know it to be truth.

That night Anna went to Paddy's Ale House in the brick built unassuming Rialto hotel. They had no "Skimpie" board so she felt safe. Inside the pub was lined with dark wood, it gave the illusion of coolness. The live band generated cheery music, even if it was not perfectly pitched. The food was delicious. It was a smorgasbord buffet. Anna ate early. She did not enjoy picked over food. She delighted in the Thai green curry. Here in this quintessential Western Australian mining town, under a wrought iron roof, she was eating Thai curry. And it was good! It seemed to Anna that most of the servers were Kiwis from New Zealand but her drink waitress was English. She was a young, newly married, athletic looking girl with a pleasing manner; she lived in Kalgoorlie and loved it. That surprised Anna. An English rose came from a lush green damp land to a red desert and loved it. The waitress said that the buildings were actually Victorian and reminded her of 'the Midlands back *"'ome'*. She said the wages were the best she had ever earned, that the Australians, not accustomed to tipping became extremely generous tippers as the nights wore on. She said they could put down more alcohol than any other species on earth. She said that early in the evening the most frequently used mode of transportation was taxi, but as it got later that changed and the most frequently used form of transportation was cop car. Anna did not know if she was joking or not when the waitress who seemed serious said,

*"It's not that they commit crimes"* she said *"it's just that they fail to keep the law"*.

That night Anna emailed Max:

*"Negative, reckless, self defeating behaviour is alive and well in these parts, fuelled by political correctness and I have fallen into the middle of it. Either I am nuts, or they are. Your opinion is not required. Love you and the boys"*.

•••••

# 32

# He Just Climbs Things

*T*hat morning was fresh and clear. There was something about the air in country towns. She could not describe it, she could just experience it. She had a leisurely shower and was about to visit the "brekkie" table when the phone rang. It was the director; she asked Anna if she would assess a male client. He had been waiting for 3 months for a psychologist's initial interview. They had a psychologist they shared with the other centres, she was .4 at Kalgoorlie when they could have used a full time clinician. He was scheduled to see her this morning but she had called in ill. He had travelled many kilometers out of country and was here for the session. Anna would be pleased to oblige. She ate her yogurt and crusty bread roll (which she removed without the tweezers) on the run and arrived in time for their 9:00 am session.

Her client was sitting on his haunches on the pavement outside the centre. She ushered him in, they walked past security and located their reserved office. No sooner had they been seated than a Police Officer knocked at the door. He was sorry but he needed the room. They had an unexpected client outside in the paddy wagon and this was the only room secure enough to hold him until the magistrate asked for him to be brought up. Anna and her client were left to find their own space. They chose the back veranda, second floor overlooking the children's play ground below. He had picked up her mobile telephone which she had left on the table in the room change. He put his name in her contact list and as he handed it to her he told her that when she was going to get rid of it to remember him, and send it back to him.

Anna had no time to read his file, nor access to it, she asked him to explain the charges against him. It was not her preferred way to begin a session as often it put the client on the defensive. However this client was so grateful for the session he did not react to that as most did, he obligingly told his story.

*"I was done for criminal trespass and stalking, and some other child abuse charges. None of them are real. They wrote a report about me, made me out to be a right nut job. Which is not real either. I am not nuts. I just climb things. And I only do that when I need to"* he said.

Anna had no way of checking his story so asked him how the Police came up with the charges. He said his missus had shot through; she had taken their two little girls with her. She had hooked up with his cousin. He was 90% pure 'bastid'. He liked the drink and would smack her around. Her client said his cousin had taken to smacking his girls around. The client said he had told the Police but because he had some assaults and domestic violence on his own record they were not about to believe him. He needed a cigarette. As smoking near a government building was banned they walked the wide street as he talked. He talked better when they walked, so they kept walking. He said,

*"I went to the Family Court to try to get my girls back. But the missus had a solicitor who had a report writer. That report writer did not believe the girls when they said they had seen my cousin smack their mother. Having been called liars once, they were not*

*going to tell the report writer that he belted them too. The report writer then interviewed the missus. Seems I was not important enough to talk to."*

He then explained that his partner accused him of stalking them and trespassing on their property. He said that was not true and claimed that all he was doing was watching out for them. Anna asked him how he did that.

*"I could not see what was happening to my girls. So whenever I was worried I climbed onto the roof of the shed in their yard and sat there. I would see through the windows and see if the girls had any tucker\*"* he said.

*"Did you do that often?"* Anna asked.

*"Just when I was worried, I got this feeling they were hungry or not looked after, then I would climb onto the shed."* Anna felt there was more.

*"And were there other places, other times you felt like you needed to check up on them?"* she asked.

*"Yes"* he answered.

*"Will you tell me about them?"*

*"I would get worried when they were at school, so I would climb the tree or onto one of the demountable class rooms in the school yard and look for them. I was checking to see if they had shoes, or their lunch, or pencils. Sometimes when it was cold they did not have warm clothes. If they needed things I would go home and get them and bring them back at play time. I always have an extra pair of shoes, or tucker for lunch or a little coat for them."*

*"Is this what they called 'trespass'?"* asked Anna.

*"Yes missus"* he said.

*"Were there other times?"* asked Anna.

*"No missus."*

*"Did you ever take anything that was not yours?"* asked Anna.

*"No Missus, I always took stuff to my girls, never from them or anyone else."*

*"Have you ever been diagnosed by a psychologist, or a doctor, any mental health professional? Has anyone ever given you a name for a disorder, or a diagnosis?"*

*"Yes missus, they said I had ADD, and ADHD"*, he paused *"OCD, way I see it I am working on t-u-v, w-x-y-z."*

Anna smiled, but she did not know the significance of his being able to recite the alphabet, even in part.

*"Did you ask to talk to the report writer?"* Anna asked.

*"No, he was not interested in talking to me"* muttered the client.

Anna did not have time to write the report and prepare for her presentation, but she did read through the solicitor's report for the Family Court and the other documents in his file.

She was not looking forward to her presentation. Her topic today was the neurological damage occurring from childhood abuse and neglect. This segment was the most easily misunderstood. She was hoping the attendees did not mirror Phyllis and think she was saying that childhood trauma excused adult wrongdoing. Before she had even completed her presentation the disputations began. It was as if they had taken Phyllis lessons in how to be oppositional. As she answered each of the questions, diverted the arguments and dismissed the attacks by ignoring them, even when they were repeated she noticed her knees were locked. She guessed that was to stop her from running. When they unlocked she realised how exhausted she was.

Too tired to explore the town or even eat dinner she retreated to her room. She walked out of her clothes, left them where they fell and slipped into bed in her underwear. No email for Max tonight. She left the television tuned to a local channel. The slower pace of the news, the advertisements for farming equipment soothed her. By 6:00 pm she was asleep, television still blaring.

She woke at 6:00 am to the sound of the early morning television news. Breakfast time, she was hungry. LeiMing was back on duty. They greeted each other. Anna was pleased to see the breakfast; she chose eggs, bacon, toast, fried potatoes and even attacked the decorative fruit bouquet.

She called home. Max was in the shower, Stu was still in bed and Lachie answered,

*"Will you be home soon mummy?"*

*"I will lovee, I will."*

*"Tomorrow?"*

*"Not tomorrow poppet, but the day after."*

*"Good, I can handle that, mum did you know that in 2 days tomorrow will be yesterday?"* Anna laughed. Her thesaurus was still working. All was well with the world. Having touched her home base, fed and content she took her laptop to the wi-fi loaded guest business room. She occupied the most luxurious chair she could find - the one by the window and began work on her report for the client she assessed yesterday. She was educating the Family Court consultant on the motives behind his choices. She knew she was countering the report of a well respected report writer. She chose not to argue with the former report but to explicitly report the situation as she saw it. The solicitors would do the arguing.

She reported the obvious, this client is an Aboriginal. He lives, with his mob, in a collection of tiny homes on the fringe of a town that was 100 kilometers north east of Kalgoorlie. It's not designated as an Aboriginal community but it functions like one. And it is dry. He was using culturally and situationally appropriate methods of checking on his children. If he were in Perth he may take an elevator to a higher floor for a clearer view. No one would consider that to be 'paranoid'. The buildings and trees were the equivalent of an elevator in Perth. In Perth you climb stairs; in the bush you climb things.

The trigger for his behaviour was that he had a feeling, a knowing, an intuition and he acted on that to protect his children. Often that intuition was correct indicating that his children needed something, like food, or clothing that he was willing to provide. He was in fact not an abusive parent but a protective one. Finding words for that to present her findings in an objective rather than an advocating tone took her some time. She checked through the solicitor ordered report and disputed the culturally insensitive interpretation of his actions. She did not know if her report would inform the court consultant at his next appearing, or assist his Probation Officer to advocate for him. At least she had given them both the tools they needed if they chose to use them.

She emailed the report to the director and to his Probation Officer. There were two hours left before she had to present. She felt no inclination to arrive at the conference room early. She did not want to encounter the attendees whom she was now viewing as opponents. She rented a car for half a day and drove the flat road out of town. The earth was deep red clay, almost purple, it appeared to be bruised. Although early morning it was hot. It had been predicted that it would be 43 degrees Celsius. A scorcher!

She cranked up the air conditioning and the radio, to a station she enjoyed and just drove. In front of her was a road train, she could not see how long it was as she was behind it. It churned up dust and gravel whenever its tyres touched the gravel shoulder. And the tyres touched the shoulder often. She pulled out to pass it and realized it was hauling 6 trailers. Suddenly she worried that she was going to be sucked under the huge wheels as her small vehicle appeared to want to head that way. Already nervous she tasted fear, worrying that she would meet oncoming traffic before she overtook it. Luckily that did not happen and after what seemed like 'too long' she did pass it successfully.

As soon as she settled her heart rate, there was a rumble and a slight dragging to the right. This had happened before, and last time the car had a flat tyre. This drive was not exactly as she had hoped. Relaxation gone she did not swear but decided to problem solve. She made a note to tell Max about that. In a land where amenities are few and far between she was lucky that a petrol* station and store were ahead. She drove in. She stopped the vehicle and inspected the front tyres. The right, front seemed to be a little deflated. She ran up to the attendant and asked him where the air was.

*"It's all around you man"* he said circling his arms and walking away. She heard him mutter,

*"Three out of four, that is 75% of the drongos* that pull in here don't know where the air is".*

Anna found the hand written sign declaring 'AIR'. She drove the car to within hose range and re-inflated the tyre. She hoped it was a slow leak and drove back to town. She turned the car in and reported the slow leak to the rental car company. The young man behind the counter listened to her story about the road train.

*"Yup those road trains have seriously tough kit\* aboard, do you know the one you passed had 2 engines? Yup one in the truck and one three trailers back. Most of the truckies are decent coves\* at heart."*

Anna was not sure why she needed to know this. She had noticed a propensity amongst the locals to inform others of unsought after facts. As it was so hot and getting hotter she asked for a ride back to the Justice Department. The female receptionist offered to take her as she was breaking for lunch anyway. Anna was appreciative. She found herself using the Kalgoorlie specific grammatically incorrect praise phrase

*"It is most excellent of you thank you"*. Funny how soon local habits rub off, next she would be dispelling all kinds of facts to the unwary.

The prime mover with its six trailers, the non helpful petrol station attendant and the willing receptionist gave her a 'most excellent' story to repeat as she began her presentation. Today she was focused on a less divisive topic, symptoms of trauma. This issue was one the attendees, including her former breakfast companion could appreciate. They approached her assignments for them with enthusiasm. Perhaps this was their apology. Perhaps it was because this session's material was pitched at the level of their understanding and provided them with some practical pointers and interventions. Whatever the reason she appreciated their cooperation and felt energized rather than depleted at the conclusion of her session.

The director called her over and thanked her for her report. The director had lived in the gold fields a long time and she knew that client was looking after his children, and she knew they needed him to do that. She told Anna that his youngest was reading delayed. As difficult as it was for him her father had taken instruction at school, had received lesson plans from the teacher and was teaching her at home. Now both she and her dad were reading at 3rd grade level. The irony was that he was illiterate yet he knew his daughter needed to learn how to read and he was going to teach her. That story struck a chord with Anna and made her trip to Kalgoorlie worthwhile. The director asked her to join her for dinner.

•••••

# 33

## Dinner with the Director

*A*nna walked to the agreed upon meeting place in another local hotel. The wind was kicking up but brought no relief from the heat. It felt as if it was hot and heavy enough to blast the paint off the buildings. She walked by the painted red "Red Dot" store, she thanked God it was not the Yellow dot store, that much yellow would be nauseating. She had not noticed the Scottish or Irish names on the buildings like McKenzie, Pattison or Murphy until now. It was sunset and the sky was on fire with reds, oranges and yellows. She stood still to take it in. The director saw her, thought she was lost and called to her to join her.

They had a pleasant chat, about family, universities attended, and mutual friends. The food was especially good, Anna ordered steak and it was melt in the mouth tender. As the director imbibed her alcohol it moved her 'don't go there' boundaries. She continued, she had been raised in Perth, attended the best girl's school. She had been born to privilege; her father was a barrister in one of the prestigious law firms in Perth. She said,

*"All my childhood I felt like Johnny Cash in some ways, my father was a solicitor and named me Sue"*. Anna did not know whether to laugh or not. She was grateful for the reprieve from the diatribe against Kalgoorlie. The relief was short lived, Sue went on to explain that she found the crude jokes, the fierce negativism

encountered in the gold fields to be wearing. There was a particular habit the locals had of praising an individual, and in the next breath verbally tearing him down. That negative interpersonal duplicity was difficult for her to tolerate. By comparison the desert, the heat, the isolation and the grinding poverty in some quarters compared to the appalling cash flow in others were all tolerable.

*"If this is Karma I must have racked up a huge debt to pay. I hope I enjoyed whatever it was I did to deserve this."* The director added, *"I think it's genetic, you have to be born here to have the gene that allows you to cope with it. I wasn't, and I don't have it."* She lowered her voice, *"I know it's not true and I castigate myself for the thought but at times I feel like I am surrounded by idiots"* she paused, *"did it tell you I don't suffer idiots well?"* That struck a funny chord with Anna, she started laughing. Sue laughed too. The laughter rescued them both from the intensity of the conversation at least temporarily.

Sue then resumed her melancholy report of life in Kalgoorlie; she did not seem to be able to help herself. Anna thought *"where is my English waitress when I need her?"* She did not know what to say so she remained silent. The director began discussing the self destructive behaviours she encountered in others, using almost the exact words Anna used in her cryptic email to Max. Despite the transition to gold field's life being difficult, the Director believed in the cause. She believed she could make a difference. Sometimes, like tonight, that belief wore thin. She understood that there was such a thing as small town mentality yet she thought what she encountered was beyond that. They were not inbred, although she had considered that to be a possibility. She ruled it out as the out of towners were worse than the locals. She blamed the alcohol as she poured them both another red wine. It was an especially delightful wine. It seemed to flirt with the palate then burst with enthusiasm and flavour. Anna did not drink alcohol often and she had never tasted anything like it. In fact, it was a wine to be experienced rather than tasted.

Anna patted Sue's hand, made supportive sounds and suggested they walk back to the hotel. They did not know enough of the same people to gossip about people so they gossiped about the Departments practices. That worked, it formed the 'us against them' bridge and allowed them to both feel safe. They giggled and joked. They both physically and psychologically relaxed. The night was still, the sky cleared and was strewn with brilliant star fire coals seemingly left over from the fiery sunset. It was warm, balmy even; the searing wind had retreated to the desert. They walked for the sake of walking. As they crisscrossed the town on foot they passed the world famous Langtree Brothel. For such a famous spot the buildings themselves were unremarkable. Sue asked Anna,

*"Did you know that individual rooms are decorated to the hostesses own taste? I mean, who knew? Whores with decorating skills? I guess if you have to look at the ceiling you want it to at least be a ceiling you like. They even have a famed domination room complete with its cuffs, and whatever else in bondage or sadism the clients want. I don't even want to go into what the dominatrix do. Oh yeah, and they have what they call the 'fantasy rooms'? "*

This was new information for Anna and she was not especially enlightened by the knowledge, but she was beginning to appreciate Sue's irreverent sense of humour. They glimpsed young women sitting in exaggerated poses behind glass in white feathers and boas. Somehow such 'Hollywood' styled nightwear and exotic erotica offered under a corrugated iron roof on the edge of the desert seemed to be a foolish proposition. They laughed until they could laugh no more. Anna peeled off, leaving the director to walk the 2 blocks home herself. Later she thought that was unwise and she should have escorted her, given the alcohol she had consumed. Despite the obvious hardships the director had encountered and the negative tone of their discussions Anna was grateful that the director had confirmed her own opinions. She was not alone; there was sanity in the world. That brought an overwhelming sense of relief. She sent Max a brief email:

*"I had a great steak, fine wine, good company (female), I'm not nuts, they are. Your opinion is still not required. I am now ready for bed, the bed and I wish you were here. Love you and the boys.*

The next day's presentation was cut short. It was planned to be a summary of what had been covered. Anna was careful to tread lightly over the neurological implications of trauma. She simply did not have the heart to cover it again. The attendees obviously felt the same and colluded with her in silence, not one question was asked, not one comment offered about that portion. As she ended her final session she received an unexpected standing ovation. That was overwhelming.

The only flight out that fitted her schedule left at 7:15 pm. She had late check out at the room. She ate an early dinner and took a taxi for the short ride to the airport. She was relieved she was the only passenger even if they did join the taxi convoy. As they drove through the flat bruised land they disturbed a flock of pink and grey galahs. These large parrots were in full flight. They flashed one way – hot pink, they wheeled around into another direction, in unison – grey –pink-grey. It was an air ballet of colour.

As they flew out Anna noted a surprising number of trees circling this town in the desert. Even the hills behind the town had the dignity to squat so as not to shame the earth for its flatness. She was glad to be going home. Her travel companions were pleased to be going home too. Most of her co-travellers smelled like they had not taken the time to shower in their haste to leave town. She was assigned a middle seat of three again. The two young men either side of her were drunk, but sleepy. In that condition 'sleepy' was good. Anna's flight arrived back in Perth at the same time as many other planes returning from the mining areas. She walked down the stairs, across the tarmac and into the building. She was confronted by a wall of passengers as the airport suddenly filled with men and women in mining clothes and working boots, talking loudly, all waiting for their bags from the same carousels. They then disgorged out to the curb to the taxi area and were ushered through the line, directed by security guards. Anna was about 50 people back from the front of the line, but the line moved quickly. She was soon seated in a rattle trap of an old taxi on her way home. She was pleased she had taken Liz's offer. She did feel refreshed and looked forward to consolidating her contact with Sue. Perhaps she could return and assist Sue and her team in the future.

●●●●●

# 34

# *Harry Makes History*

*H*arry Browning was an unlikely student of history. Nevertheless he had a well defined interest in specific historic incidents. For example, the account of an accidental explosion on April 16th, 1947 at the dock at Texas City had long intrigued him. For years he ruminated over the thought that two ships had cargoes which were filled with ammonia nitrate fertilizer and sulfur. His readings suggested that a cigarette sparked a small fire that initially blew the ship's hatches. The fire raged and the fertilizer eventually exploded with such force that pedestrians 10 kilometers away were knocked clear off their feet and individuals 150 kilometers away heard the explosions. The port was destroyed, hundreds of vehicles were incinerated. Two airplanes were unceremoniously ripped out of the sky and oil tanks spontaneously ignited. The stories of hundreds of deaths and thousands of good citizens being injured along with billions of dollars of property damage excited him to the point of ejaculation.

On April 19, 1995, murderers parked a rented truck stuffed with only slightly modified ammonium nitrate fertilizer in front of an Oklahoma City office building and ignited it. Browning was furious that someone did it before him. Now he had a target and a plan. The cops took his livelihood, his stash of weapons and explosives. But he still held sole title to his motive.

His unauthorized nocturnal visits to the storage sheds of nearby stations*, near his community provided him with the older style fertilizer, Ammonium Nitrate which he would later soak in diesel fuel. The bang was in the mix and he intended it to give him the maximum bang for other people's buck. He illegally procured the detonating caps and cylinders, cords, flammable fuses for the detonating caps and dynamite boosters from the mining camps. The cigarettes and a passion for revenge he came by honestly. No one could stop him. They found his explosives last time and that uniform. He was better prepared this time with the fertilizer, rat poison, nails, diesel fuel, blasting paraphernalia on board his Holden ute*, covered by a modified beaten up, not worth a second look, camper top. It rode low but no one would suspect anything was amiss when a scruffy lonely looking man packed his belongings and left Fitzroy Crossing. His plan now had wheels and those wheels were pointed south. Revenge had a physical address and he was on the way to it.

He would embed the nails in the rat poison. He had read that Hamas used this against Israel. When nail shrapnel was reinforced with the rat poison the wounds bled beyond treatment. He had not been able to test this, but would use it for good measure. He had long practiced with different detonating caps and cords, wicks and ignition substances. He knew how long it would take for the ignition to reach the first detonating cap, to give him 15 minutes to flee the scene by the free city bus.

As soon as he arrived in Fremantle he stole a vehicle from the late night shopping area parking lot. It was a van. He placed the plates from his ute on it, that should buy him time enough. He sweat with the exertion of stacking the van with almost 1800 kilos of fertilizer, and soaking it all with diesel fuel. He spaced the bags carefully, wrapping them in the detonating cords and peppering the blasting caps throughout his van bomb. He wound the windows down to provide sufficient oxygen for the fuse leading to the detonating caps. He had the exact length of wick he needed and he artistically placed it, leaving 15 minutes of burning between the tip of the wick and the detonating cap.

He was glad he did not have to drive far in those fumes. He was beginning to feel light headed. He drove to the Department's reserved parking area. At 8:00 am Tuesday, he parked the van in the 'Employee of the Month' parking spot. It was closest to the door, and under the glassed overhang. He drove it further forward than employees who parked there did. He intended to undermine the foundations of the building. He lit the carefully measured wick with a cigarette. He tore open the top of a few bags of fertilizer and placed additional diesel soaked rags carefully around these fuel soaked paper sacks. He dug out small trenches in the fuelled fertilizer, filled it with rat poison and threw hands full of nails inside the sacks. He checked the placement of the detonating caps and cords. He opened the windows and closed the van doors. He hopped onto the free city bus down to the safety of the Port area. He stood to afford a pregnant woman a seat. He congratulated himself on his mannerly action telling himself he was a *"good mate"*. She thanked him, believing him to be kindly.

At 8:05 am PP sat at his computer and turned on the slow to boot machine. He had unlocked all of the interior doors according to his individualized sequence. He was preparing to make his morning perimeter check, he just needed to log onto his computer first. It took forever to load.

At 8:08 am Barbara arrived at the front doors and fumbled with her swipe. She finally activated the release and opened the front doors.

At 8:10 am Charlotte was at her desk. Her office window overlooked the glass overhang but she had no time for window gazing this morning. She painstakingly combed through the reports from the Probation Officers. These were to be presented to the Magistrates and she felt it her honor bound duty to track down every errant comma and full stop*, even when the authors' grammatical skills and education outweighed her own. Charlotte had been at her desk for over an hour and was not yet half way through the pile of reports.

At 8:12 am Sophie, who often acted as manager, who actually was the employee of the month tried to park her nifty red Holden Commodore in the exalted, much coveted spot. She swore when she saw the old junker van there, and drove to a 'pay for parking' five level parking tower some streets away. She only prepaid for 2 hours parking as she intended to have that van towed. She was busy trawling through the phone book on her mobile telephone to find the Ranger's number. Distracted, she did not notice the angry contorted face of the scruffy lonely looking man high in the window of the free bus as it passed. He thought he recognized her and wished she would hurry to work.

At 8:13 Harry descended the steps of the free bus at the Port stop. There he waited. At that precise moment Sophie hurried along the sidewalk to work. Scurrying along she called the Ranger's office. She was eager to ask the Ranger to remove the van so she could park there later in the day. The morning was cool; she pulled her suit jacket around her. She tripped on the uneven pavement. The trip caused her to stand still for her own safety; today she could not walk and talk at the same time. The phone rang out, there was no one there. This action delayed her arrival at the Centre. She crossed the road for better reception away from the buildings and tried again. Same non response. She decided to call the Ranger again from her office desk.

At 8:14 am Ben hung up from a mobile telephone call to his son. Tonight was his night to take Calvin to the movies. Mummy was off to a scrap booking class that night. She did that every Monday night and Ben and Calvin enjoyed their 'boy' time together. Ben slipped the phone into his pocket and activated the back door with his swipe. Once inside he began climbing the two flights of stairs up to his office. He stopped on the landing and bought a can of Coke from the drink dispenser. He stood there as he drank it. He often told himself that when he grew up he'd have coffee like every other adult, until then, Coke was his morning beverage.

At 8:15 Harry was anxious,

*"What happened? Where the fuck is the explosion?"* He had miscalculated the time it would take for the flaming petrol filled rags to actually spark the explosion in the fertilizer.

At 8:16 am the early morning janitor held the side door open for the secretary. He was a political refugee from Iraq, his given name was Mahmoud. He didn't use it as when he did others treated him with fear so he called himself Joe. Most Australians did not understand that as a converted Christian and a political dissident he had much more to fear from Taliban terrorists than they did from him. He thought he smelled fumes and smoke. He was distracted when he saw the secretary struggling along the sidewalk. She was loaded down with plastic bags bulging with biscuits, tea, coffee and sugar replacements for the lunch room. Her ungainly packages of groceries made it physically impossible to hold them, locate and use her own swipe so she was grateful for Joe's help. She walked through the door he held open and thanked him. She gave him a chocolate Tim Tam biscuit.

At 8:18 am The young female with a habit of accidentally stabbing her male partners was early for her session with Anna. She sat on the wooden bench outside the front door, about 20 feet from a junker van she had never seen before. As she lit a cigarette she told herself it was bad for her health. The message would not change her behavior but it made her feel better to say it. She was alone today as her male partner was working. She leant back against the outer wall of the Department, crossed her legs at the ankles and drew in the nicotine. Waiting never bothered her. She noticed Albert Dixon walk by and sit opposite her. She did not know him but she did not like him. He had to return some paperwork for his file. He'd only be here a minute or two.

At 8:20 am Anna parked her car on Abernathy Street. She found a closer park than usual, just above the office. She was anxious to get to work to catch up on all that was waiting for her after her week away in Kalgoorlie. She walked quickly around to the rear of the vehicle, as her high heels clicked against the pavement she removed her 'office on wheels' from the boot.

At 8:21 am the janitor, Joe, remembered to check on the burning smell. He approached the rear end of the unknown van parked in the 'Employee of the Month' parking bay. As he reached for the rear door handle he felt heat. He noticed smoke coming from the front windows. He remembered the smell. From Baghdad. He started screaming bloody murder. In Arabic.

Albert Dixon was in no mood for theatrics, he stalked toward Joe ordering him to *"shut the fuck up"*. Anna's female client sensed danger and started running. Away.

'Ausbruch' is the German word for explosion. And it was a magnificent 'ausbruch'. Onlookers described a black smoke plume that erupted into a strange murderous orange flame; they said it looked *"almost beautiful"*. Those who lost loved ones called it *"a tragedy"* and those who saw the aerial view of the exploded area called it *"a bomb created wasteland"*. Once the dust settled and the ability to think returned the city of Fremantle began to cry, then sob, then wail, and the wailing continued through the night, and day and night.

From her place high on Abernathy Street and at that point in time Anna did not know what to call it. She heard it first. Eardrum bursting savage sound. Then she felt it. Her car rocked violently. She feared being run down by her own driverless vehicle, and the one parked behind it. She was protected from the full force of the negative pressure wave by the incline of the hill and the door of her vehicle's boot.

The explosion blasted every thought, even the ability to think, from her mind. Once she regained her balance she just stood there staring, trying not to look, unable to look away. No one emerged from the smoking rubble. Sirens, fire engines with no fire to extinguish, ambulances with no wounded yet to tend came from kilometers around.

Max's heart sank when he heard the explosion announced on the radio news. In a panic he had a colleague drive him to Anna's usual parking area and prayed she had not gone to work early. He called her mobile phone incessantly, on spontaneous redial. She could not remember how to answer it. He was becoming frantic. She did not hear him approach and did not know why he was there but when Max came behind her and grabbed her, her knees unlocked and she fell against him. She took him down with her. They sobbed together as they lay shaking, on the sidewalk.

The traffic helicopter for the Channel 12 news room was filming the area for traffic news, flying above the Ministry of Prisons and Corrections on Abernathy Street Fremantle at 8:20 am. The last image it captured was of a janitor at the back of an abandoned van, at the Ministry of Prisons and Corrections. He was screaming. Those images, later titled 'Hero Screaming', were transmitted live to the television station that was broadcasting them. A wife and mother was cleaning up the children's breakfast dishes, and preparing an early lunch for her husband Mahmoud. He worked at the Ministry of Prisons and Corrections and would be home soon. She noticed the screaming man. Was that Mahmoud? She walked over to the television to see if it was her Mahmoud. Her television screen blacked without warning. So did all of the televisions tuned into that station. Temporarily. Until the pretty girl came on to apolo-gize for the technical difficulties. The helicopter unceremoniously rocked in place before it was savagely sucked out of the sky and hurled into the ground with a tremendous force of a negative pressure wave of the blast. No survivors. A woman's voice screeched *"Oh my God"*. It was the most appalling application of the human voice.

The façade of the top floor of the Ministry of Prisons and Corrections crushed the fleeing young Aboriginal woman mid stride. Albert Dixon's ash remains floated, unnoted, back to earth. Distance from the Ministry was Sophie's salvation. She was not within the immediate blast or lethal area of the explosion. But she was within the evacuation area and her head felt as it was being crushed. She was flung onto the pavement by an unseen hand. She lay there paralyzed with terror, too frightened to move, wondering if that was what it felt like to die. She was close enough to hear the screams, the twisting and metal and concrete, the exploding impact of the helicopter as it smashed to earth. She thought it was an earthquake. When they found her she was covered in dust, traumatized, repeatedly demanding to know what had happened, even after she had been told.

Fremantle's emergency response teams were overwhelmed. Those citizens far enough from the blast to survive but close enough to be torn by it walked or were carried to the local hospital. One after the other these wounded aliens cloaked in concrete dust and blood staggered or were carried or dragged into the doctors' sterile field. The doctors could not stop the bleeding of the shrapnel wounds. They had never encountered anything like it. They shouted for information. A nurse who had worked in Tel Aviv Emergency Rooms as part of her training knew what it was and ran to assist.

One blood covered patient arrived bundled into a shopping trolley cart pushed by a stranger. The stranger decided hospital was the only place for her to be and the trolley was the only way to get her there. There were too many walk ins or carried ins or pushed ins for the beds, they fell where they stood and littered the highly polished floor. The telephone systems both land line and mobile collapsed under the load. Rescuers didn't need the phone directions, they drove toward the smoke. They arrived in asbestos protective suits. The silver suited men and women crawled over the mountainous wreckage of the buildings looking for life. Some had dogs. The dogs found the scent of life. Ben who had been protected by the stairwell was unconscious and broken was gingerly plucked from the wretched rubble 6 hours later. When the rescuers were sure there were no more live survivors in the rubble the Coroner's Disaster Response Team arrived. First they looked for bodies, then body parts, then a finger, then a skin fragment, to be picked up reverently, bagged and carefully taken to the Coroner's laboratory.

The last images filmed by the helicopter crew were played over and over again. The pain of watching it did not abate even with repeat viewings. Each time the images were broadcast they had the same chilling effect on the watchers as they did the first time. Utter horror. Later a television news reader announced that Ben had died on his way to hospital. He did not regain consciousness, not that they knew anyway. Given his horrendous burn injuries his partner hoped they were right. Calvin kept asking when daddy would be home. They had plans that night and daddy had promised. Daddy never broke a promise.

PP, Sue, Charlotte, the secretary, the young Aboriginal woman, the janitor Joe and Barbara were amongst the missing. As were the mother with the broad Australian accent from one of the row houses, and the stupid boy who would not wear his 'jumpuh'. Not even a skin fragment remained of the boy. And the Disaster Identification Teams looked. Ben was found, but then gone. So too were the staff from the television helicopter. 56 neighbors, employees and offenders all told, the watchers and winos and unknown others who were walking or driving by were never seen again. Some were reverently pieced together in small piles. The Ministry of Prisons and Corrections in Fremantle, the offices Births Deaths and Marriages, the Justice of the Peace, the Office of Transport, the Police Station and the neighboring the row houses lost their street facades and suffered varying degrees of damage. Confidential paper files became confetti; carefully kept document stashes were strewn. Within the immediate blast area, besides Ben, there were no intact bodies. The photographs of loved ones stuck to nearly all the computer screens were gone. Windows 4 blocks away were blown out or smashed by flying debris. While the primary damage occurred within a radius of 60 meters, shrapnel from the blast was found over 825 meters away.

The Disaster Identification Team did find Barbara's necklace. It was a puffy gold heart on a chain. It had been damaged. With every good intention the team tracked down its owner, had it repaired and personally returned it to Barbara's mother. Her mother cried when she saw it. The deliverer thought they were tears of joy. They were not. The golden heart had been repaired. Years before the puffy heart had been chewed by both Barbara's girls, McKenzie and Imogene, when they were teething. Those bites had imprinted the heart with tiny teeth marks. Barbara knew which imprint belonged to which girl. The loss of those teeth prints underscored the total loss of all things Barbara and the severing of yet one more a tie between her and the girls. Her mother tried to be grateful but she could not stop the tears. Wiping them, chiding herself, apologizing, all made it worse. The Disaster Identification Team psychologist who delivered the necklace to Barbara's mother cried too.

The citizens of Fremantle and surrounds came to look at the remaining 3 walled shell of the government buildings and row houses. The good and the bad came, the young and the old. They just stood in silence and locked. At first the Police feared trouble from the onlookers but they feared it unnecessarily. The crowd just stood, reverently, some cried. Most didn't. Local, national then international news broadcasters reported on the strange Australian phenomenon of *"Silent Mourning"*, or *"Wordless Grieving"*. One international newspaper headlines screamed *"Aussies in Fremantle lose their 'Oi Oi Oi'"*. Most Aussies thought that to be a stupid comment, but in true Australian form, once stated their opinion was soon forgotten. No malice. No one, including those who stood, even knew why they were there or what they were supposed to do. They just stood and looked. And looked and stood. Standing. Looking. Hundreds became thousands in rotating lines; some left flowers, but most did not. This was not a Lady Di death moment.

It was 3 days before Anna fully stopped the shaking and anguished crying. Strange tearless crying that hemorrhaged from her soul rather than her eyes, with a voice she had never heard before. A part of her died in the flame of the 'ausbruch' and it would forever stay dead. The pain began in her lower jaw and filled the space between her jaw and her diaphragm. At first it was constant, then it came in intermittent unpredictable waves. She thought that must be what it felt like to feel 'gutted'. Sometimes it felt as if her heart would stop, sometimes she wanted it to. She surrendered to it, submitting her body to total collapse, willing it to stop functioning. Other times it felt as if she was progressing through the pain. Until yet another emotion laden tsunami dispelled the myth that she was healing in any measure.

Some days were what she called 'can do days'. Often as she lay in bed she would think what she could not do and those thoughts would strangle her motivation and sap her strength,

*"I cannot think, I cannot understand this, I cannot go back to work, I can't even mother".* The 'can't do days' were burying her. She flipped it to,

*"What can I do today? Can I get out of bed? Yes I can do that. Can I brush my teeth and hair? Yes I can do that?"* And so on as she coached herself through the mundane tasks of 'can do days' as she tried to claw her way up the slippery walls of depression, one inch forward, two back. Searching her strength she asked herself,

*"Can I get dressed today?"*

Sometimes the answer was *"no"* so she would ask *"Can I sit up today? Yes I can do that. Can I put my feet on the floor? Yes I can do that."* Smaller steps. She coached and coaxed herself from the bed to the floor, from the floor to the shower, from the shower to the mirror and so on and so on. It was a full week before she could eat. And it was 2 weeks before she could ask *"Why? Who?"* The Police visited and asked her what she knew. Harry Browning was their person of interest. Anna did not know him. She only knew what she had been told by the Police since the explosion and what Charlotte and the Police told the department before the explosion.

Anna's life was now divided into two parts by the timeline 'before the explosion and after the explosion'. Anna's voice was unusually high pitched; she could get no bass to it, no depth. Her sister told her she needed to go into a room and scream. But scream what? How would she get the energy to scream? Anna decided that time and quiet would bring back the tone to her voice, not screaming.

Structural engineers would later say that besides the buildings across the street that were destroyed, 4 adjoining and nearby buildings suffered significant damage although thankfully, none collapsed. Their non collapse spared the occupants from being crushed. Had they collapsed there would have been many more fatalities. This fact did not escape the survivors. Shrapnel caused the majority of injuries and deaths outside of the lethal radius of the initial blast. The death toll was as high as it was because so many were passing by that office, parking in the area, crossing through the park or arriving at their work stations at that time.

A temporary correction's office was set up closer to the port itself in an area inaccessible to road vehicles. Office furniture and computers were scavenged from closets, back rooms, and anywhere else in government buildings. None of it matched, chairs were too big for desks, desks were too small for chairs, the scavenged telephone system was outdated 10 years ago, and it had too few extensions, but it would do for now, until the rented one could be installed. There were no files, Liz's cyber files had to be printed and compiled. The office was temporarily staffed by volunteers from surrounding offices. There were so many volunteers from other centres wanting to lend a hand that they could not all be accommodated. No one complained about the furniture, the phones, the computers or the vehicular inconvenience. Ironically Liz's much resented new data bank of information was accessible and was all that remained of the documents about Fremantle's offenders and staff. It was now a vital resource, the only comprehensive testimony to their existence hung unseen and voiceless in cyber space.

Every other Centre under the Directorate's supervision, including the jails and prisons went into emergency mode, fearing copy cat attacks. A web of lanky cyclone fences were erected and chained together. Not trusting the security of the swipes security guards ensured that only identified staff members were allowed to park behind the locked gates. Close vehicular access was denied to all others.

Each morning Max found flowers on the doorstep addressed to Anna. They were home grown roses and hibiscus, daisies and other garden-variety plants. Some tied with ribbon, some crunched together with cooking foil, others in jam jars with their own water supply. Neighbors left their floral tributes to wordlessly express *"Sorry, we're so sorry"*. Almost every day following the blast there was a new supply of fresh flowers. Flowers for the broken hearted. One morning Max found a six pack of Bourbon amongst the flowers with a note from Sean O'Connor *"when all else fails"*. Anna was too shattered to react to this intrusion or to think through what it meant. Despite Directorate instructions that staff must return all gifts from offenders, she and Max, who seldom drank alcohol, drank the booze in one sitting.

The good people of the area, and the bad, left photographs of their missing and dead stapled, nailed, stuck, taped to the wooden telephone poles along both sides of Abernathy Street in Fremantle. These poles became silent sentries of grief. The photographs were covered in plastic zip loc bags, or plastic wrap. No one disturbed them. If one was knocked loose or fell to the ground, an unacknowledged hand reverently replaced it, back in place with the others. The crime rate plummeted to almost zero. Passersby greeted total strangers in the street. Almost everyone, even estranged relatives telephoned their family members and friends, reconnecting in the presence of an eternal disconnect.

Anna's sister took the boys home with her, planning to keep them for a couple of weeks. It sounded like a good idea in theory. Anna did not want them to see her in her present state. But Stu and

Lachie begged to be taken home that first evening to be with their mum, and they were.

When the engineers had combed through the rubble of the buildings and located the axle of the stolen van they also found the remains of a Police truncheon. Enough of the number engraved on the inner metal core survived the blast and identified it as the truncheon Harry Browning stole.

Six weeks later there was a memorial service held at the Port. Reporters from almost every nation on earth were there eagerly waiting for images to broadcast to their local audiences. The world's fascination with things Australian was heightened by the tragedy that rocked what was usually called 'the lucky country'.

On the morning of the service the entrance to the dock was emblazoned by officers from the local Army Barracks in their full dress regalia. The officers, themselves veterans of war and foreign political upheaval, saluted as Anna, still numb, Sophie and the others walked to their places. Sophie, her partner and 4 year old son, Max and Anna stood in the early summer sunshine with thousands of others. Those in the inner circle were ashen faced. Some had to be supported to stand. Dignitaries spoke. One was the commander from the local Special Forces Army Squadron. He referred to the employees of the Directorate as,

*"Civilian warriors fighting a war for good against the armies of crime".* That was the undoing of Anna, she was grateful to be distracted from that thought when the children sang and a Priest and Rabbi prayed.

The names of the dead and missing were read by family members, one after the other. Every name brought a face to mind for Anna or at least one of the other mourners. Her knees buckled when PP's real name was read. A sole piper in a kilt arm wrestled "Amazing Grace" from his bag pipes.

While Lachie and Stuart were not there, two little girls were. McKenzie and Imogene. The petite daughters of Barbara now clung to the skirted legs of their silent grandmother. The three of them looked absolutely lost. Each girl held a ribbon attached to a heart shaped helium filled balloon with a note attached to the ribbon string. Both notes were addressed to *"My Mummy"*. McKenzie's was written in a child's hand. She had written *"Mummy if I don't fite with immie will you come home? Plees?"* and Imogene's was a drawing of a red headed Barbara surrounded by hearts and cross kisses.

56 Roses, one for each of the lost, were released upon the waves of the Indian Ocean to float out from the port into the unknown vastness beyond. Two helium filled balloons with their little notes, 56 butterflies and 56 white doves were released to the sky. Anna spotted the partner of her young female Aboriginal client in the crowd. He was expressionless. Tear streams had dried on his cheeks. Anna slept for 2 days and nights following the service. Once she awoke her usual voice was back. Perhaps it was because when she woke she found Stuart and Lachie beside her in bed; each boy had an arm around her. Lachie pressed the full length of his body against his mum, gently patted her shoulder and purred in soothing tones,

*"There there, there there"* as she had to done to them when they were babies. Stu, silent, barely breathing had her hand pressed against his cheek. She wanted to crush both boys to her chest and wail in that alien voice birthed on the sidewalk above the initial blast but she knew that would terrify them. Instead, mercifully she

held their hands, kissed them and said.

*"My beautiful beautiful boys"*. She wanted them to know how much they were contributing to her healing without putting that burden upon them. Max was making coffee. Her family knew that when her schedule allowed it, her definition of luxury was to stay in bed long enough to eat a raisin scone from the local bakery and read the paper. Seven days later there were 7 unread papers and 7 white paper bags containing 7 untouched scones in a temporary pile beside her bed. It was a silent, sweet testament to their willing her well. She loved them all the more. Her family had willingly become her conduit to her own life, even when the dead part surfaced.

Prior to the committal ceremony Harry Browning bought every newspaper he could that described the tragedy in Fremantle. His eyes consumed every delicious word, over and over. He laughed at McKenzie and Imogene's notes to their mother. He savored and delighted in each story of pain, much like a murderer who revisits the scene of the murder to roll in the dust. However after the funerals and final ceremony he felt unsettled, rattled even and decided to hide out in Kuala Lumpur. He had friends there, and thought that he could hide amongst the teeming international populace without detection. He did not like foreigners when they were in Australia, but he didn't mind them if they stayed in their place, their own country.

He told his friends on the community that he was going to work for a company in Asia known as RTS. They were impressed. His friends did not know that was Singaporean slang for *"Run The Streets"*. Anyone who is unemployed and without easily identifiable means of support in Singapore will say they are *"employed by RTS"*. Head shaved bald and face clean shaven again, losing weight and without the limp he booked a flight through Singapore. Due to the lateness of the booking he had an 8 hour layover in Singapore. Instead of taking one of the free city sightseeing tours he would use the time to nap, freshen up and change into clean, neatly pressed dress clothes. Going where he was going, having done what he had done, watching his own metamorphous seeing what he looked like and how he looked now, he congratulated himself on committing the perfect crime.

No crime is ever perfect. Harry Browning's partner sobbed as she read the newspaper article about McKenzie's *"Note to Mummy"*. She was a mother. Not of Harry's children, but a mother no less. She had two daughters, aged 3 and 5. She had partnered with a psychopath, but she was not a psychopath. She picked up the telephone and placed a call. She quietly requested to speak to the lead detective on the case.

•••••

# 35

# *An International Pick Up*

*A*mongst the myriad of perfectly choreographed landings and take offs of airplanes negotiating Singapore, and the local university students who came to the airport to study, scurrying travelers, with the lights, the fantastic design, the busyness, the shopping and the glamour of one of the most impressive airports in the world slept a mass murderer. The Singaporean Police woke then arrested Mr.Harold Butler, aka Harry Browning in one of the many napping areas at Changi airport in Singapore. They handed him to the Australian Federal Police Liaison stationed in Singapore. Australia had joined forces with Singapore as part of an International agreement to rid the world of the rats that hide or run through the secret back alleys and airports of the Global Village. The Aussies escorted the decidedly reluctant and constantly morphing Harry Browning back to Perth. Barbara's mother told the newspaper reporter that she cursed the law change of 1984 when the death penalty was abolished in WA. She said she wished they lived in Texas because then Browning would *"fry"*.

• • • • •

# 36

## Family Day

*E*merging from the faces and voices that played in her head day and night, awake or asleep, exhausted beyond sleep, fearing sleep, desperately needing sleep, slowly Anna returned, especially on 'can do days' which were coming much more frequently now. The first thing she wanted to do was to pick up her end of the parenting spectrum. She and Lachie were walking home from the local tennis courts. He had just played and won and was feeling especially good. He asked her,

*"Mum are the clouds thrombolites?"*

*"These ones look like it lovee. What made you think of thrombolites?"*

*"Peter and I have to do a project next term on thrombolites. I was just thinking about them."*

*"Would you like to go to Lake Clifton to see them?"*

*"Can Pete come?"*

*"Yes."*

*"Okay, wizard."*

Anna did not feel stable enough to drive the 2 hours it would take to go to Lake Clifton. Max took the day off work; it was a pupil free day for Stuart, Lachie and Peter. The three boys piled into the back seat of the car. Anna took cold drinks and a picnic basket. As the boys began chatting Anna closed her eyes. Lachie and Peter were discussing the best and worst years of their lives. Stuart entered the conversation and said that 9 was his worst year of his entire life. Anna and Max could not think why, they managed not to ask. He expounded on how at that age he was neither a child nor a teenager. He wanted to stay a child but adults expected more than childish behaviour from him. Then when he wanted to be a teenager he was treated like a child. He said he found it very difficult. The three old souls in the back seat continued their sage like analysis of the ages of child hood. After the road trip Anna realised that when Stuart was 9 Lachlan was born, and she was sure that factored into his *"worst year"* in my entire life discourse. This was the year he had to share the throne to his parents' hearts. She knew which was the worst year in her life.

They picnicked at the Mandurah foreshore. The water was especially vibrant turquoise today and being a work day the crowds were thin. A double bonus. St. Bennies along with the other private colleges had a pupil free day today prior to the long summer holidays. Those children who attended public schools were still in class. There were few children at the foreshore. George the Pelican showed up and helped himself to some ham from Lachie's sandwich. Lake Clifton was a short drive away from their picnic spot. They made their way along the short sandy pathway to the wooden walkway built over the fresh lake to protect the thrombolites. Lachie eagerly read the information board pro-claimed that the micro-organisms that formed the rocks also released oxygen into the atmosphere. Stuart told him not to bring 'the gasping' patients for help with their breathing. He said the oxygen releasing thrombolites grew 1 millimetre a year. That's a long time to wait for a breath.

The thrombolites looked like dome or pancake shaped rocks. Lachie said he thought they looked like piles of cow poop. They were easily seen along the lake's edge. There was not a human habitat to be seen. The area looked as it might have pre man, except for the winding wooden viewing platform. Peter began reading from his notes and said that,

*"These thrombolites were built by miniscule micro-organisms. Being too small for the eye to see they lived in communities with as many as 3000 of these living rock forming creatures per square meter. Lake Clifton is one of only a few places in Western Australia where living thrombolites survive. The thrombolites are the only form of life on Earth from 3500 million to 650 million years ago to survive to the present. There are remains of other thrombolites to be seen at nearby Lake Preston."* Peter finally took a breath. Stuart changed the subject.

Lachie and Stuart took photos of the strange looking rocks. Peter drew a cartoon rendition of them. Lachie squatted down on his haunches, with his head between his knees staring into the brackish water. He was silent and still. Both were strange for him.

*"Dad?"*

*"Yeah Mate."*

*"Did you say these rocks are alive?"*

*"Yes mate."*

*"How would you know?"*

*"What do you mean?"*

*"I've been watching this hummer for ages and it hasn't done anything 'living'."*

*"Well not that you can see mate, but it is growing there under the water, those micro-organisms are as busy as."*

*"You kiddin' me?"*

*"Nope."*

*"You wouldn't lie to me?"*

*"No mate. Well, not on a Friday anyway."*

*"Dad?"*

*"Yep."*

*"Today is Wednesday."*

Anna asked if the boys wanted to go to Lake Preston to see the dead thrombolites. Stuart was quick to answer,

*"With as lively as the living ones aren't I think the dead ones would be a real yawner."* That was taken as a family vote. Satisfied they had enough for their project for now, the boys asked to go back to the foreshore. There was a movie they wanted to see and they happened to notice it was playing there. While they watched their movie Anna napped on the grass of the foreshore, head on Max's legs. Max just watched her stroking her hair.

On the way home the boys connected their hand held computer games and systematically saved and destroyed the world. Lachie was not pleased that Stuart kept 'killing him'. On the other hand Peter was feeling left out because he had not been 'killed' in an hour. Anna asked why they had to play such violent games. Stu told her that just as soon as the controls were modified to include 'International Diplomacy' and 'Treaties Without Violence' the kids of the world would rush to use them. Anna answered *"As they would"*. She and Max decided to let the boys sort out who would kill whom, in the interim, as they waited for the new control functions. It was far too complex an issue for adult involvement.

Although Anna had time to think during her stress leave she was disappointed at how fatigued she still was. Day after day she lay on her bed watching the sun scoot the shadows across the yard as it moved through the sky. The element of the scene that amazed her most was that she had time to watch it, and that she even wanted to. Today's clouds looked like thrombolites again. She could not bring herself to voluntarily think about those that were lost in the explosion, nor the brutality of the action that caused such senseless loss of life and destruction. Not only were buildings, homes and offices blown to pieces so were families, dreams and hearts.

A psychologist, who formerly worked in the Directorate, was re-employed to back fill for her, to allow Anna to have as much time to heal as she needed. Her replacement would contact Anna now and then, mainly for procedural assistance as the protocols had changed in the 3 years since the temporary employee decided to stay at home with her three children. She often needed help with the data bank. It had never occurred to Anna that she could stay home as her replacement had. Until now, when it dawned on Anna that she would probably never 'heal', that there was no statute of limitations on grief and trauma. Sometimes when bits die they stay dead. Sometimes she asked Max,

*"What if this is as good as I get?"*

His response was to hold her.

●●●●●

# 37

# A Report for the Directorate

*A*nna did not think it reckless at the time. Later she would know it was. She woke from an afternoon nap and without thought robotically text messaged Liz *"Harry Browning was a psychopath"*. Anna started writing a report to the Directorate. She began with the statistics, the fact that 1% of the population is over represented in the prison population. These are the psychopaths, these are the murderers, the bludgeoners, the rapists, the frickin' drug lords and the bikies that commit 50% of the crimes yet there were no protocols in place to even assess them. She demanded to know why they were treated the same as a man whose only crime, as bad as it was, was smacking his wife and violating the restraining order when the Judge said the wife did all she could to coerce him into doing both? She begged them to consider why the punishment given to a young man who drank alchohol, then drove, recently killing a family was more severe than the punishment metered out to a habituated criminal. She demanded to know if he should be treated the same way as a hardened criminal who inflicted pain gratuitously replacing any goodness in his life with violence. Anna ranted that if the Department differentiated between crimes of stupidity crimes or crimes where trauma was the criminogenic variable and crimes of true criminality or psychopathic variables the offenders could then be effectively treated.

Anna's argument was that by treating all of the offenders as though they were rational and wanted to break their offending cycle, that they would even if they could, was purely ludicrous. Anna's anguish raged. The 'one size fits all' philosophy was ineffective. The current approach involved respect and an empathetic understanding of the impact of their troubled childhoods on their adult crimes. However it did not include accurately assessing the offending behaviour. By not doing this the Department offered the devious amongst them a well oiled loophole through which to slide. And the reluctance to violate them was the push they needed to ride that loop. She was not suggesting that the Directorate instruct its employees to be disrespectful to offenders. She was shouting at them to understand that to have insufficient doubt about the offenders' inherent goodness sabotaged the department's attempts to really help them. She wrote

*"There is nothing rehabilitative in pretending we were helping. We have to understand who they are before we can help them."*

To support that argument Anna stated that by underestimating the criminal mind and failing to accurately assess each offender on his or her own merits means the worst amongst them are able to run free amongst the best of them. Enabled by that freedom and released to community based orders some criminals posed a threat to everybody in the department who served them, including the security guards, the Probation Officers, other offenders and the administrative staff, as Harry Browning proved. She wrote the report quickly, with expletives, slang words, namelessly quoting from the lives of the mason, Albert Dixon, Jack Williams and Sean

O'Connor comparing them with Crystal and others in a manner that indicated they cannot be compared to each other.

The report needed to be reworked into the accepted departmental numbered, indented format and language but she did not have the stamina for it. Anna vomited the passion and the disgust, the frustration and the terror through words onto the paper and she sent it in before she could change her mind. She ended it with a plea

*"Please do the right thing"*. And she typed these words in size 8 font so that they would have to enlarge it to read it and thereby take notice. When she finished she was sobbing, swearing out loud and trembling to the point she asked Stu to print off the report, fold it and place it in the envelope with the thumb drive version. These final tasks were beyond her.

•••••

# 38

# *Summer Christmas*

*T*he boys had another 7 weeks of school holidays and Christmas was coming. Anna usually decorated every room throughout the month of December until their entire home was a tribute to Christmas. It was a custom she picked up when she worked in America. This year the thought of getting the Christmas tree out and decorating it overwhelmed her. Stuart and Lachie dragged the tree down from the loft in the garage. They put it together, L branch to L groove, K branch to K groove and so on and so on. And as they did they played Christmas carols and drank spiders (ice cream floating in coke). These were Anna's customs, she had no idea they even noticed or that they could reproduce the scene. Once the boys had carefully set the atmosphere they decorated the tree. They planned their strategy, one boy on each side. The tree looked perfect. All the decorations were on the lower right hand side of the tree on Lachie's side. Stu's side was more equally decorated, with the larger decorations on the lower branches and the smaller ones at the top. The angel was carefully propped at a perilous angle on its apex.

One of Anna's friends said she should move the tree to the family room and put a 'properly decorated tree' in the formal front lounge room. Anna could not think of a way to more 'properly' decorate a tree and left it exactly where it was. Non symmetric distribution of decorations, non decorated areas, and lop sided angel notwithstanding. Max knew Anna did not have the strength to Christmas shop so together the family went through the newspaper advertisements and chose gifts for everyone on their list, plus a few. And Max did the buying. He definitely knew why he usually left that task to her. Once the gifts were home, Anna locked their bedroom door and did the wrapping. Hours of it. It exhausted her but she refused all offers of help.

Christmas Day promised to be over 43 degrees Celsius so Anna decided they would have their actual Christmas celebration on Christmas Eve. The family was pleased to oblige, just to have her up and functioning as "mum" meant the world to them. Anna utilised the cooler temperatures of the night to have a candle lit dinner of beef, chicken and Stuart caught ocean fish. There were prawns aplenty with Max's secret sauce and of course a Pavlova dessert. They were joined by family and friends, including thrombolite studying Peter and his family. They had a genuinely pleasant time. The next morning the boys opened their gifts. By 6:00 am it was already 38 degrees Celsius. They ate leftovers at a picnic under the shade of weeping gum trees by the Swan River. It was cooler than anywhere else. Not quite, but it was an almost perfect Christmas.

Anna and Sophie had not been close. Anna had always appreciated the way Sophie ran the team meetings and the calm her approach brought. Sophie admired the way Anna could focus on treating the offenders even amongst the political uproar of the Centre. But they did not really 'know' each other; they had not made the time to connect socially. So when Sophie text messaged Anna's mobile telephone with the invitation *"want 2 get 2gether?"* she responded more from surprise than a real desire to, with

*"Yes whr?"* Sophie nominated *"Dome, Napoleon Street, 2moro @ 10:00am."*

Anna did not know why she arrived early, but she did. She often came here, she loved the combination of sidewalk dining behind protective screens and comfortable wooden panels inside and addictive aromas occupying both areas. So did Sophie. Usually the patrons of the Dome placed their orders at the counter then selected a seat. Being a warm summer's morning the two survivors wordlessly and unanimously chose to sit outside under the umbrellas. They did not go to the counter. They did not order. Neither computed or remembered that process. The young male waiter Tim knew them both and came to their tables with their favourites. Tim was not an ingratiating in your face *"How are you and the children Mrs. Lennox?"* type of waiter, but he always managed to make them feel genuinely welcome and remembered. Anna smiled at Tim, oblivious to the fact that she had not ordered. One cappuccino, low fat milk and a latte – Irish Cream, no sugar and blue berry cheese cake for both. He thought they looked like they needed some comfort food. The conversation started hesitatingly as Sophie asked

*"How?"* followed by silence.

Anna slowly answered

*"Sometimes?"* more silence.

Sophie asked *"Do you?"*

*"Yes, you? Often?"* said Anna.

*" Most days, no tears,"* offered Sophie.

*"I still  do -  tears,"* added Anna.

*"Dreams?"*

*"Way beyond dreams, night terrors really, and I don't have to be asleep to see them,"* whispered Anna.

Silence.

*"Smell, sounds?"*asked Sohpie.

*"Concrete, taste dust – still."*

*"What is the worst?"* asked Sophie.

Anna couldn't answer until she gained control of her quivering lips and recalcitrant tongue. When finally she could speak she said.

*"The balloons?"*

*"MacKenzie's and Immies?"* Sophie asked.

*"Yes. Those,"* said Anna.

*"For me too,"*said Sophie.

Silence.

More silence.

*"And now?"* asked Anna.

*"Guilt,"*offered Sophie.

*"Oh yeah,"* responded Anna.

*"Do you think we will ever want sex again?"*asked Sophie.

They both laughed. Sophie's breathing then became noisily shallow. The rhythm was somehow comforting. At least she and Anna were still breathing. Anna's mascara was obviously not water-proof. Sophie's was. Nevertheless tears tracked irreverently down both women's cheeks. The tears left only water marks on Sophie's cheeks, and dark tiny rivers on Anna's. They extended their hands toward each other at the same time. Their fingers brushed, they were both self conscious about it but held hands anyway. Sometimes the need for comfort supersedes embarrassment. Neither spoke, they were almost crying. They sat at the sidewalk table, in the early sunshine for an hour. They would have stayed longer but left before it became too hot to enjoy the sidewalk location. The waiter paid their bill from his tips. They did not even notice. Days later Anna remembered she had not ordered nor paid for her coffee and snack. Max called the Dome and was informed of Tim's schedule. He drove there at the appointed time. He easily parked and found Tim, thanked him and tried to pay him with a sizeable tip. Tim would have none of it and wished Max a happy new year.

The weather was increasingly warm. They had the typical summer heat wave of 10 days over 40 degrees Celsius. Living where they did the nights were cooler with the sea breeze. This breeze had a name, the locals dubbed it 'The Fremantle Doctor' as it blew through Fremantle and was 'what the doctor ordered'. Anna preferred to sleep the day and function in the cooler night. This did not work with the boys' schedule. They loved the daylight hours that seemed to extend with daylight saving. So she adapted. When they were not at their friend's homes or at tennis or cricket camp she endured the heat of the day with them. She was surprised at her reaction to the heat as she usually enjoyed the Australian summer. Now she avoided doing her laundry and hanging the clothes on the line until at least 10:00 pm.

She remembered that when she was a young bride living in South Australia, she would hang her clothes under early morning skies in distinct order on her revolving Hills Hoist. If she hung longer garments near the centre pole they perilously wrapped themselves around the pole and became tangled and damaged in the wind. She soon learned to hang first socks (no way they could entangle themselves around that pole), then underwear, the small hand towels, then shorter garments, on out until the sheets and towels hung on the outside lines, away from that menacing centre pole. Then she would use the handle to hoist the entire wet flapping load out of the dog's way and high enough to 'catch the wind'. She enjoyed it when her neighbour called out "Nice line Mrs. Lennox", for indeed it was. Then when Alice Butler did the same she would return the compliment by chirping, "Nice line Mrs. Butler". However, these days there was no one out at 10:00 pm to judge her line. Usually she enjoyed the sun dried freshness of her clothing but for now the night drying worked. Nothing was the same. What had that murdering Harry Browning aka Butler done to her life?

• • • • •

# 39

## Going to Work

*I*t was the 2nd week on February before Anna's psyche could drag itself from the dust and wreckage of the buildings up on its feet to return to work. The ash clung to her. She could taste it, smell it and wore it as a grey mask under her face. It coated her bones. She asked Liz for permission to reduce her work week to 3 days. Liz agreed and assigned her back to Port Stirling as she knew the staff and offenders there. Not only that, she had worked hard to liaise with local mental health facilities who could support her at this time. She did not feel safe to drive so caught the train again. There was only one seat, by a dirty man in dirty clothes in his mid 40's. When she sat by him other commuters looked at her with expressions that silently shouted *"what are you doing?"* At first the journey was silent then he began to talk. He told of his life as a child in Western Europe as his father worked in Tuscany for an international winery. She asked him to speak Italian, more to test his story than anything. And he did, and as far as she could tell it was an accomplished Italian, not a school boy's halting attempt.

He had an encyclopaedic knowledge of movies, who wrote them, where they were filmed. He said that the young man on the train with the US flag embroidered on his coat sleeve was probably an officer from the visiting US Navy ship. He said he was probably an officer and a gentleman and asked if she had been to Port

Townsend. She said she had for that is where the movie by that title was filmed. He seemed surprised she knew that and commented that it made her a good citizen, he had a citizen watch and did she know about Citizen Kane? His tangential connections seemingly had a life of their own and wove themselves throughout the story of his life. When Anna stood to leave the same commuters who looked at her with danger signs in their eyes now looked at her questioningly *"what did you not understand about him before she sat down?"* At least he had stopped her thinking. She smiled at his stories.

She was not yet stable enough to offer offender care so she tidied her cabinet drawers, redesigned and reprinted forms and strengthened her alliances with the community based mental health care givers. She found it to be ironic that when she actually changed the forms they would remain the way she designed them, without Charlotte's heavy handed editing. There was not as much joy in that as she once thought there might have been. She reviewed Cory's progress notes. He appeared to have engaged with Lorraine. Through the way Lorraine tracked and recorded his therapeutic work she could not tell how the business was progressing.Lorraine's notes were purely clinical, addressing only Cory's psychological progress. Anna thought she must adopt that style when she began to see clients again. Cory had not consulted with Lorraine for 3 weeks. He was obviously doing well enough to reduce his intervention.

She had been working for a week before Liz telephoned her. Liz sounded formal and as if she was on a mission. She said that on behalf of the Directorate she was inviting Anna to meet with the Best Practice Committee concerning the report she submitted to them.

Tomorrow. Liz told Anna that it was not compulsory she attend, but that she should be aware of who issued the invitation. Anna would attend. 'Tomorrow' came slowly. But come it did. Anna took the train to the City of Perth. Today she took no interest in those who rode with her. It was a short walk from the train station to the high rise building that housed the Directorate. She did not enjoy this stroll as she had previously, in fact she did not remember seeing any of the usual land marks. She did not even feel the ever present breeze or enjoy the sunshine. She passed through the tight security of the Directorate and took the elevator to the 28th floor. She did wonder why the directors who never encountered a criminal were protected by layers of security while those who actually dealt with criminals on a daily basis had no such protections.

A pleasant receptionist greeted her, asked her to sign in and gave her a temporary day pass to wear that said 'Visitor". Anna was then ushered into a large carpeted room with Liz and Katherine Bourke. Anna had expected to see a group, to see the Director herself. She wondered when or how these two women became the Best Practice Committee. Liz barely acknowledged Anna. That was not a good sign. There was no face recognition of Ms. Bourke as up till that time Anna had not yet met her. When she heard the name she remembered her email about *"reinventing the wheel"* as the Mastermind Program was initially proposed. Katherine was elegant, hair swept up into a tight rolled bun. She moved slowly, wore an electric blue rayon dress in a Department where dresses were rare. Especially party type blue ones. She had a male secretary. He watched her face constantly for cues to obey. He fluttered around her, remaining physically close to her. He was appropriately shorter than Katherine and buzzed around dutifully. It was like a Yul Brunner, Deborah Kerr moment, but gender reversed. Anna found him to be aggravating.

Ms. Bourke welcomed her, thanked her for coming. The male secretary took Anna's order for coffee and obediently disappeared. Ms. Bourke patronizingly explained that the department believed strongly in line management. Anna's situation, as tragic as it was, did not change that. They had granted her some leeway due to her obvious trauma. However Ms. Bourke pointed out that Liz was Anna's line manager, as if Anna had missed that point. If Anna's proposals or concerns were to be considered then they would need to be presented, in appropriate format and language to Liz first for her review. If Liz thought them appropriate she would then escalate them to her line manager, and so on, and so on. Not once did Ms. Bourke look at Anna. Ms. Bourke handed Anna's report back to her in its original envelope. She thanked Anna for her service, assured her of the Directorate's full support and gratitude. She called her a *"hero"* and excused herself. The receptionist came to remove her 'Visitor' pass. The interview was over. As Anna rode the elevator down to the ground floor she was numb. The one isolated thought that dared show itself on the empty terrain of her mind was,

*"It took her 3 months not to read my report"*. It was then she realised 'his maleness' took her coffee order but never did bring the coffee.

Ms. Bourke watched from her 28th floor window as Anna tossed the unopened report and thumb drive into the nearest rubbish bin she passed. Ms. Bourke smiled. She turned to Liz and reminded her that Anna's contract was ending in 6 months. As Anna had been judged 'non competitive' by a more experienced Principle Forensic Psychologist she was sure Liz would not consider offering Anna a contract extension. Liz excused herself and left.

Anna told Max that Ms. Bourke's insulting speech was 'junk food for the mindless'.

•••••

# 40

## *The Con*

Anna was feeling stronger. She was finally sleeping through most nights, and felt refreshed most mornings. She was working 3 days a week for 2 weeks. Due to her absence she had a new case load, and spent time acquainting herself with their details. As she ploughed through yet another life on paper Cory's Probation Officer asked her for an appointment. Anna was only seeing 3 clients a day, in total, per doctor's orders. She booked her in after the 3rd and last client of the day. Anna poured them both a cup of coffee, dragged out the 'good' biscuits and removed her shoes.

Cory's Probation Officer sat silently for several minutes then she quietly said,

*"Cory is in jail?"* Anna had had enough of drama and trauma, obviously he was in for something minor so why the big lead up?

*"Where is Sam?"* she asked, her annoyance evident.

*"The cops shot him."* A jagged pang of knowing ripped through her. The dogs died only when the owner really angered the cops beyond sanity. Katy now had her full attention.

*"Cory in jail, why?"*

*"Remember that huge drug haul I told you about before the Freo-Browning explosion? Well, he was the lead dog. I saw him yesterday in Hakea Prison for his Pre Sentence Report. He said to*

*tell you it had been a hell of a ride, and that he and Mervyn thank you for the trip to Asia and for all of your business guidance and contacts. He said you helped him become the Drug Premier he will continue to work on becoming the Prime Minister...and what else? Oh yeah, and that his skills really were transferable."*

•••••

# Australian Words Explained

**Ambos** - ambulance drivers, paramedics

**Barrack** - root (as for a team)

**Biscuits** - cookies

**Blokes** - guys

**Boot** - trunk of car

**Chockers** - crowded

**Chuck** - toss

**Cobbas** - friends

**Coppers** - police officers

**Coves** - guys

**Cuppa** - cup of tea or coffee

**Do his block** - have a tantrum

**Dodgy** - suspect

**Drongo** - fool

**Firies** - firemen

**Full stop** - period

**Gite** - French county house for rent

**Jumpuh** - sweater

**Kit** - equipment

**Mobile telephones** - cell phones

**Pansy** – wimp

**Petrol** - gasoline

**Pinnie** - apron

**Pom, pommie** – British people

**Poofter** – weak one (as used)

**Preggers** - pregnant

**Rottie** - Rottweiler

**State school** – public school

**Station** – large ranch

**Tradies** - tradesmen

**Tucker** - food

**Ute** – pickup truck

**Yarning** - talking

# THE CON

ISBN 978-1-935434-53-5

*Gael McCarte*

Fact●ion
...fiction based on fact
an imprint of GEA Press

www.ingramcontent.com/pod-product-compliance
Lightning Source LLC
Chambersburg PA
CBHW031501270326
41930CB00006B/189